THE PRETRIAL PROCESS
DOCUMENT SUPPLEMENT

THE PRETRIAL PROCESS
Second Edition

2015 Document Supplement

James Alexander Tanford
Professor of Law
Indiana University—Bloomington

Layne S. Keele
Associate Professor of Law
Faulkner University

ISBN: 978-1-6328-4508-5 (print)
ISBN: 978-1-6328-4509-2 (eBook)

NOTE TO USERS

To ensure that you are using the latest materials available in this area, please be sure to periodically check the LexisNexis® Law School web site for downloadable updates and supplements at www.lexisnexis. com/lawschool.

Editorial Offices
630 Central Ave., New Providence, NJ 07974 (908) 464-6800
www.lexisnexis.com

MATTHEW BENDER   (Pub. 03160)

TABLE OF CONTENTS

FEDERAL RULES OF CIVIL PROCEDURE

(Including Amendments through Dec. 1, 2015)

TITLE V. DISCLOSURES AND DISCOVERY

TITLE VI. TRIALS

TITLE VII. JUDGMENT

TITLE VIII. PROVISIONAL AND FINAL REMEDIES

TITLE IX. SPECIAL PROCEEDINGS

TITLE X. DISTRICT COURTS AND CLERKS: CONDUCTING BUSINESS; ISSUING ORDERS

TITLE I. SCOPE OF RULES; FORM OF ACTION

Rule 1. Scope and Purpose

These rules govern the procedure in all civil actions and proceedings in the United States district courts, except as stated in Rule 81. They should be construed, administered, and employed by the court and the parties to secure the just, speedy, and inexpensive determination of every action and proceeding.

Rule 2. One Form of Action

There is one form of action—the civil action.

TITLE II. COMMENCING AN ACTION; SERVICE OF PROCESS, PLEADINGS, MOTIONS, AND ORDERS

Rule 3. Commencing an Action

A civil action is commenced by filing a complaint with the court.

Rule 4. Summons

(a) Contents; Amendments.

    (1) *Contents.* A summons must:

        (A) name the court and the parties;

        (B) be directed to the defendant;

        (C) state the name and address of the plaintiff's attorney or—if unrepresented—of the plaintiff;

        (D) state the time within which the defendant must appear and defend;

        (E) notify the defendant that a failure to appear and defend will result in a default judgment against the defendant for the relief demanded in the complaint;

        (F) be signed by the clerk; and

        (G) bear the court's seal.

    (2) *Amendments.* The court may permit a summons to be amended.

(b) Issuance. On or after filing the complaint, the plaintiff may present a summons to the clerk for signature and seal. If the summons is properly completed, the clerk must sign, seal, and issue it to the plaintiff for service on the defendant. A summons—or a copy of a summons that is addressed to multiple defendants—must be issued for each defendant to be served.

(c) Service.

    (1) *In General.* A summons must be served with a copy of the complaint. The plaintiff is responsible for having the summons and complaint served within the time allowed by Rule 4(m) and must furnish the necessary copies to the person who makes service.

(2) *By Whom.* Any person who is at least 18 years old and not a party may serve a summons and complaint.

(3) *By a Marshal or Someone Specially Appointed.* At the plaintiff's request, the court may order that service be made by a United States marshal or deputy marshal or by a person specially appointed by the court. The court must so order if the plaintiff is authorized to proceed in forma pauperis under 28 U.S.C. § 1915 or as a seaman under 28 U.S.C. § 1916.

(d) Waiving Service.

(1) *Requesting a Waiver.* An individual, corporation, or association that is subject to service under Rule 4(e), (f), or (h) has a duty to avoid unnecessary expenses of serving the summons. The plaintiff may notify such a defendant that an action has been commenced and request that the defendant waive service of a summons. The notice and request must:

    (A) be in writing and be addressed:

        (i)   to the individual defendant; or

        (ii)   for a defendant subject to service under Rule 4(h), to an officer, a managing or general agent, or any other agent authorized by appointment or by law to receive service of process;

    (B) name the court where the complaint was filed;

    (C) be accompanied by a copy of the complaint, 2 copies of the waiver form appended to this Rule 4, and a prepaid means for returning the form;

    (D) inform the defendant, using the form appended to this Rule 4, of the consequences of waiving and not waiving service;

    (E) state the date when the request is sent;

    (F) give the defendant a reasonable time of at least 30 days after the request was sent—or at least 60 days if sent to the defendant outside any judicial district of the United States—to return the waiver; and

    (G) be sent by first-class mail or other reliable means.

(2) *Failure to Waive.* If a defendant located within the United States fails, without good cause, to sign and return a waiver requested by a plaintiff located within the United States, the court must impose on the defendant:

    (A) the expenses later incurred in making service; and

    (B) the reasonable expenses, including attorney's fees, of any motion required to collect those service expenses.

(3) *Time to Answer After a Waiver.* A defendant who, before being served with process, timely returns a waiver need not serve an answer to the complaint until 60 days after the request was sent—or until 90 days after it was sent to the defendant outside any judicial district of the United States.

(4) *Results of Filing a Waiver.* When the plaintiff files a waiver, proof of service is not required and these rules apply as if a summons and complaint had been served at the time of filing the waiver.

(5) *Jurisdiction and Venue Not Waived.* Waiving service of a summons does not waive any objection to personal jurisdiction or to venue.

(e) Serving an Individual within a Judicial District of the United States. Unless federal law provides otherwise, an individual—other than a minor, an incompetent person, or a person whose waiver has been filed—may be served in a judicial district of the United States by:

> (1) following state law for serving a summons in an action brought in courts of general jurisdiction in the state where the district court is located or where service is made; or

> (2) doing any of the following:

>> (A) delivering a copy of the summons and of the complaint to the individual personally;

>> (B) leaving a copy of each at the individual's dwelling or usual place of abode with someone of suitable age and discretion who resides there; or

>> (C) delivering a copy of each to an agent authorized by appointment or by law to receive service of process.

(f) Serving an Individual in a Foreign Country. Unless federal law provides otherwise, an individual—other than a minor, an incompetent person, or a person whose waiver has been filed—may be served at a place not within any judicial district of the United States:

> (1) by any internationally agreed means of service that is reasonably calculated to give notice, such as those authorized by the Hague Convention on the Service Abroad of Judicial and Extrajudicial Documents;

> (2) if there is no internationally agreed means, or if an international agreement allows but does not specify other means, by a method that is reasonably calculated to give notice:

>> (A) as prescribed by the foreign country's law for service in that country in an action in its courts of general jurisdiction;

>> (B) as the foreign authority directs in response to a letter rogatory or letter of request; or

>> (C) unless prohibited by the foreign country's law, by:

>>> (i) delivering a copy of the summons and of the complaint to the individual personally; or

>>> (ii) using any form of mail that the clerk addresses and sends to the individual and that requires a signed receipt; or

> (3) by other means not prohibited by international agreement, as the court orders.

(g) Serving a Minor or an Incompetent Person. A minor or an incompetent person in a judicial district of the United States must be served by following state law for serving a summons or like process on such a defendant in an action brought in the courts of general jurisdiction of the state where service is made. A minor or an incompetent person who is not within any judicial district of the United States must be served in the manner prescribed by Rule 4(f)(2)(A), (f)(2)(B), or (f)(3).

(h) Serving a Corporation, Partnership, or Association. Unless federal law provides otherwise or the defendant's waiver has been filed, a domestic or foreign corporation, or a partnership or other unincorporated association that is subject to suit under a common name, must be served:

> (1) in a judicial district of the United States:

>> (A) in the manner prescribed by Rule 4(e)(1) for serving an individual; or

>> (B) by delivering a copy of the summons and of the complaint to an officer, a managing or general agent, or any other agent authorized by appointment or by law to receive

service of process and—if the agent is one authorized by statute and the statute so requires—by also mailing a copy of each to the defendant; or

(2) at a place not within any judicial district of the United States, in any manner prescribed by Rule 4(f) for serving an individual, except personal delivery under (f)(2)(C)(i).

(i) Serving the United States and its Agencies, Corporations, Officers, or Employees.

(1) *United States.* To serve the United States, a party must:

(A)

(i) deliver a copy of the summons and of the complaint to the United States attorney for the district where the action is brought—or to an assistant United States attorney or clerical employee whom the United States attorney designates in a writing filed with the court clerk—or

(ii) send a copy of each by registered or certified mail to the civil-process clerk at the United States attorney's office;

(B) send a copy of each by registered or certified mail to the Attorney General of the United States at Washington, D.C.; and

(C) if the action challenges an order of a nonparty agency or officer of the United States, send a copy of each by registered or certified mail to the agency or officer.

(2) *Agency; Corporation; Officer or Employee Sued in an Official Capacity.* To serve a United States agency or corporation, or a United States officer or employee sued only in an official capacity, a party must serve the United States and also send a copy of the summons and of the complaint by registered or certified mail to the agency, corporation, officer, or employee.

(3) *Officer or Employee Sued Individually.* To serve a United States officer or employee sued in an individual capacity for an act or omission occurring in connection with duties performed on the United States' behalf (whether or not the officer or employee is also sued in an official capacity), a party must serve the United States and also serve the officer or employee under Rule 4(e), (f), or (g).

(4) *Extending Time.* The court must allow a party a reasonable time to cure its failure to:

(A) serve a person required to be served under Rule 4(i)(2), if the party has served either the United States attorney or the Attorney General of the United States; or

(B) serve the United States under Rule 4(i)(3), if the party has served the United States officer or employee.

(j) Serving a Foreign, State, or Local Government.

(1) *Foreign State.* A foreign state or its political subdivision, agency, or instrumentality must be served in accordance with 28 U.S.C. § 1608.

(2) *State or Local Government.* A state, a municipal corporation, or any other state-created governmental organization that is subject to suit must be served by:

(A) delivering a copy of the summons and of the complaint to its chief executive officer; or

(B) serving a copy of each in the manner prescribed by that state's law for serving a summons or like process on such a defendant.

(k) Territorial Limits of Effective Service.

    (1) *In General.* Serving a summons or filing a waiver of service establishes personal jurisdiction over a defendant:

        (A) who is subject to the jurisdiction of a court of general jurisdiction in the state where the district court is located;

        (B) who is a party joined under Rule 14 or 19 and is served within a judicial district of the United States and not more than 100 miles from where the summons was issued; or

        (C) when authorized by a federal statute.

    (2) *Federal Claim Outside State-Court Jurisdiction.* For a claim that arises under federal law, serving a summons or filing a waiver of service establishes personal jurisdiction over a defendant if:

        (A) the defendant is not subject to jurisdiction in any state's courts of general jurisdiction; and

        (B) exercising jurisdiction is consistent with the United States Constitution and laws.

(l) Proving Service.

    (1) *Affidavit Required.* Unless service is waived, proof of service must be made to the court. Except for service by a United States marshal or deputy marshal, proof must be by the server's affidavit.

    (2) *Service Outside the United States.* Service not within any judicial district of the United States must be proved as follows:

        (A) if made under Rule 4(f)(1), as provided in the applicable treaty or convention; or

        (B) if made under Rule 4(f)(2) or (f)(3), by a receipt signed by the addressee, or by other evidence satisfying the court that the summons and complaint were delivered to the addressee.

    (3) *Validity of Service; Amending Proof.* Failure to prove service does not affect the validity of service. The court may permit proof of service to be amended.

(m) Time Limit for Service. If a defendant is not served within 90 days after the complaint is filed, the court—on motion or on its own after notice to the plaintiff—must dismiss the action without prejudice against that defendant or order that service be made within a specified time. But if the plaintiff shows good cause for the failure, the court must extend the time for service for an appropriate period. This subdivision (m) does not apply to service in a foreign country under Rule 4(f) or 4(j)(1) or to service of a notice under Rule 71.1(d)(3)(A).

(n) Asserting Jurisdiction over Property or Assets.

    (1) *Federal Law.* The court may assert jurisdiction over property if authorized by a federal statute. Notice to claimants of the property must be given as provided in the statute or by serving a summons under this rule.

    (2) *State Law.* On a showing that personal jurisdiction over a defendant cannot be obtained in the district where the action is brought by reasonable efforts to serve a summons under this rule, the court may assert jurisdiction over the defendant's assets found in the district. Jurisdiction is acquired by seizing the assets under the circumstances and in the manner provided by state law in that district.

Rule 4 Notice of a Lawsuit and Request to Waive Service of Summons.

(Caption)

To (*name the defendant or – if the defendant is a corporation, partnership, or association – name an officer or agent authorized to receive service*):

Why are you getting this?

A lawsuit has been filed against you, or the entity you represent, in this court under the number shown above. A copy of the complaint is attached.

This is not a summons, or an official notice from the court. It is a request that, to avoid expenses, you waive the formal service of a summons by signing and returning the enclosed waiver. To avoid these expenses, you must return the signed waiver within (*give at least 30 days or at least 60 days if the defendant is outside any judicial district of the United States*) from the date shown below, which is the date this notice was sent. Two copies of the waiver form are enclosed, along with a stamped, self-addressed envelope or other prepaid means for returning one copy. You may keep the other copy.

What happens next?

If you return the signed waiver, I will file it with the court. The action will then proceed as if you had been served on the date the waiver is filed, but no summons will be served on you and you will have 60 days from the date this notice is sent (see the date below) to answer the complaint (or 90 days if this notice is sent to you outside any judicial district of the United States).

If you do not return the signed waiver within the time indicated, I will arrange to have the summons and complaint served on you. And I will ask the court to require you, or the entity you represent, to pay the expenses of making service.

Please read the enclosed statement about the duty to avoid unnecessary expenses.

I certify that this request is being sent to you on the date below.

Date: _____

_____

(Signature of the attorney
or unrepresented party)

_____

(Printed name)

_____

(Address)

_____

(E-mail address)

_____

(Telephone number)

Rule 4 Waiver of the Service of Summons.

(Caption)

To (*name the plaintiff's attorney or the unrepresented plaintiff*):

I have received your request to waive service of a summons in this action along with a copy of the complaint, two copies of this waiver form, and a prepaid means of returning one signed copy of the form to you.

I, or the entity I represent, agree to save the expense of serving a summons and complaint in this case.

I understand that I, or the entity I represent, will keep all defenses or objections to the lawsuit, the court's jurisdiction, and the venue of the action, but that I waive any objections to the absence of a summons or of service.

I also understand that I, or the entity I represent, must file and serve an answer or a motion under Rule 12 within 60 days from _____, the date when this request was sent (or 90 days if it was sent outside the United States). If I fail to do so, a default judgment will be entered against me or the entity I represent.

Date: _____

_____
(Signature of the attorney
or unrepresented party)

_____
(Printed Name)

_____
(Address)

_____
(E-mail address)

_____
(Telephone number)

(Attach the following)

Duty to Avoid Unnecessary Expenses
of Serving a Summons

Rule 4 of the Federal Rules of Civil Procedure requires certain defendants to cooperate in saving unnecessary expenses of serving a summons and complaint. A defendant who is located in the United States and who fails to return a signed waiver of service requested by a plaintiff located in the United States will be required to pay the expenses of service, unless the defendant shows good cause for the failure.

"Good cause" does not include a belief that the lawsuit is groundless, or that it has been brought in an improper venue, or that the court has no jurisdiction over this matter or over the defendant or the defendant's property.

If the waiver is signed and returned, you can still make these and all other defenses and objections, but you cannot object to the absence of a summons or of service.

If you waive service, then you must, within the time specified on the waiver form, serve an answer or a motion under Rule 12 on the plaintiff and file a copy with the court. By signing and returning the waiver form, you are allowed more time to respond than if a summons had been served.

Rule 4.1. Serving Other Process

(a) In General. Process—other than a summons under Rule 4 or a subpoena under Rule 45—must be served by a United States marshal or deputy marshal or by a person specially appointed for that purpose. It may be served anywhere within the territorial limits of the state where the district court is located and, if authorized by a federal statute, beyond those limits. Proof of service must be made under Rule 4(*l*).

(b) Enforcing Orders: Committing For Civil Contempt. An order committing a person for civil contempt of a decree or injunction issued to enforce federal law may be served and enforced in any district. Any other order in a civil-contempt proceeding may be served only in the state where the issuing court is located or elsewhere in the United States within 100 miles from where the order was issued.

Rule 5. Serving and Filing Pleadings and Other Papers

(a) Service: When Required.

(1) *In General.* Unless these rules provide otherwise, each of the following papers must be served on every party:

(A) an order stating that service is required;

(B) a pleading filed after the original complaint, unless the court orders otherwise under Rule 5(c) because there are numerous defendants;

(C) a discovery paper required to be served on a party, unless the court orders otherwise;

(D) a written motion, except one that may be heard ex parte; and

(E) a written notice, appearance, demand, or offer of judgment, or any similar paper.

(2) *If a Party Fails to Appear.* No service is required on a party who is in default for failing to appear. But a pleading that asserts a new claim for relief against such a party must be served on that party under Rule 4.

(3) *Seizing Property.* If an action is begun by seizing property and no person is or need be named as a defendant, any service required before the filing of an appearance, answer, or claim must be made on the person who had custody or possession of the property when it was seized.

(b) Service: How Made.

(1) *Serving an Attorney.* If a party is represented by an attorney, service under this rule must be made on the attorney unless the court orders service on the party.

(2) *Service in General.* A paper is served under this rule by:

    (A) handing it to the person;

    (B) leaving it:

        (i) at the person's office with a clerk or other person in charge or, if no one is in charge, in a conspicuous place in the office; or

        (ii) if the person has no office or the office is closed, at the person's dwelling or usual place of abode with someone of suitable age and discretion who resides there;

    (C) mailing it to the person's last known address—in which event service is complete upon mailing;

    (D) leaving it with the court clerk if the person has no known address;

    (E) sending it by electronic means if the person consented in writing—in which event service is complete upon transmission, but is not effective if the serving party learns that it did not reach the person to be served; or

    (F) delivering it by any other means that the person consented to in writing—in which event service is complete when the person making service delivers it to the agency designated to make delivery.

(3) *Using Court Facilities.* If a local rule so authorizes, a party may use the court's transmission facilities to make service under Rule 5(b)(2)(E).

(c) Serving Numerous Defendants.

(1) *In General.* If an action involves an unusually large number of defendants, the court may, on motion or on its own, order that:

    (A) defendants' pleadings and replies to them need not be served on other defendants;

    (B) any crossclaim, counterclaim, avoidance, or affirmative defense in those pleadings and replies to them will be treated as denied or avoided by all other parties; and

    (C) filing any such pleading and serving it on the plaintiff constitutes notice of the pleading to all parties.

(2) *Notifying Parties.* A copy of every such order must be served on the parties as the court directs.

(d) Filing.

(1) *Required Filings; Certificate of Service.* Any paper after the complaint that is required to be served—together with a certificate of service—must be filed within a reasonable time after service. But disclosures under Rule 26(a)(1) or (2) and the following discovery requests and responses must not be filed until they are used in the proceeding or the court orders filing: depositions, interrogatories, requests for documents or tangible things or to permit entry onto land, and requests for admission.

(2) *How Filing Is Made—In General.* A paper is filed by delivering it:

    (A) to the clerk; or

    (B) to a judge who agrees to accept it for filing, and who must then note the filing date on the paper and promptly send it to the clerk.

(3) *Electronic Filing, Signing, or Verification.* A court may, by local rule, allow papers to be filed, signed, or verified by electronic means that are consistent with any technical standards established by the Judicial Conference of the United States. A local rule may require electronic

filing only if reasonable exceptions are allowed. A paper filed electronically in compliance with a local rule is a written paper for purposes of these rules.

(4) *Acceptance by the Clerk.* The clerk must not refuse to file a paper solely because it is not in the form prescribed by these rules or by a local rule or practice.

Rule 5.1. Constitutional Challenge to a Statute—Notice, Certification, and Intervention

(a) Notice by a Party. A party that files a pleading, written motion, or other paper drawing into question the constitutionality of a federal or state statute must promptly:

(1) file a notice of constitutional question stating the question and identifying the paper that raises it, if:

(A) a federal statute is questioned and the parties do not include the United States, one of its agencies, or one of its officers or employees in an official capacity; or

(B) a state statute is questioned and the parties do not include the state, one of its agencies, or one of its officers or employees in an official capacity; and

(2) serve the notice and paper on the Attorney General of the United States if a federal statute is questioned—or on the state attorney general if a state statute is questioned—either by certified or registered mail or by sending it to an electronic address designated by the attorney general for this purpose.

(b) Certification by the Court. The court must, under 28 U.S.C. § 2403, certify to the appropriate attorney general that a statute has been questioned.

(c) Intervention; Final Decision on the Merits. Unless the court sets a later time, the attorney general may intervene within 60 days after the notice is filed or after the court certifies the challenge, whichever is earlier. Before the time to intervene expires, the court may reject the constitutional challenge, but may not enter a final judgment holding the statute unconstitutional.

(d) No Forfeiture. A party's failure to file and serve the notice, or the court's failure to certify, does not forfeit a constitutional claim or defense that is otherwise timely asserted.

Rule 5.2. Privacy Protection For Filings Made with the Court

(a) Redacted Filings. Unless the court orders otherwise, in an electronic or paper filing with the court that contains an individual's social-security number, taxpayer-identification number, or birth date, the name of an individual known to be a minor, or a financial-account number, a party or nonparty making the filing may include only:

(1) the last four digits of the social-security number and taxpayer-identification number;

(2) the year of the individual's birth;

(3) the minor's initials; and

(4) the last four digits of the financial-account number.

(b) Exemptions from the Redaction Requirement. The redaction requirement does not apply to the following:

(1) a financial-account number that identifies the property allegedly subject to forfeiture in a forfeiture proceeding;

    (2) the record of an administrative or agency proceeding;

    (3) the official record of a state-court proceeding;

    (4) the record of a court or tribunal, if that record was not subject to the redaction requirement when originally filed;

    (5) a filing covered by Rule 5.2(c) or (d); and

    (6) a pro se filing in an action brought under 28 U.S.C. §§ 2241, 2254, or 2255.

(c) Limitations on Remote Access to Electronic Files; Social-Security Appeals and Immigration Cases. Unless the court orders otherwise, in an action for benefits under the Social Security Act, and in an action or proceeding relating to an order of removal, to relief from removal, or to immigration benefits or detention, access to an electronic file is authorized as follows:

    (1) the parties and their attorneys may have remote electronic access to any part of the case file, including the administrative record;

    (2) any other person may have electronic access to the full record at the courthouse, but may have remote electronic access only to:

        (A) the docket maintained by the court; and

        (B) an opinion, order, judgment, or other disposition of the court, but not any other part of the case file or the administrative record.

(d) Filings Made Under Seal. The court may order that a filing be made under seal without redaction. The court may later unseal the filing or order the person who made the filing to file a redacted version for the public record.

(e) Protective Orders. For good cause, the court may by order in a case:

    (1) require redaction of additional information; or

    (2) limit or prohibit a nonparty's remote electronic access to a document filed with the court.

(f) Option for Additional Unredacted Filing Under Seal. A person making a redacted filing may also file an unredacted copy under seal. The court must retain the unredacted copy as part of the record.

(g) Option for Filing a Reference List. A filing that contains redacted information may be filed together with a reference list that identifies each item of redacted information and specifies an appropriate identifier that uniquely corresponds to each item listed. The list must be filed under seal and may be amended as of right. Any reference in the case to a listed identifier will be construed to refer to the corresponding item of information.

(h) Waiver of Protection of Identifiers. A person waives the protection of Rule 5.2(a) as to the person's own information by filing it without redaction and not under seal.

Rule 6. Computing and Extending Time; Time for Motion Papers

(a) Computing Time. The following rules apply in computing any time period specified in these rules, in any local rule or court order, or in any statute that does not specify a method of computing time.

    (1) *Period Stated in Days or a Longer Unit.* When the period is stated in days or a longer unit of time:

        (A) exclude the day of the event that triggers the period;

        (B) count every day, including intermediate Saturdays, Sundays, and legal holidays; and

(C) include the last day of the period, but if the last day is a Saturday, Sunday, or legal holiday, the period continues to run until the end of the next day that is not a Saturday, Sunday, or legal holiday.

(2) *Period Stated in Hours.* When the period is stated in hours:

(A) begin counting immediately on the occurrence of the event that triggers the period;

(B) count every hour, including hours during intermediate Saturdays, Sundays, and legal holidays; and

(C) if the period would end on a Saturday, Sunday, or legal holiday, the period continues to run until the same time on the next day that is not a Saturday, Sunday, or legal holiday.

(3) *Inaccessibility of the Clerk's Office.* Unless the court orders otherwise, if the clerk's office is inaccessible:

(A) on the last day for filing under Rule 6(a)(1), then the time for filing is extended to the first accessible day that is not a Saturday, Sunday, or legal holiday; or

(B) during the last hour for filing under Rule 6(a)(2), then the time for filing is extended to the same time on the first accessible day that is not a Saturday, Sunday, or legal holiday.

(4) *"Last Day" Defined.* Unless a different time is set by a statute, local rule, or court order, the last day ends:

(A) for electronic filing, at midnight in the court's time zone; and

(B) for filing by other means, when the clerk's office is scheduled to close.

(5) *"Next Day" Defined.* The "next day" is determined by continuing to count forward when the period is measured after an event and backward when measured before an event.

(6) *"Legal Holiday" Defined.* "Legal holiday" means:

(A) the day set aside by statute for observing New Year's Day, Martin Luther King Jr.'s Birthday, Washington's Birthday, Memorial Day, Independence Day, Labor Day, Columbus Day, Veterans' Day, Thanksgiving Day, or Christmas Day;

(B) any day declared a holiday by the President or Congress; and

(C) for periods that are measured after an event, any other day declared a holiday by the state where the district court is located.

(b) Extending Time.

(1) *In General.* When an act may or must be done within a specified time, the court may, for good cause, extend the time:

(A) with or without motion or notice if the court acts, or if a request is made, before the original time or its extension expires; or

(B) on motion made after the time has expired if the party failed to act because of excusable neglect.

(2) *Exceptions.* A court must not extend the time to act under Rules 50(b) and (d), 52(b), 59(b), (d), and (e), and 60(b).

(c) Motions, Notices of Hearing, and Affidavits.

(1) *In General.* A written motion and notice of the hearing must be served at least 14 days before the time specified for the hearing, with the following exceptions:

    (A) when the motion may be heard ex parte;

    (B) when these rules set a different time; or

    (C) when a court order—which a party may, for good cause, apply for ex parte—sets a different time.

(2) *Supporting Affidavit.* Any affidavit supporting a motion must be served with the motion. Except as Rule 59(c) provides otherwise, any opposing affidavit must be served at least 7 days before the hearing, unless the court permits service at another time.

(d) Additional Time After Certain Kinds of Service. When a party may or must act within a specified time after service and service is made under Rule 5(b)(2)(C), (D), (E), or (F), 3 days are added after the period would otherwise expire under Rule 6(a).

TITLE III. PLEADINGS AND MOTIONS

Rule 7. Pleadings Allowed; Form of Motions and Other Papers

(a) Pleadings. Only these pleadings are allowed:

    (1) a complaint;

    (2) an answer to a complaint;

    (3) an answer to a counterclaim designated as a counterclaim;

    (4) an answer to a crossclaim;

    (5) a third-party complaint;

    (6) an answer to a third-party complaint; and

    (7) if the court orders one, a reply to an answer.

(b) Motions and Other Papers.

(1) *In General.* A request for a court order must be made by motion. The motion must:

    (A) be in writing unless made during a hearing or trial;

    (B) state with particularity the grounds for seeking the order; and

    (C) state the relief sought.

(2) *Form.* The rules governing captions and other matters of form in pleadings apply to motions and other papers.

Rule 7.1. Disclosure Statement

(a) Who Must File; Contents. A nongovernmental corporate party must file 2 copies of a disclosure statement that:

    (1) identifies any parent corporation and any publicly held corporation owning 10% or more of its stock; or

    (2) states that there is no such corporation.

(b) Time To File; Supplemental Filing. A party must:

    (1) file the disclosure statement with its first appearance, pleading, petition, motion, response, or other request addressed to the court; and

    (2) promptly file a supplemental statement if any required information changes.

Rule 8. General Rules of Pleading

(a) Claim for Relief. A pleading that states a claim for relief must contain:

    (1) a short and plain statement of the grounds for the court's jurisdiction, unless the court already has jurisdiction and the claim needs no new jurisdictional support;

    (2) a short and plain statement of the claim showing that the pleader is entitled to relief; and

    (3) a demand for the relief sought, which may include relief in the alternative or different types of relief.

(b) Defenses; Admissions and Denials.

    (1) *In General.* In responding to a pleading, a party must:

        (A) state in short and plain terms its defenses to each claim asserted against it; and

        (B) admit or deny the allegations asserted against it by an opposing party.

    (2) *Denials—Responding to the Substance.* A denial must fairly respond to the substance of the allegation.

    (3) *General and Specific Denials.* A party that intends in good faith to deny all the allegations of a pleading—including the jurisdictional grounds—may do so by a general denial. A party that does not intend to deny all the allegations must either specifically deny designated allegations or generally deny all except those specifically admitted.

    (4) *Denying Part of an Allegation.* A party that intends in good faith to deny only part of an allegation must admit the part that is true and deny the rest.

    (5) *Lacking Knowledge or Information.* A party that lacks knowledge or information sufficient to form a belief about the truth of an allegation must so state, and the statement has the effect of a denial.

    (6) *Effect of Failing to Deny.* An allegation—other than one relating to the amount of damages—is admitted if a responsive pleading is required and the allegation is not denied. If a responsive pleading is not required, an allegation is considered denied or avoided.

(c) Affirmative Defenses.

    (1) *In General.* In responding to a pleading, a party must affirmatively state any avoidance or affirmative defense, including:

        • accord and satisfaction;

        • arbitration and award;

        • assumption of risk;

        • contributory negligence;

        • duress;

        • estoppel;

- failure of consideration;
- fraud;
- illegality;
- injury by fellow servant;
- laches;
- license;
- payment;
- release;
- res judicata;
- statute of frauds;
- statute of limitations; and
- waiver.

(2) *Mistaken Designation.* If a party mistakenly designates a defense as a counterclaim, or a counterclaim as a defense, the court must, if justice requires, treat the pleading as though it were correctly designated, and may impose terms for doing so.

(d) Pleading to be Concise And Direct; Alternative Statements; Inconsistency.

(1) *In General.* Each allegation must be simple, concise, and direct. No technical form is required.

(2) *Alternative Statements of a Claim or Defense.* A party may set out 2 or more statements of a claim or defense alternatively or hypothetically, either in a single count or defense or in separate ones. If a party makes alternative statements, the pleading is sufficient if any one of them is sufficient.

(3) *Inconsistent Claims or Defenses.* A party may state as many separate claims or defenses as it has, regardless of consistency.

(e) Construing Pleadings. Pleadings must be construed so as to do justice.

Rule 9. Pleading Special Matters

(a) Capacity or Authority to Sue; Legal Existence.

(1) *In General.* Except when required to show that the court has jurisdiction, a pleading need not allege:

(A) a party's capacity to sue or be sued;

(B) a party's authority to sue or be sued in a representative capacity; or

(C) the legal existence of an organized association of persons that is made a party.

(2) *Raising Those Issues.* To raise any of those issues, a party must do so by a specific denial, which must state any supporting facts that are peculiarly within the party's knowledge.

(b) Fraud or Mistake; Conditions of Mind. In alleging fraud or mistake, a party must state with particularity the circumstances constituting fraud or mistake. Malice, intent, knowledge, and other conditions of a person's mind may be alleged generally.

(c) Conditions Precedent. In pleading conditions precedent, it suffices to allege generally that all conditions precedent have occurred or been performed. But when denying that a condition precedent has occurred or been performed, a party must do so with particularity.

(d) Official Document or Act. In pleading an official document or official act, it suffices to allege that the document was legally issued or the act legally done.

(e) Judgment. In pleading a judgment or decision of a domestic or foreign court, a judicial or quasi-judicial tribunal, or a board or officer, it suffices to plead the judgment or decision without showing jurisdiction to render it.

(f) Time and Place. An allegation of time or place is material when testing the sufficiency of a pleading.

(g) Special Damages. If an item of special damage is claimed, it must be specifically stated.

(h) Admiralty Or Maritime Claim.

> (1) *How Designated.* If a claim for relief is within the admiralty or maritime jurisdiction and also within the court's subject-matter jurisdiction on some other ground, the pleading may designate the claim as an admiralty or maritime claim for purposes of Rules 14(c), 38(e), and 82 and the Supplemental Rules for Admiralty or Maritime Claims and Asset Forfeiture Actions. A claim cognizable only in the admiralty or maritime jurisdiction is an admiralty or maritime claim for those purposes, whether or not so designated.

> (2) *Designation for Appeal.* A case that includes an admiralty or maritime claim within this subdivision (h) is an admiralty case within 28 U.S.C. § 1292(a)(3).

Rule 10. Form of Pleadings

(a) Caption; Names of Parties. Every pleading must have a caption with the court's name, a title, a file number, and a Rule 7(a) designation. The title of the complaint must name all the parties; the title of other pleadings, after naming the first party on each side, may refer generally to other parties.

(b) Paragraphs; Separate Statements. A party must state its claims or defenses in numbered paragraphs, each limited as far as practicable to a single set of circumstances. A later pleading may refer by number to a paragraph in an earlier pleading. If doing so would promote clarity, each claim founded on a separate transaction or occurrence—and each defense other than a denial—must be stated in a separate count or defense.

(c) Adoption By Reference; Exhibits. A statement in a pleading may be adopted by reference elsewhere in the same pleading or in any other pleading or motion. A copy of a written instrument that is an exhibit to a pleading is a part of the pleading for all purposes.

Rule 11. Signing Pleadings, Motions, and Other Papers; Representations to the Court; Sanctions

(a) Signature. Every pleading, written motion, and other paper must be signed by at least one attorney of record in the attorney's name—or by a party personally if the party is unrepresented. The paper must state the signer's address, e-mail address, and telephone number. Unless a rule or statute specifically states otherwise, a pleading need not be verified or accompanied by an affidavit. The court must strike an unsigned paper unless the omission is promptly corrected after being called to the attorney's or party's attention.

(b) Representations to the Court. By presenting to the court a pleading, written motion, or other paper—whether by signing, filing, submitting, or later advocating it—an attorney or unrepresented party certifies that to the best of the person's knowledge, information, and belief, formed after an inquiry reasonable under the circumstances:

(1) it is not being presented for any improper purpose, such as to harass, cause unnecessary delay, or needlessly increase the cost of litigation;

(2) the claims, defenses, and other legal contentions are warranted by existing law or by a nonfrivolous argument for extending, modifying, or reversing existing law or for establishing new law;

(3) the factual contentions have evidentiary support or, if specifically so identified, will likely have evidentiary support after a reasonable opportunity for further investigation or discovery; and

(4) the denials of factual contentions are warranted on the evidence or, if specifically so identified, are reasonably based on belief or a lack of information.

(c) Sanctions.

(1) *In General.* If, after notice and a reasonable opportunity to respond, the court determines that Rule 11(b) has been violated, the court may impose an appropriate sanction on any attorney, law firm, or party that violated the rule or is responsible for the violation. Absent exceptional circumstances, a law firm must be held jointly responsible for a violation committed by its partner, associate, or employee.

(2) *Motion for Sanctions.* A motion for sanctions must be made separately from any other motion and must describe the specific conduct that allegedly violates Rule 11(b). The motion must be served under Rule 5, but it must not be filed or be presented to the court if the challenged paper, claim, defense, contention, or denial is withdrawn or appropriately corrected within 21 days after service or within another time the court sets. If warranted, the court may award to the prevailing party the reasonable expenses, including attorney's fees, incurred for the motion.

(3) *On the Court's Initiative.* On its own, the court may order an attorney, law firm, or party to show cause why conduct specifically described in the order has not violated Rule 11(b).

(4) *Nature of a Sanction.* A sanction imposed under this rule must be limited to what suffices to deter repetition of the conduct or comparable conduct by others similarly situated. The sanction may include nonmonetary directives; an order to pay a penalty into court; or, if imposed on motion and warranted for effective deterrence, an order directing payment to the movant of part or all of the reasonable attorney's fees and other expenses directly resulting from the violation.

(5) *Limitations on Monetary Sanctions.* The court must not impose a monetary sanction:

(A) against a represented party for violating Rule 11(b)(2); or

(B) on its own, unless it issued the show-cause order under Rule 11(c)(3) before voluntary dismissal or settlement of the claims made by or against the party that is, or whose attorneys are, to be sanctioned.

(6) *Requirements for an Order.* An order imposing a sanction must describe the sanctioned conduct and explain the basis for the sanction.

(d) Inapplicability to Discovery. This rule does not apply to disclosures and discovery requests, responses, objections, and motions under Rules 26 through 37.

Rule 12. Defenses and Objections: When and How Presented; Motion for Judgment on the Pleadings; Consolidating Motions; Waiving Defenses; Pretrial Hearing

(a) Time to Serve a Responsive Pleading.

(1) *In General.* Unless another time is specified by this rule or a federal statute, the time for serving a responsive pleading is as follows:

(A) A defendant must serve an answer:

(i) within 21 days after being served with the summons and complaint; or

(ii) if it has timely waived service under Rule 4(d), within 60 days after the request for a waiver was sent or within 90 days after it was sent to the defendant outside any judicial district of the United States.

(B) A party must serve an answer to a counterclaim or crossclaim within 21 days after being served with the pleading that states the counterclaim or crossclaim.

(C) A party must serve a reply to an answer within 21 days after being served with an order to reply, unless the order specifies a different time.

(2) *United States and Its Agencies, Officers, or Employees Sued in an Official Capacity.* The United States, a United States agency, or a United States officer or employee sued only in an official capacity must serve an answer to a complaint, counterclaim, or crossclaim within 60 days after service on the United States attorney.

(3) *United States Officers or Employees Sued in an Individual Capacity.* A United States officer or employee sued in an individual capacity for an act or omission occurring in connection with duties performed on the United States' behalf must serve an answer to a complaint, counterclaim, or crossclaim within 60 days after service on the officer or employee or service on the United States attorney, whichever is later.

(4) *Effect of a Motion.* Unless the court sets a different time, serving a motion under this rule alters these periods as follows:

(A) if the court denies the motion or postpones its disposition until trial, the responsive pleading must be served within 14 days after notice of the court's action; or

(B) if the court grants a motion for a more definite statement, the responsive pleading must be served within 14 days after the more definite statement is served.

(b) How to Present Defenses. Every defense to a claim for relief in any pleading must be asserted in the responsive pleading if one is required. But a party may assert the following defenses by motion:

(1) lack of subject-matter jurisdiction;

(2) lack of personal jurisdiction;

(3) improper venue;

(4) insufficient process;

(5) insufficient service of process;

(6) failure to state a claim upon which relief can be granted; and

(7) failure to join a party under Rule 19.

A motion asserting any of these defenses must be made before pleading if a responsive pleading is allowed. If a pleading sets out a claim for relief that does not require a responsive pleading, an opposing party may assert at trial any defense to that claim. No defense or objection is waived by joining it with one or more other defenses or objections in a responsive pleading or in a motion.

(c) Motion for Judgment on the Pleadings. After the pleadings are closed—but early enough not to delay trial—a party may move for judgment on the pleadings.

(d) Result of Presenting Matters Outside the Pleadings. If, on a motion under Rule 12(b)(6) or 12(c), matters outside the pleadings are presented to and not excluded by the court, the motion must be treated as one for summary judgment under Rule 56. All parties must be given a reasonable opportunity to present all the material that is pertinent to the motion.

(e) Motion for a More Definite Statement. A party may move for a more definite statement of a pleading to which a responsive pleading is allowed but which is so vague or ambiguous that the party cannot reasonably prepare a response. The motion must be made before filing a responsive pleading and must point out the defects complained of and the details desired. If the court orders a more definite statement and the order is not obeyed within 14 days after notice of the order or within the time the court sets, the court may strike the pleading or issue any other appropriate order.

(f) Motion to Strike. The court may strike from a pleading an insufficient defense or any redundant, immaterial, impertinent, or scandalous matter. The court may act:

(1) on its own; or

(2) on motion made by a party either before responding to the pleading or, if a response is not allowed, within 21 days after being served with the pleading.

(g) Joining Motions.

(1) *Right to Join.* A motion under this rule may be joined with any other motion allowed by this rule.

(2) *Limitation on Further Motions.* Except as provided in Rule 12(h)(2) or (3), a party that makes a motion under this rule must not make another motion under this rule raising a defense or objection that was available to the party but omitted from its earlier motion.

(h) Waiving and Preserving Certain Defenses.

(1) *When Some Are Waived.* A party waives any defense listed in Rule 12(b)(2)–(5) by:

(A) omitting it from a motion in the circumstances described in Rule 12(g)(2); or

(B) failing to either:

(i) make it by motion under this rule; or

(ii) include it in a responsive pleading or in an amendment allowed by Rule 15(a)(1) as a matter of course.

(2) *When to Raise Others.* Failure to state a claim upon which relief can be granted, to join a person required by Rule 19(b), or to state a legal defense to a claim may be raised:

(A) in any pleading allowed or ordered under Rule 7(a);

(B) by a motion under Rule 12(c); or

(C) at trial.

(3) *Lack of Subject-Matter Jurisdiction.* If the court determines at any time that it lacks subject-matter jurisdiction, the court must dismiss the action.

(i) Hearing Before Trial. If a party so moves, any defense listed in Rule 12(b)(1)–(7)—whether made in a pleading or by motion— and a motion under Rule 12(c) must be heard and decided before trial unless the court orders a deferral until trial.

Rule 13. Counterclaim and Crossclaim

(a) Compulsory Counterclaim.

(1) *In General.* A pleading must state as a counterclaim any claim that—at the time of its service—the pleader has against an opposing party if the claim:

(A) arises out of the transaction or occurrence that is the subject matter of the opposing party's claim; and

(B) does not require adding another party over whom the court cannot acquire jurisdiction.

(2) *Exceptions.* The pleader need not state the claim if:

(A) when the action was commenced, the claim was the subject of another pending action; or

(B) the opposing party sued on its claim by attachment or other process that did not establish personal jurisdiction over the pleader on that claim, and the pleader does not assert any counterclaim under this rule.

(b) Permissive Counterclaim. A pleading may state as a counterclaim against an opposing party any claim that is not compulsory.

(c) Relief Sought in a Counterclaim. A counterclaim need not diminish or defeat the recovery sought by the opposing party. It may request relief that exceeds in amount or differs in kind from the relief sought by the opposing party.

(d) Counterclaim Against the United States. These rules do not expand the right to assert a counterclaim—or to claim a credit—against the United States or a United States officer or agency.

(e) Counterclaim Maturing or Acquired After Pleading. The court may permit a party to file a supplemental pleading asserting a counterclaim that matured or was acquired by the party after serving an earlier pleading.

(f) [Abrogated.]

(g) Crossclaim Against a Coparty. A pleading may state as a crossclaim any claim by one party against a coparty if the claim arises out of the transaction or occurrence that is the subject matter of the original action or of a counterclaim, or if the claim relates to any property that is the subject matter of the original action. The crossclaim may include a claim that the coparty is or may be liable to the crossclaimant for all or part of a claim asserted in the action against the crossclaimant.

(h) Joining Additional Parties. Rules 19 and 20 govern the addition of a person as a party to a counterclaim or crossclaim.

(i) Separate Trials; Separate Judgments. If the court orders separate trials under Rule 42(b), it may enter judgment on a counterclaim or crossclaim under Rule 54(b) when it has jurisdiction to do so, even if the opposing party's claims have been dismissed or otherwise resolved.

Rule 14. Third-Party Practice

(a) When a Defending Party May Bring in a Third Party.

(1) *Timing of the Summons and Complaint.* A defending party may, as third-party plaintiff, serve a summons and complaint on a nonparty who is or may be liable to it for all or part of the claim against it. But the third-party plaintiff must, by motion, obtain the court's leave if it files the third-party complaint more than 14 days after serving its original answer.

(2) *Third-Party Defendant's Claims and Defenses.* The person served with the summons and third-party complaint—the "third-party defendant":

> (A) must assert any defense against the third-party plaintiff's claim under Rule 12;
>
> (B) must assert any counterclaim against the third-party plaintiff under Rule 13(a), and may assert any counterclaim against the third-party plaintiff under Rule 13(b) or any crossclaim against another third-party defendant under Rule 13(g);
>
> (C) may assert against the plaintiff any defense that the third-party plaintiff has to the plaintiff's claim; and
>
> (D) may also assert against the plaintiff any claim arising out of the transaction or occurrence that is the subject matter of the plaintiff's claim against the third-party plaintiff.

(3) *Plaintiff's Claims Against a Third-Party Defendant.* The plaintiff may assert against the third-party defendant any claim arising out of the transaction or occurrence that is the subject matter of the plaintiff's claim against the third-party plaintiff. The third-party defendant must then assert any defense under Rule 12 and any counterclaim under Rule 13(a), and may assert any counterclaim under Rule 13(b) or any crossclaim under Rule 13(g).

(4) *Motion to Strike, Sever, or Try Separately.* Any party may move to strike the third-party claim, to sever it, or to try it separately.

(5) *Third-Party Defendant's Claim Against a Nonparty.* A third-party defendant may proceed under this rule against a non-party who is or may be liable to the third-party defendant for all or part of any claim against it.

(6) *Third-Party Complaint In Rem.* If it is within the admiralty or maritime jurisdiction, a third-party complaint may be in rem. In that event, a reference in this rule to the "summons" includes the warrant of arrest, and a reference to the defendant or third-party plaintiff includes, when appropriate, a person who asserts a right under Supplemental Rule C(6)(a)(i) in the property arrested.

(b) When a Plaintiff May Bring in a Third Party. When a claim is asserted against a plaintiff, the plaintiff may bring in a third party if this rule would allow a defendant to do so.

(c) Admiralty or Maritime Claim.

(1) *Scope of Impleader.* If a plaintiff asserts an admiralty or maritime claim under Rule 9(h), the defendant or a person who asserts a right under Supplemental Rule C(6)(a)(i) may, as a third-party plaintiff, bring in a third-party defendant who may be wholly or partly liable— either to the plaintiff or to the third-party plaintiff—for remedy over, contribution, or otherwise on account of the same transaction, occurrence, or series of transactions or occurrences.

(2) *Defending Against a Demand for Judgment for the Plaintiff.* The third-party plaintiff may demand judgment in the plaintiff's favor against the third-party defendant. In that event, the third-party defendant must defend under Rule 12 against the plaintiff's claim as well as the third-party plaintiff's claim; and the action proceeds as if the plaintiff had sued both the third-party defendant and the third-party plaintiff.

Rule 15. Amended and Supplemental Pleadings

(a) Amendments Before Trial.

(1) *Amending as a Matter of Course.* A party may amend its pleading once as a matter of course within:

      (A) 21 days after serving it, or

      (B) if the pleading is one to which a responsive pleading is required, 21 days after service of a responsive pleading or 21 days after service of a motion under Rule 12(b), (e), or (f), whichever is earlier.

(2) *Other Amendments.* In all other cases, a party may amend its pleading only with the opposing party's written consent or the court's leave. The court should freely give leave when justice so requires.

(3) *Time to Respond.* Unless the court orders otherwise, any required response to an amended pleading must be made within the time remaining to respond to the original pleading or within 14 days after service of the amended pleading, whichever is later.

(b) Amendments During and After Trial.

(1) *Based on an Objection at Trial.* If, at trial, a party objects that evidence is not within the issues raised in the pleadings, the court may permit the pleadings to be amended. The court should freely permit an amendment when doing so will aid in presenting the merits and the objecting party fails to satisfy the court that the evidence would prejudice that party's action or defense on the merits. The court may grant a continuance to enable the objecting party to meet the evidence.

(2) *For Issues Tried by Consent.* When an issue not raised by the pleadings is tried by the parties' express or implied consent, it must be treated in all respects as if raised in the pleadings. A party may move—at any time, even after judgment— to amend the pleadings to conform them to the evidence and to raise an unpleaded issue. But failure to amend does not affect the result of the trial of that issue.

(c) Relation Back of Amendments.

(1) *When an Amendment Relates Back.* An amendment to a pleading relates back to the date of the original pleading when:

      (A) the law that provides the applicable statute of limitations allows relation back;

      (B) the amendment asserts a claim or defense that arose out of the conduct, transaction, or occurrence set out—or attempted to be set out—in the original pleading; or

      (C) the amendment changes the party or the naming of the party against whom a claim is asserted, if Rule 15(c)(1)(B) is satisfied and if, within the period provided by Rule 4(m) for serving the summons and complaint, the party to be brought in by amendment:

            (i)   received such notice of the action that it will not be prejudiced in defending on the merits; and

            (ii)   knew or should have known that the action would have been brought against it, but for a mistake concerning the proper party's identity.

(2) *Notice to the United States.* When the United States or a United States officer or agency is added as a defendant by amendment, the notice requirements of Rule 15(c)(1)(C)(i) and (ii) are satisfied if, during the stated period, process was delivered or mailed to the United States attorney or the United States attorney's designee, to the Attorney General of the United States, or to the officer or agency.

(d) Supplemental Pleadings. On motion and reasonable notice, the court may, on just terms, permit a party to serve a supplemental pleading setting out any transaction, occurrence, or event that happened after the date of the pleading to be supplemented. The court may permit supplementation even though the original pleading is defective in stating a claim or defense. The court may order that the opposing party plead to the supplemental pleading within a specified time.

Rule 16. Pretrial Conferences; Scheduling; Management

(a) Purposes of a Pretrial Conference. In any action, the court may order the attorneys and any unrepresented parties to appear for one or more pretrial conferences for such purposes as:

(1) expediting disposition of the action;

(2) establishing early and continuing control so that the case will not be protracted because of lack of management;

(3) discouraging wasteful pretrial activities;

(4) improving the quality of the trial through more thorough preparation; and

(5) facilitating settlement.

(b) Scheduling.

(1) *Scheduling Order.* Except in categories of actions exempted by local rule, the district judge—or a magistrate judge when authorized by local rule—must issue a scheduling order:

(A) after receiving the parties' report under Rule 26(f); or

(B) after consulting with the parties' attorneys and any unrepresented parties at a scheduling conference.

(2) *Time to Issue.* The judge must issue the scheduling order as soon as practicable, but unless the judge finds good cause for delay, the judge must issue it within the earlier of 90 days after any defendant has been served with the complaint or 60 days after any defendant has appeared.

(3) *Contents of the Order.*

(A) *Required Contents.* The scheduling order must limit the time to join other parties, amend the pleadings, complete discovery, and file motions.

(B) *Permitted Contents.* The scheduling order may:

(i) modify the timing of disclosures under Rules 26(a) and 26(e)(1);

(ii) modify the extent of discovery;

(iii) provide for disclosure, discovery, or preservation of electronically stored information;

(iv) include any agreements the parties reach for asserting claims of privilege or of protection as trial-preparation material after information is produced, including agreements reached under Federal Rule of Evidence 502;

(v) direct that before moving for an order relating to discovery, the movant must request a conference with the court;

(vi) set dates for pretrial conferences and for trial; and

(vii) include other appropriate matters.

(4) *Modifying a Schedule.* A schedule may be modified only for good cause and with the judge's consent.

(c) Attendance and Matters for Consideration at a Pretrial Conference.

(1) *Attendance.* A represented party must authorize at least one of its attorneys to make stipulations and admissions about all matters that can reasonably be anticipated for discussion at a pretrial conference. If appropriate, the court may require that a party or its representative be present or reasonably available by other means to consider possible settlement.

(2) *Matters for Consideration.* At any pretrial conference, the court may consider and take appropriate action on the following matters:

(A) formulating and simplifying the issues, and eliminating frivolous claims or defenses;

(B) amending the pleadings if necessary or desirable;

(C) obtaining admissions and stipulations about facts and documents to avoid unnecessary proof, and ruling in advance on the admissibility of evidence;

(D) avoiding unnecessary proof and cumulative evidence, and limiting the use of testimony under Federal Rule of Evidence 702;

(E) determining the appropriateness and timing of summary adjudication under Rule 56;

(F) controlling and scheduling discovery, including orders affecting disclosures and discovery under Rule 26 and Rules 29 through 37;

(G) identifying witnesses and documents, scheduling the filing and exchange of any pretrial briefs, and setting dates for further conferences and for trial;

(H) referring matters to a magistrate judge or a master;

(I) settling the case and using special procedures to assist in resolving the dispute when authorized by statute or local rule;

(J) determining the form and content of the pretrial order;

(K) disposing of pending motions;

(L) adopting special procedures for managing potentially difficult or protracted actions that may involve complex issues, multiple parties, difficult legal questions, or unusual proof problems;

(M) ordering a separate trial under Rule 42(b) of a claim, counterclaim, crossclaim, third-party claim, or particular issue;

(N) ordering the presentation of evidence early in the trial on a manageable issue that might, on the evidence, be the basis for a judgment as a matter of law under Rule 50(a) or a judgment on partial findings under Rule 52(c);

(O) establishing a reasonable limit on the time allowed to present evidence; and

(P) facilitating in other ways the just, speedy, and inexpensive disposition of the action.

(d) Pretrial Orders. After any conference under this rule, the court should issue an order reciting the action taken. This order controls the course of the action unless the court modifies it.

(e) Final Pretrial Conference and Orders. The court may hold a final pretrial conference to formulate a trial plan, including a plan to facilitate the admission of evidence. The conference must be held as close to the start of trial as is reasonable, and must be attended by at least one attorney who will conduct the trial for each party and by any unrepresented party. The court may modify the order issued after a final pretrial conference only to prevent manifest injustice.

(f) Sanctions.

(1) *In General.* On motion or on its own, the court may issue any just orders, including those authorized by Rule 37(b)(2)(A)(ii)-(vii), if a party or its attorney:

(A) fails to appear at a scheduling or other pretrial conference;

(B) is substantially unprepared to participate—or does not participate in good faith—in the conference; or

(C) fails to obey a scheduling or other pretrial order.

(2) *Imposing Fees and Costs.* Instead of or in addition to any other sanction, the court must order the party, its attorney, or both to pay the reasonable expenses—including attorney's fees—incurred because of any noncompliance with this rule, unless the noncompliance was substantially justified or other circumstances make an award of expenses unjust.

TITLE IV. PARTIES

Rule 17. Plaintiff and Defendant; Capacity; Public Officers

(a) Real Party in Interest.

(1) *Designation in General.* An action must be prosecuted in the name of the real party in interest. The following may sue in their own names without joining the person for whose benefit the action is brought:

(A) an executor;

(B) an administrator;

(C) a guardian;

(D) a bailee;

(E) a trustee of an express trust;

(F) a party with whom or in whose name a contract has been made for another's benefit; and

(G) a party authorized by statute.

(2) *Action in the Name of the United States for Another's Use or Benefit.* When a federal statute so provides, an action for another's use or benefit must be brought in the name of the United States.

(3) *Joinder of the Real Party in Interest.* The court may not dismiss an action for failure to prosecute in the name of the real party in interest until, after an objection, a reasonable time has been allowed for the real party in interest to ratify, join, or be substituted into the action. After ratification, joinder, or substitution, the action proceeds as if it had been originally commenced by the real party in interest.

(b) Capacity to Sue or Be Sued. Capacity to sue or be sued is determined as follows:

(1) for an individual who is not acting in a representative capacity, by the law of the individual's domicile;

(2) for a corporation, by the law under which it was organized; and

(3) for all other parties, by the law of the state where the court is located, except that:

    (A) a partnership or other unincorporated association with no such capacity under that state's law may sue or be sued in its common name to enforce a substantive right existing under the United States Constitution or laws; and

    (B) 28 U.S.C. §§ 754 and 959(a) govern the capacity of a receiver appointed by a United States court to sue or be sued in a United States court.

(c) Minor or Incompetent Person.

(1) *With a Representative.* The following representatives may sue or defend on behalf of a minor or an incompetent person:

    (A) a general guardian;

    (B) a committee;

    (C) a conservator; or

    (D) a like fiduciary.

(2) *Without a Representative.* A minor or an incompetent person who does not have a duly appointed representative may sue by a next friend or by a guardian ad litem. The court must appoint a guardian ad litem—or issue another appropriate order—to protect a minor or incompetent person who is unrepresented in an action.

(d) Public Officer's Title And Name. A public officer who sues or is sued in an official capacity may be designated by official title rather than by name, but the court may order that the officer's name be added.

Rule 18. Joinder of Claims

(a) In General. A party asserting a claim, counterclaim, crossclaim, or third-party claim may join, as independent or alternative claims, as many claims as it has against an opposing party.

(b) Joinder of Contingent Claims. A party may join two claims even though one of them is contingent on the disposition of the other; but the court may grant relief only in accordance with the parties' relative substantive rights. In particular, a plaintiff may state a claim for money and a claim to set aside a conveyance that is fraudulent as to that plaintiff, without first obtaining a judgment for the money.

Rule 19. Required Joinder of Parties

(a) Persons Required to Be Joined if Feasible.

(1) *Required Party.* A person who is subject to service of process and whose joinder will not deprive the court of subjectmatter jurisdiction must be joined as a party if:

    (A) in that person's absence, the court cannot accord complete relief among existing parties; or

    (B) that person claims an interest relating to the subject of the action and is so situated that disposing of the action in the person's absence may:

        (i) as a practical matter impair or impede the person's ability to protect the interest; or

(ii) leave an existing party subject to a substantial risk of incurring double, multiple, or otherwise inconsistent obligations because of the interest.

(2) *Joinder by Court Order.* If a person has not been joined as required, the court must order that the person be made a party. A person who refuses to join as a plaintiff may be made either a defendant or, in a proper case, an involuntary plaintiff.

(3) *Venue.* If a joined party objects to venue and the joinder would make venue improper, the court must dismiss that party.

(b) When Joinder Is Not Feasible. If a person who is required to be joined if feasible cannot be joined, the court must determine whether, in equity and good conscience, the action should proceed among the existing parties or should be dismissed. The factors for the court to consider include:

(1) the extent to which a judgment rendered in the person's absence might prejudice that person or the existing parties;

(2) the extent to which any prejudice could be lessened or avoided by:

(A) protective provisions in the judgment;

(B) shaping the relief; or

(C) other measures;

(3) whether a judgment rendered in the person's absence would be adequate; and

(4) whether the plaintiff would have an adequate remedy if the action were dismissed for nonjoinder.

(c) Pleading the Reasons for Nonjoinder. When asserting a claim for relief, a party must state:

(1) the name, if known, of any person who is required to be joined if feasible but is not joined; and

(2) the reasons for not joining that person.

(d) Exception For Class Actions. This rule is subject to Rule 23.

Rule 20. Permissive Joinder of Parties

(a) Persons Who May Join or be Joined.

(1) *Plaintiffs.* Persons may join in one action as plaintiffs if:

(A) they assert any right to relief jointly, severally, or in the alternative with respect to or arising out of the same transaction, occurrence, or series of transactions or occurrences; and

(B) any question of law or fact common to all plaintiffs will arise in the action.

(2) *Defendants.* Persons—as well as a vessel, cargo, or other property subject to admiralty process in rem—may be joined in one action as defendants if:

(A) any right to relief is asserted against them jointly, severally, or in the alternative with respect to or arising out of the same transaction, occurrence, or series of transactions or occurrences; and

(B) any question of law or fact common to all defendants will arise in the action.

(3) *Extent of Relief.* Neither a plaintiff nor a defendant need be interested in obtaining or defending against all the relief demanded. The court may grant judgment to one or more plaintiffs according to their rights, and against one or more defendants according to their liabilities.

(b) Protective Measures. The court may issue orders—including an order for separate trials—to protect a party against embarrassment, delay, expense, or other prejudice that arises from including a person against whom the party asserts no claim and who asserts no claim against the party.

Rule 21. Misjoinder and Nonjoinder of Parties

Misjoinder of parties is not a ground for dismissing an action. On motion or on its own, the court may at any time, on just terms, add or drop a party. The court may also sever any claim against a party.

Rule 22. Interpleader

(a) Grounds.

> (1) *By a Plaintiff.* Persons with claims that may expose a plaintiff to double or multiple liability may be joined as defendants and required to interplead. Joinder for interpleader is proper even though:
>
> > (A) the claims of the several claimants, or the titles on which their claims depend, lack a common origin or are adverse and independent rather than identical; or
> >
> > (B) the plaintiff denies liability in whole or in part to any or all of the claimants.
>
> (2) *By a Defendant.* A defendant exposed to similar liability may seek interpleader through a crossclaim or counterclaim.

(b) Relation to Other Rules and Statutes. This rule supplements—and does not limit—the joinder of parties allowed by Rule 20. The remedy this rule provides is in addition to—and does not supersede or limit—the remedy provided by 28 U.S.C. §§ 1335, 1397, and 2361. An action under those statutes must be conducted under these rules.

Rule 23. Class Actions

(a) Prerequisites. One or more members of a class may sue or be sued as representative parties on behalf of all members only if:

> (1) the class is so numerous that joinder of all members is impracticable;
>
> (2) there are questions of law or fact common to the class; (3) the claims or defenses of the representative parties are typical of the claims or defenses of the class; and
>
> (4) the representative parties will fairly and adequately protect the interests of the class.

(b) Types of Class Actions. A class action may be maintained if Rule 23(a) is satisfied and if:

> (1) prosecuting separate actions by or against individual class members would create a risk of:
>
> > (A) inconsistent or varying adjudications with respect to individual class members that would establish incompatible standards of conduct for the party opposing the class; or
> >
> > (B) adjudications with respect to individual class members that, as a practical matter, would be dispositive of the interests of the other members not parties to the individual adjudications or would substantially impair or impede their ability to protect their interests;

(2) the party opposing the class has acted or refused to act on grounds that apply generally to the class, so that final injunctive relief or corresponding declaratory relief is appropriate respecting the class as a whole; or

(3) the court finds that the questions of law or fact common to class members predominate over any questions affecting only individual members, and that a class action is superior to other available methods for fairly and efficiently adjudicating the controversy. The matters pertinent to these findings include:

(A) the class members' interests in individually controlling the prosecution or defense of separate actions;

(B) the extent and nature of any litigation concerning the controversy already begun by or against class members;

(C) the desirability or undesirability of concentrating the litigation of the claims in the particular forum; and

(D) the likely difficulties in managing a class action.

(c) Certification Order; Notice to Class Members; Judgment; Issues Classes; Subclasses.

(1) *Certification Order.*

(A) *Time to Issue.* At an early practicable time after a person sues or is sued as a class representative, the court must determine by order whether to certify the action as a class action.

(B) *Defining the Class; Appointing Class Counsel.* An order that certifies a class action must define the class and the class claims, issues, or defenses, and must appoint class counsel under Rule 23(g).

(C) *Altering or Amending the Order.* An order that grants or denies class certification may be altered or amended before final judgment.

(2) *Notice.*

(A) *For (b)(1) or (b)(2) Classes.* For any class certified under Rule 23(b)(1) or (b)(2), the court may direct appropriate notice to the class.

(B) *For (b)(3) Classes.* For any class certified under Rule 23(b)(3), the court must direct to class members the best notice that is practicable under the circumstances, including individual notice to all members who can be identified through reasonable effort. The notice must clearly and concisely state in plain, easily understood language:

(i) the nature of the action;

(ii) the definition of the class certified;

(iii) the class claims, issues, or defenses;

(iv) that a class member may enter an appearance through an attorney if the member so desires;

(v) that the court will exclude from the class any member who requests exclusion;

(vi) the time and manner for requesting exclusion; and

(vii) the binding effect of a class judgment on members under Rule 23(c)(3).

(3) *Judgment*. Whether or not favorable to the class, the judgment in a class action must:

(A) for any class certified under Rule 23(b)(1) or (b)(2), include and describe those whom the court finds to be class members; and

(B) for any class certified under Rule 23(b)(3), include and specify or describe those to whom the Rule 23(c)(2) notice was directed, who have not requested exclusion, and whom the court finds to be class members.

(4) *Particular Issues*. When appropriate, an action may be brought or maintained as a class action with respect to particular issues.

(5) *Subclasses*. When appropriate, a class may be divided into subclasses that are each treated as a class under this rule.

(d) Conducting the Action.

(1) *In General*. In conducting an action under this rule, the court may issue orders that:

(A) determine the course of proceedings or prescribe measures to prevent undue repetition or complication in presenting evidence or argument;

(B) require—to protect class members and fairly conduct the action—giving appropriate notice to some or all class members of:

(i) any step in the action;

(ii) the proposed extent of the judgment; or

(iii) the members' opportunity to signify whether they consider the representation fair and adequate, to intervene and present claims or defenses, or to otherwise come into the action;

(C) impose conditions on the representative parties or on intervenors;

(D) require that the pleadings be amended to eliminate allegations about representation of absent persons and that the action proceed accordingly; or

(E) deal with similar procedural matters.

(2) *Combining and Amending Orders*. An order under Rule 23(d)(1) may be altered or amended from time to time and may be combined with an order under Rule 16.

(e) Settlement, Voluntary Dismissal, or Compromise. The claims, issues, or defenses of a certified class may be settled, voluntarily dismissed, or compromised only with the court's approval. The following procedures apply to a proposed settlement, voluntary dismissal, or compromise:

(1) The court must direct notice in a reasonable manner to all class members who would be bound by the proposal.

(2) If the proposal would bind class members, the court may approve it only after a hearing and on finding that it is fair, reasonable, and adequate.

(3) The parties seeking approval must file a statement identifying any agreement made in connection with the proposal.

(4) If the class action was previously certified under Rule 23(b)(3), the court may refuse to approve a settlement unless it affords a new opportunity to request exclusion to individual class members who had an earlier opportunity to request exclusion but did not do so.

(5) Any class member may object to the proposal if it requires court approval under this subdivision (e); the objection may be withdrawn only with the court's approval.

(f) Appeals. A court of appeals may permit an appeal from an order granting or denying class-action certification under this rule if a petition for permission to appeal is filed with the circuit clerk within 14 days after the order is entered. An appeal does not stay proceedings in the district court unless the district judge or the court of appeals so orders.

(g) Class Counsel.

(1) *Appointing Class Counsel.* Unless a statute provides otherwise, a court that certifies a class must appoint class counsel. In appointing class counsel, the court:

(A) must consider:

(i) the work counsel has done in identifying or investigating potential claims in the action;

(ii) counsel's experience in handling class actions, other complex litigation, and the types of claims asserted in the action;

(iii) counsel's knowledge of the applicable law; and

(iv) the resources that counsel will commit to representing the class;

(B) may consider any other matter pertinent to counsel's ability to fairly and adequately represent the interests of the class;

(C) may order potential class counsel to provide information on any subject pertinent to the appointment and to propose terms for attorney's fees and nontaxable costs;

(D) may include in the appointing order provisions about the award of attorney's fees or nontaxable costs under Rule 23(h); and

(E) may make further orders in connection with the appointment.

(2) *Standard for Appointing Class Counsel.* When one applicant seeks appointment as class counsel, the court may appoint that applicant only if the applicant is adequate under Rule 23(g)(1) and (4). If more than one adequate applicant seeks appointment, the court must appoint the applicant best able to represent the interests of the class.

(3) *Interim Counsel.* The court may designate interim counsel to act on behalf of a putative class before determining whether to certify the action as a class action.

(4) *Duty of Class Counsel.* Class counsel must fairly and adequately represent the interests of the class.

(h) Attorney's Fees and Nontaxable Costs. In a certified class action, the court may award reasonable attorney's fees and non-taxable costs that are authorized by law or by the parties' agreement. The following procedures apply:

(1) A claim for an award must be made by motion under Rule 54(d)(2), subject to the provisions of this subdivision (h), at a time the court sets. Notice of the motion must be served on all parties and, for motions by class counsel, directed to class members in a reasonable manner.

(2) A class member, or a party from whom payment is sought, may object to the motion.

(3) The court may hold a hearing and must find the facts and state its legal conclusions under Rule 52(a).

(4) The court may refer issues related to the amount of the award to a special master or a magistrate judge, as provided in Rule 54(d)(2)(D).

Rule 23.1. Derivative Actions

(a) Prerequisites. This rule applies when one or more shareholders or members of a corporation or an unincorporated association bring a derivative action to enforce a right that the corporation or association may properly assert but has failed to enforce. The derivative action may not be maintained if it appears that the plaintiff does not fairly and adequately represent the interests of shareholders or members who are similarly situated in enforcing the right of the corporation or association.

(b) Pleading Requirements. The complaint must be verified and must:

    (1) allege that the plaintiff was a shareholder or member at the time of the transaction complained of, or that the plaintiff's share or membership later devolved on it by operation of law;

    (2) allege that the action is not a collusive one to confer jurisdiction that the court would otherwise lack; and

    (3) state with particularity:

        (A) any effort by the plaintiff to obtain the desired action from the directors or comparable authority and, if necessary, from the shareholders or members; and

        (B) the reasons for not obtaining the action or not making the effort.

(c) Settlement, Dismissal, and Compromise. A derivative action may be settled, voluntarily dismissed, or compromised only with the court's approval. Notice of a proposed settlement, voluntary dismissal, or compromise must be given to shareholders or members in the manner that the court orders.

Rule 23.2. Actions Relating to Unincorporated Associations

This rule applies to an action brought by or against the members of an unincorporated association as a class by naming certain members as representative parties. The action may be maintained only if it appears that those parties will fairly and adequately protect the interests of the association and its members. In conducting the action, the court may issue any appropriate orders corresponding with those in Rule 23(d), and the procedure for settlement, voluntary dismissal, or compromise must correspond with the procedure in Rule 23(e).

Rule 24. Intervention

(a) Intervention of Right. On timely motion, the court must permit anyone to intervene who:

    (1) is given an unconditional right to intervene by a federal statute; or

    (2) claims an interest relating to the property or transaction that is the subject of the action, and is so situated that disposing of the action may as a practical matter impair or impede the movant's ability to protect its interest, unless existing parties adequately represent that interest.

(b) Permissive Intervention.

    (1) *In General.* On timely motion, the court may permit anyone to intervene who:

        (A) is given a conditional right to intervene by a federal statute; or

        (B) has a claim or defense that shares with the main action a common question of law or fact.

(2) *By a Government Officer or Agency.* On timely motion, the court may permit a federal or state governmental officer or agency to intervene if a party's claim or defense is based on:

> (A) a statute or executive order administered by the officer or agency; or

> (B) any regulation, order, requirement, or agreement issued or made under the statute or executive order.

(3) *Delay or Prejudice.* In exercising its discretion, the court must consider whether the intervention will unduly delay or prejudice the adjudication of the original parties' rights.

(c) Notice and Pleading Required. A motion to intervene must be served on the parties as provided in Rule 5. The motion must state the grounds for intervention and be accompanied by a pleading that sets out the claim or defense for which intervention is sought.

Rule 25. Substitution of Parties

(a) Death.

> (1) *Substitution if the Claim Is Not Extinguished.* If a party dies and the claim is not extinguished, the court may order substitution of the proper party. A motion for substitution may be made by any party or by the decedent's successor or representative. If the motion is not made within 90 days after service of a statement noting the death, the action by or against the decedent must be dismissed.

> (2) *Continuation Among the Remaining Parties.* After a party's death, if the right sought to be enforced survives only to or against the remaining parties, the action does not abate, but proceeds in favor of or against the remaining parties. The death should be noted on the record.

> (3) *Service.* A motion to substitute, together with a notice of hearing, must be served on the parties as provided in Rule 5 and on nonparties as provided in Rule 4. A statement noting death must be served in the same manner. Service may be made in any judicial district.

(b) Incompetency. If a party becomes incompetent, the court may, on motion, permit the action to be continued by or against the party's representative. The motion must be served as provided in Rule 25(a)(3).

(c) Transfer Of Interest. If an interest is transferred, the action may be continued by or against the original party unless the court, on motion, orders the transferee to be substituted in the action or joined with the original party. The motion must be served as provided in Rule 25(a)(3).

(d) Public Officers; Death or Separation from Office. An action does not abate when a public officer who is a party in an official capacity dies, resigns, or otherwise ceases to hold office while the action is pending. The officer's successor is automatically substituted as a party. Later proceedings should be in the substituted party's name, but any misnomer not affecting the parties' substantial rights must be disregarded. The court may order substitution at any time, but the absence of such an order does not affect the substitution.

TITLE V. DISCLOSURES AND DISCOVERY

Rule 26. Duty to Disclose; General Provisions Governing Discovery

(a) Required Disclosures.

> (1) *Initial Disclosure.*

(A) *In General.* Except as exempted by Rule 26(a)(1)(B) or as otherwise stipulated or ordered by the court, a party must, without awaiting a discovery request, provide to the other parties:

> **(i)** the name and, if known, the address and telephone number of each individual likely to have discoverable information—along with the subjects of that information—that the disclosing party may use to support its claims or defenses, unless the use would be solely for impeachment;

> **(ii)** a copy—or a description by category and location—of all documents, electronically stored information, and tangible things that the disclosing party has in its possession, custody, or control and may use to support its claims or defenses, unless the use would be solely for impeachment;

> **(iii)** a computation of each category of damages claimed by the disclosing party—who must also make available for inspection and copying as under Rule 34 the documents or other evidentiary material, unless privileged or protected from disclosure, on which each computation is based, including materials bearing on the nature and extent of injuries suffered; and

> **(iv)** for inspection and copying as under Rule 34, any insurance agreement under which an insurance business may be liable to satisfy all or part of a possible judgment in the action or to indemnify or reimburse for payments made to satisfy the judgment.

(B) *Proceedings Exempt from Initial Disclosure.* The following proceedings are exempt from initial disclosure:

> **(i)** an action for review on an administrative record;

> **(ii)** a forfeiture action in rem arising from a federal statute;

> **(iii)** a petition for habeas corpus or any other proceeding to challenge a criminal conviction or sentence;

> **(iv)** an action brought without an attorney by a person in the custody of the United States, a state, or a state subdivision;

> **(v)** an action to enforce or quash an administrative summons or subpoena;

> **(vi)** an action by the United States to recover benefit payments;

> **(vii)** an action by the United States to collect on a student loan guaranteed by the United States;

> **(viii)** a proceeding ancillary to a proceeding in another court; and

> **(ix)** an action to enforce an arbitration award.

(C) *Time for Initial Disclosures—In General.* A party must make the initial disclosures at or within 14 days after the parties' Rule 26(f) conference unless a different time is set by stipulation or court order, or unless a party objects during the conference that initial disclosures are not appropriate in this action and states the objection in the proposed discovery plan. In ruling on the objection, the court must determine what disclosures, if any, are to be made and must set the time for disclosure.

(D) *Time for Initial Disclosures—For Parties Served or Joined Later.* A party that is first served or otherwise joined after the Rule 26(f) conference must make the initial disclosures within 30 days after being served or joined, unless a different time is set by stipulation or court order.

(E) *Basis for Initial Disclosure; Unacceptable Excuses.* A party must make its initial disclosures based on the information then reasonably available to it. A party is not excused from making its disclosures because it has not fully investigated the case or because it challenges the sufficiency of another party's disclosures or because another party has not made its disclosures.

(2) *Disclosure of Expert Testimony.*

(A) *In General.* In addition to the disclosures required by Rule 26(a)(1), a party must disclose to the other parties the identity of any witness it may use at trial to present evidence under Federal Rule of Evidence 702, 703, or 705.

(B) *Witnesses Who Must Provide a Written Report.* Unless otherwise stipulated or ordered by the court, this disclosure must be accompanied by a written report— prepared and signed by the witness—if the witness is one retained or specially employed to provide expert testimony in the case or one whose duties as the party's employee regularly involve giving expert testimony. The report must contain:

> (i) a complete statement of all opinions the witness will express and the basis and reasons for them;

> (ii) the facts or data considered by the witness in forming them;

> (iii) any exhibits that will be used to summarize or support them;

> (iv) the witness's qualifications, including a list of all publications authored in the previous 10 years;

> (v) a list of all other cases in which, during the previous 4 years, the witness testified as an expert at trial or by deposition; and

> (vi) a statement of the compensation to be paid for the study and testimony in the case.

(C) *Witnesses Who Do Not Provide a Written Report.* Unless otherwise stipulated or ordered by the court, if the witness is not required to provide a written report, this disclosure must state:

> (i) the subject matter on which the witness is expected to present evidence under Federal Rule of Evidence 702, 703, or 705; and

> (ii) a summary of the facts and opinions to which the witness is expected to testify.

(D) *Time to Disclose Expert Testimony.* A party must make these disclosures at the times and in the sequence that the court orders. Absent a stipulation or a court order, the disclosures must be made:

> (i) at least 90 days before the date set for trial or for the case to be ready for trial; or

> (ii) if the evidence is intended solely to contradict or rebut evidence on the same subject matter identified by another party under Rule 26(a)(2)(B) or (C), within 30 days after the other party's disclosure.

(E) *Supplementing the Disclosure.* The parties must supplement these disclosures when required under Rule 26(e).

(3) *Pretrial Disclosures.*

(A) *In General.* In addition to the disclosures required by Rule 26(a)(1) and (2), a party must provide to the other parties and promptly file the following information about the evidence that it may present at trial other than solely for impeachment:

(i) the name and, if not previously provided, the address and telephone number of each witness—separately identifying those the party expects to present and those it may call if the need arises;

(ii) the designation of those witnesses whose testimony the party expects to present by deposition and, if not taken stenographically, a transcript of the pertinent parts of the deposition; and

(iii) an identification of each document or other exhibit, including summaries of other evidence—separately identifying those items the party expects to offer and those it may offer if the need arises.

(B) *Time for Pretrial Disclosures; Objections.* Unless the court orders otherwise, these disclosures must be made at least 30 days before trial. Within 14 days after they are made, unless the court sets a different time, a party may serve and promptly file a list of the following objections: any objections to the use under Rule 32(a) of a deposition designated by another party under Rule 26(a)(3)(A)(ii); and any objection, together with the grounds for it, that may be made to the admissibility of materials identified under Rule 26(a)(3)(A)(iii). An objection not so made—except for one under Federal Rule of Evidence 402 or 403—is waived unless excused by the court for good cause.

(4) *Form of Disclosures.* Unless the court orders otherwise, all disclosures under Rule 26(a) must be in writing, signed, and served.

(b) Discovery Scope and Limits.

(1) *Scope in General.* Unless otherwise limited by court order, the scope of discovery is as follows: Parties may obtain discovery regarding any nonprivileged matter that is relevant to any party's claim or defense and proportional to the needs of the case, considering the importance of the issues at stake in the action, the amount in controversy, the parties' relative access to relevant information, the parties' resources, the importance of the discovery in resolving the issues, and whether the burden or expense of the proposed discovery outweighs its likely benefit. Information within this scope of discovery need not be admissible in evidence to be discoverable.

(2) *Limitations on Frequency and Extent.*

(A) *When Permitted.* By order, the court may alter the limits in these rules on the number of depositions and interrogatories or on the length of depositions under Rule 30. By order or local rule, the court may also limit the number of requests under Rule 36.

(B) *Specific Limitations on Electronically Stored Information.* A party need not provide discovery of electronically stored information from sources that the party identifies as not reasonably accessible because of undue burden or cost. On motion to compel discovery or for a protective order, the party from whom discovery is sought must show that the information is not reasonably accessible because of undue burden or cost. If that showing is made, the court may nonetheless order discovery from such sources if the requesting party shows good cause, considering the limitations of Rule 26(b)(2)(C). The court may specify conditions for the discovery.

(C) *When Required*. On motion or on its own, the court must limit the frequency or extent of discovery otherwise allowed by these rules or by local rule if it determines that:

> (i)   the discovery sought is unreasonably cumulative or duplicative, or can be obtained from some other source that is more convenient, less burdensome, or less expensive;
>
> (ii)   the party seeking discovery has had ample opportunity to obtain the information by discovery in the action; or
>
> (iii)   the proposed discovery is outside the scope permitted by Rule 26(b)(1).

(3) *Trial Preparation: Materials.*

> (A) *Documents and Tangible Things*. Ordinarily, a party may not discover documents and tangible things that are prepared in anticipation of litigation or for trial by or for another party or its representative (including the other party's attorney, consultant, surety, indemnitor, insurer, or agent). But, subject to Rule 26(b)(4), those materials may be discovered if:
>
> > (i)   they are otherwise discoverable under Rule 26(b)(1); and
> >
> > (ii)   the party shows that it has substantial need for the materials to prepare its case and cannot, without undue hardship, obtain their substantial equivalent by other means.
>
> (B) *Protection Against Disclosure*. If the court orders discovery of those materials, it must protect against disclosure of the mental impressions, conclusions, opinions, or legal theories of a party's attorney or other representative concerning the litigation.
>
> (C) *Previous Statement*. Any party or other person may, on request and without the required showing, obtain the person's own previous statement about the action or its subject matter. If the request is refused, the person may move for a court order, and Rule 37(a)(5) applies to the award of expenses. A previous statement is either:
>
> > (i)   a written statement that the person has signed or otherwise adopted or approved; or
> >
> > (ii)   a contemporaneous stenographic, mechanical, electrical, or other recording—or a transcription of it—that recites substantially verbatim the person's oral statement.

(4) *Trial Preparation: Experts.*

> (A) *Deposition of an Expert Who May Testify*. A party may depose any person who has been identified as an expert whose opinions may be presented at trial. If Rule 26(a)(2)(B) requires a report from the expert, the deposition may be conducted only after the report is provided.
>
> (B) *Trial-Preparation Protection for Draft Reports or Disclosures*. Rules 26(b)(3)(A) and (B) protect drafts of any report or disclosure required under Rule 26(a)(2), regardless of the form in which the draft is recorded.
>
> (C) *Trial-Preparation Protection for Communications Between a Party's Attorney and Expert Witnesses*. Rules 26(b)(3)(A) and (B) protect communications between the party's

attorney and any witness required to provide a report under Rule 26(a)(2)(B), regardless of the form of the communications, except to the extent that the communications:

    (i)   relate to compensation for the expert's study or testimony;

    (ii)   identify facts or data that the party's attorney provided and that the expert considered in forming the opinions to be expressed; or

    (iii)   identify assumptions that the party's attorney provided and that the expert relied on in forming the opinions to be expressed.

    (D) *Expert Employed Only for Trial Preparation.* Ordinarily, a party may not, by interrogatories or deposition, discover facts known or opinions held by an expert who has been retained or specially employed by another party in anticipation of litigation or to prepare for trial and who is not expected to be called as a witness at trial. But a party may do so only:

    (i)   as provided in Rule 35(b); or

    (ii)   on showing exceptional circumstances under which it is impracticable for the party to obtain facts or opinions on the same subject by other means.

    (E) *Payment.* Unless manifest injustice would result, the court must require that the party seeking discovery:

    (i)   pay the expert a reasonable fee for time spent in responding to discovery under Rule 26(b)(4)(A) or (D); and

    (ii)   for discovery under (D), also pay the other party a fair portion of the fees and expenses it reasonably incurred in obtaining the expert's facts and opinions.

  (5) *Claiming Privilege or Protecting Trial-Preparation Materials.*

    (A) *Information Withheld.* When a party withholds information otherwise discoverable by claiming that the information is privileged or subject to protection as trial-preparation material, the party must:

    (i)   expressly make the claim; and

    (ii)   describe the nature of the documents, communications, or tangible things not produced or disclosed—and do so in a manner that, without revealing information itself privileged or protected, will enable other parties to assess the claim.

    (B) *Information Produced.* If information produced in discovery is subject to a claim of privilege or of protection as trial-preparation material, the party making the claim may notify any party that received the information of the claim and the basis for it. After being notified, a party must promptly return, sequester, or destroy the specified information and any copies it has; must not use or disclose the information until the claim is resolved; must take reasonable steps to retrieve the information if the party disclosed it before being notified; and may promptly present the information to the court under seal for a determination of the claim. The producing party must preserve the information until the claim is resolved.

(c) Protective Orders.

  (1) *In General.* A party or any person from whom discovery is sought may move for a protective order in the court where the action is pending—or as an alternative on matters relating to a deposition, in the court for the district where the deposition will be taken. The motion must include a certification that the movant has in good faith conferred or attempted to confer with other affected parties in an effort to resolve the dispute without court action. The court may, for good cause, issue an order to protect a party or person from annoyance, embarrassment, oppression, or undue burden or expense, including one or more of the following:

    (A) forbidding the disclosure or discovery;

    (B) specifying terms, including time and place or the allocation of expenses, for the disclosure or discovery;

    (C) prescribing a discovery method other than the one selected by the party seeking discovery;

    (D) forbidding inquiry into certain matters, or limiting the scope of disclosure or discovery to certain matters;

    (E) designating the persons who may be present while the discovery is conducted;

    (F) requiring that a deposition be sealed and opened only on court order;

    (G) requiring that a trade secret or other confidential research, development, or commercial information not be revealed or be revealed only in a specified way; and

    (H) requiring that the parties simultaneously file specified documents or information in sealed envelopes, to be opened as the court directs.

  (2) *Ordering Discovery.* If a motion for a protective order is wholly or partly denied, the court may, on just terms, order that any party or person provide or permit discovery.

  (3) *Awarding Expenses.* Rule 37(a)(5) applies to the award of expenses.

(d) Timing and Sequence of Discovery.

  (1) *Timing.* A party may not seek discovery from any source before the parties have conferred as required by Rule 26(f), except in a proceeding exempted from initial disclosure under Rule 26(a)(1)(B), or when authorized by these rules, by stipulation, or by court order.

  (2) *Early Rule 34 Requests.*

    (A) *Time to Deliver.* More than 21 days after the summons and complaint are served on a party, a request under Rule 34 may be delivered:

        (i)   to that party by any other party, and

        (ii)   by that party to any plaintiff or to any other party that has been served.

    (B) *When Considered Served.* The request is considered to have been served at the first Rule 26(f) conference.

  (3) *Sequence.* Unless the parties stipulate or the court orders otherwise for the parties' and witnesses' convenience and in the interests of justice:

    (A) methods of discovery may be used in any sequence; and

    (B) discovery by one party does not require any other party to delay its discovery.

(e) Supplementing Disclosures and Responses.

  (1) *In General.* A party who has made a disclosure under Rule 26(a)—or who has responded to an interrogatory, request for production, or request for admission—must supplement or correct its disclosure or response:

(A) in a timely manner if the party learns that in some material respect the disclosure or response is incomplete or incorrect, and if the additional or corrective information has not otherwise been made known to the other parties during the discovery process or in writing; or

(B) as ordered by the court.

(2) *Expert Witness.* For an expert whose report must be disclosed under Rule 26(a)(2)(B), the party's duty to supplement extends both to information included in the report and to information given during the expert's deposition. Any additions or changes to this information must be disclosed by the time the party's pretrial disclosures under Rule 26(a)(3) are due.

(f) Conference of the Parties; Planning for Discovery.

(1) *Conference Timing.* Except in a proceeding exempted from initial disclosure under Rule 26(a)(1)(B) or when the court orders otherwise, the parties must confer as soon as practicable—and in any event at least 21 days before a scheduling conference is to be held or a scheduling order is due under Rule 16(b).

(2) *Conference Content; Parties' Responsibilities.* In conferring, the parties must consider the nature and basis of their claims and defenses and the possibilities for promptly settling or resolving the case; make or arrange for the disclosures required by Rule 26(a)(1); discuss any issues about preserving discoverable information; and develop a proposed discovery plan. The attorneys of record and all unrepresented parties that have appeared in the case are jointly responsible for arranging the conference, for attempting in good faith to agree on the proposed discovery plan, and for submitting to the court within 14 days after the conference a written report outlining the plan. The court may order the parties or attorneys to attend the conference in person.

(3) *Discovery Plan.* A discovery plan must state the parties' views and proposals on:

(A) what changes should be made in the timing, form, or requirement for disclosures under Rule 26(a), including a statement of when initial disclosures were made or will be made;

(B) the subjects on which discovery may be needed, when discovery should be completed, and whether discovery should be conducted in phases or be limited to or focused on particular issues;

(C) any issues about disclosure, discovery, or preservation of electronically stored information, including the form or forms in which it should be produced;

(D) any issues about claims of privilege or of protection as trial-preparation materials, including—if the parties agree on a procedure to assert these claims after production—whether to ask the court to include their agreement in an order under Federal Rule of Evidence 502;

(E) what changes should be made in the limitations on discovery imposed under these rules or by local rule, and what other limitations should be imposed; and

(F) any other orders that the court should issue under Rule 26(c) or under Rule 16(b) and (c).

(4) *Expedited Schedule.* If necessary to comply with its expedited schedule for Rule 16(b) conferences, a court may by local rule:

(A) require the parties' conference to occur less than 21 days before the scheduling conference is held or a scheduling order is due under Rule 16(b); and

(B) require the written report outlining the discovery plan to be filed less than 14 days after the parties' conference, or excuse the parties from submitting a written report and permit them to report orally on their discovery plan at the Rule 16(b) conference.

(g) Signing Disclosures and Discovery Requests, Responses, and Objections.

(1) *Signature Required; Effect of Signature.* Every disclosure under Rule 26(a)(1) or (a)(3) and every discovery request, response, or objection must be signed by at least one attorney of record in the attorney's own name—or by the party personally, if unrepresented—and must state the signer's address, e-mail address, and telephone number. By signing, an attorney or party certifies that to the best of the person's knowledge, information, and belief formed after a reasonable inquiry:

(A) with respect to a disclosure, it is complete and correct as of the time it is made; and

(B) with respect to a discovery request, response, or objection, it is:

(i) consistent with these rules and warranted by existing law or by a nonfrivolous argument for extending, modifying, or reversing existing law, or for establishing new law;

(ii) not interposed for any improper purpose, such as to harass, cause unnecessary delay, or needlessly increase the cost of litigation; and

(iii) neither unreasonable nor unduly burdensome or expensive, considering the needs of the case, prior discovery in the case, the amount in controversy, and the importance of the issues at stake in the action.

(2) *Failure to Sign.* Other parties have no duty to act on an unsigned disclosure, request, response, or objection until it is signed, and the court must strike it unless a signature is promptly supplied after the omission is called to the attorney's or party's attention.

(3) *Sanction for Improper Certification.* If a certification violates this rule without substantial justification, the court, on motion or on its own, must impose an appropriate sanction on the signer, the party on whose behalf the signer was acting, or both. The sanction may include an order to pay the reasonable expenses, including attorney's fees, caused by the violation.

Rule 27. Depositions to Perpetuate Testimony

(a) Before an Action Is Filed.

(1) *Petition.* A person who wants to perpetuate testimony about any matter cognizable in a United States court may file a verified petition in the district court for the district where any expected adverse party resides. The petition must ask for an order authorizing the petitioner to depose the named persons in order to perpetuate their testimony. The petition must be titled in the petitioner's name and must show:

(A) that the petitioner expects to be a party to an action cognizable in a United States court but cannot presently bring it or cause it to be brought;

(B) the subject matter of the expected action and the petitioner's interest;

(C) the facts that the petitioner wants to establish by the proposed testimony and the reasons to perpetuate it;

(D) the names or a description of the persons whom the petitioner expects to be adverse parties and their addresses, so far as known; and

(E) the name, address, and expected substance of the testimony of each deponent.

(2) *Notice and Service.* At least 21 days before the hearing date, the petitioner must serve each expected adverse party with a copy of the petition and a notice stating the time and place of the hearing. The notice may be served either inside or outside the district or state in the manner provided in Rule 4. If that service cannot be made with reasonable diligence on an expected adverse party, the court may order service by publication or otherwise. The court must appoint an attorney to represent persons not served in the manner provided in Rule 4 and to cross-examine the deponent if an unserved person is not otherwise represented. If any expected adverse party is a minor or is incompetent, Rule 17(c) applies.

(3) *Order and Examination.* If satisfied that perpetuating the testimony may prevent a failure or delay of justice, the court must issue an order that designates or describes the persons whose depositions may be taken, specifies the subject matter of the examinations, and states whether the depositions will be taken orally or by written interrogatories. The depositions may then be taken under these rules, and the court may issue orders like those authorized by Rules 34 and 35. A reference in these rules to the court where an action is pending means, for purposes of this rule, the court where the petition for the deposition was filed.

(4) *Using the Deposition.* A deposition to perpetuate testimony may be used under Rule 32(a) in any later-filed districtcourt action involving the same subject matter if the deposition either was taken under these rules or, although not so taken, would be admissible in evidence in the courts of the state where it was taken.

(b) Pending Appeal.

(1) *In General.* The court where a judgment has been rendered may, if an appeal has been taken or may still be taken, permit a party to depose witnesses to perpetuate their testimony for use in the event of further proceedings in that court.

(2) *Motion.* The party who wants to perpetuate testimony may move for leave to take the depositions, on the same notice and service as if the action were pending in the district court. The motion must show:

> (A) the name, address, and expected substance of the testimony of each deponent; and
>
> (B) the reasons for perpetuating the testimony.

(3) *Court Order.* If the court finds that perpetuating the testimony may prevent a failure or delay of justice, the court may permit the depositions to be taken and may issue orders like those authorized by Rules 34 and 35. The depositions may be taken and used as any other deposition taken in a pending district-court action.

(c) Perpetuation By an Action. This rule does not limit a court's power to entertain an action to perpetuate testimony.

Rule 28. Persons Before Whom Depositions May Be Taken

(a) Within the United States.

(1) *In General.* Within the United States or a territory or insular possession subject to United States jurisdiction, a deposition must be taken before:

> (A) an officer authorized to administer oaths either by federal law or by the law in the place of examination; or
>
> (B) a person appointed by the court where the action is pending to administer oaths and take testimony.

(2) *Definition of "Officer."* The term "officer" in Rules 30, 31, and 32 includes a person appointed by the court under this rule or designated by the parties under Rule 29(a).

(b) In a foreign country.

(1) *In General.* A deposition may be taken in a foreign country:

(A) under an applicable treaty or convention;

(B) under a letter of request, whether or not captioned a "letter rogatory";

(C) on notice, before a person authorized to administer oaths either by federal law or by the law in the place of examination; or

(D) before a person commissioned by the court to administer any necessary oath and take testimony.

(2) *Issuing a Letter of Request or a Commission.* A letter of request, a commission, or both may be issued:

(A) on appropriate terms after an application and notice of it; and

(B) without a showing that taking the deposition in another manner is impracticable or inconvenient.

(3) *Form of a Request, Notice, or Commission.* When a letter of request or any other device is used according to a treaty or convention, it must be captioned in the form prescribed by that treaty or convention. A letter of request may be addressed "To the Appropriate Authority in [name of country]." A deposition notice or a commission must designate by name or descriptive title the person before whom the deposition is to be taken.

(4) *Letter of Request—Admitting Evidence.* Evidence obtained in response to a letter of request need not be excluded merely because it is not a verbatim transcript, because the testimony was not taken under oath, or because of any similar departure from the requirements for depositions taken within the United States.

(c) Disqualification. A deposition must not be taken before a person who is any party's relative, employee, or attorney; who is related to or employed by any party's attorney; or who is financially interested in the action.

Rule 29. Stipulations About Discovery Procedure

Unless the court orders otherwise, the parties may stipulate that:

(a) a deposition may be taken before any person, at any time or place, on any notice, and in the manner specified—in which event it may be used in the same way as any other deposition; and

(b) other procedures governing or limiting discovery be modified—but a stipulation extending the time for any form of discovery must have court approval if it would interfere with the time set for completing discovery, for hearing a motion, or for trial.

Rule 30. Depositions by Oral Examination

(a) When a Deposition May Be Taken.

(1) *Without Leave.* A party may, by oral questions, depose any person, including a party, without leave of court except as provided in Rule 30(a)(2). The deponent's attendance may be compelled by subpoena under Rule 45.

(2) *With Leave.* A party must obtain leave of court, and the court must grant leave to the extent consistent with Rule 26(b)(1) and (2):

    (A) if the parties have not stipulated to the deposition and:

        (i)   the deposition would result in more than 10 depositions being taken under this rule or Rule 31 by the plaintiffs, or by the defendants, or by the third-party defendants;

        (ii)   the deponent has already been deposed in the case; or

        (iii) the party seeks to take the deposition before the time specified in Rule 26(d), unless the party certifies in the notice, with supporting facts, that the deponent is expected to leave the United States and be unavailable for examination in this country after that time; or

    (B) if the deponent is confined in prison.

(b) Notice of the Deposition; Other Formal Requirements.

(1) *Notice in General.* A party who wants to depose a person by oral questions must give reasonable written notice to every other party. The notice must state the time and place of the deposition and, if known, the deponent's name and address. If the name is unknown, the notice must provide a general description sufficient to identify the person or the particular class or group to which the person belongs.

(2) *Producing Documents.* If a subpoena duces tecum is to be served on the deponent, the materials designated for production, as set out in the subpoena, must be listed in the notice or in an attachment. The notice to a party deponent may be accompanied by a request under Rule 34 to produce documents and tangible things at the deposition.

(3) *Method of Recording.*

    (A) *Method Stated in the Notice.* The party who notices the deposition must state in the notice the method for recording the testimony. Unless the court orders otherwise, testimony may be recorded by audio, audiovisual, or stenographic means. The noticing party bears the recording costs. Any party may arrange to transcribe a deposition.

    (B) *Additional Method.* With prior notice to the deponent and other parties, any party may designate another method for recording the testimony in addition to that specified in the original notice. That party bears the expense of the additional record or transcript unless the court orders otherwise.

(4) *By Remote Means.* The parties may stipulate—or the court may on motion order—that a deposition be taken by telephone or other remote means. For the purpose of this rule and Rules 28(a), 37(a)(2), and 37(b)(1), the deposition takes place where the deponent answers the questions.

(5) *Officer's Duties.*

    (A) *Before the Deposition.* Unless the parties stipulate otherwise, a deposition must be conducted before an officer appointed or designated under Rule 28. The officer must begin the deposition with an on-the-record statement that includes:

        (i)   the officer's name and business address;

        (ii)   the date, time, and place of the deposition;

        (iii) the deponent's name;

> > (iv) the officer's administration of the oath or affirmation to the deponent; and
> >
> > (v) the identity of all persons present.
>
> **(B)** *Conducting the Deposition; Avoiding Distortion.* If the deposition is recorded nonstenographically, the officer must repeat the items in Rule 30(b)(5)(A)(i)-(iii) at the beginning of each unit of the recording medium. The deponent's and attorneys' appearance or demeanor must not be distorted through recording techniques.
>
> **(C)** *After the Deposition.* At the end of a deposition, the officer must state on the record that the deposition is complete and must set out any stipulations made by the attorneys about custody of the transcript or recording and of the exhibits, or about any other pertinent matters.

(6) *Notice or Subpoena Directed to an Organization.* In its notice or subpoena, a party may name as the deponent a public or private corporation, a partnership, an association, a governmental agency, or other entity and must describe with reasonable particularity the matters for examination. The named organization must then designate one or more officers, directors, or managing agents, or designate other persons who consent to testify on its behalf; and it may set out the matters on which each person designated will testify. A subpoena must advise a nonparty organization of its duty to make this designation. The persons designated must testify about information known or reasonably available to the organization. This paragraph (6) does not preclude a deposition by any other procedure allowed by these rules.

(c) Examination and Cross-Examination; Record of the Examination; Objections; Written Questions.

(1) *Examination and Cross-Examination.* The examination and cross-examination of a deponent proceed as they would at trial under the Federal Rules of Evidence, except Rules 103 and 615. After putting the deponent under oath or affirmation, the officer must record the testimony by the method designated under Rule 30(b)(3)(A). The testimony must be recorded by the officer personally or by a person acting in the presence and under the direction of the officer.

(2) *Objections.* An objection at the time of the examination—whether to evidence, to a party's conduct, to the officer's qualifications, to the manner of taking the deposition, or to any other aspect of the deposition—must be noted on the record, but the examination still proceeds; the testimony is taken subject to any objection. An objection must be stated concisely in a nonargumentative and nonsuggestive manner. A person may instruct a deponent not to answer only when necessary to preserve a privilege, to enforce a limitation ordered by the court, or to present a motion under Rule 30(d)(3).

(3) *Participating Through Written Questions.* Instead of participating in the oral examination, a party may serve written questions in a sealed envelope on the party noticing the deposition, who must deliver them to the officer. The officer must ask the deponent those questions and record the answers verbatim.

(d) Duration; Sanction; Motion to Terminate or Limit.

(1) *Duration.* Unless otherwise stipulated or ordered by the court, a deposition is limited to 1 day of 7 hours. The court must allow additional time consistent with Rule 26(b)(1) and (2) if needed to fairly examine the deponent or if the deponent, another person, or any other circumstance impedes or delays the examination.

(2) *Sanction.* The court may impose an appropriate sanction—including the reasonable expenses and attorney's fees incurred by any party—on a person who impedes, delays, or frustrates the fair examination of the deponent.

    (3) *Motion to Terminate or Limit.*

        (A) *Grounds.* At any time during a deposition, the deponent or a party may move to terminate or limit it on the ground that it is being conducted in bad faith or in a manner that unreasonably annoys, embarrasses, or oppresses the deponent or party. The motion may be filed in the court where the action is pending or the deposition is being taken. If the objecting deponent or party so demands, the deposition must be suspended for the time necessary to obtain an order.

        (B) *Order.* The court may order that the deposition be terminated or may limit its scope and manner as provided in Rule 26(c). If terminated, the deposition may be resumed only by order of the court where the action is pending.

        (C) *Award of Expenses.* Rule 37(a)(5) applies to the award of expenses.

(e) Review by the Witness; Changes.

    (1) *Review; Statement of Changes.* On request by the deponent or a party before the deposition is completed, the deponent must be allowed 30 days after being notified by the officer that the transcript or recording is available in which:

        (A) to review the transcript or recording; and

        (B) if there are changes in form or substance, to sign a statement listing the changes and the reasons for making them.

    (2) *Changes Indicated in the Officer's Certificate.* The officer must note in the certificate prescribed by Rule 30(f)(1) whether a review was requested and, if so, must attach any changes the deponent makes during the 30-day period.

(f) Certification and Delivery; Exhibits; Copies of the Transcript or Recording; Filing.

    (1) *Certification and Delivery.* The officer must certify in writing that the witness was duly sworn and that the deposition accurately records the witness's testimony. The certificate must accompany the record of the deposition. Unless the court orders otherwise, the officer must seal the deposition in an envelope or package bearing the title of the action and marked "Deposition of [witness's name]" and must promptly send it to the attorney who arranged for the transcript or recording. The attorney must store it under conditions that will protect it against loss, destruction, tampering, or deterioration.

    (2) *Documents and Tangible Things.*

        (A) *Originals and Copies.* Documents and tangible things produced for inspection during a deposition must, on a party's request, be marked for identification and attached to the deposition. Any party may inspect and copy them. But if the person who produced them wants to keep the originals, the person may:

            (i) offer copies to be marked, attached to the deposition, and then used as originals—after giving all parties a fair opportunity to verify the copies by comparing them with the originals; or

            (ii) give all parties a fair opportunity to inspect and copy the originals after they are marked—in which event the originals may be used as if attached to the deposition.

        (B) *Order Regarding the Originals.* Any party may move for an order that the originals be attached to the deposition pending final disposition of the case.

    (3) *Copies of the Transcript or Recording.* Unless otherwise stipulated or ordered by the court, the officer must retain the stenographic notes of a deposition taken stenographically or a copy

of the recording of a deposition taken by another method. When paid reasonable charges, the officer must furnish a copy of the transcript or recording to any party or the deponent.

(4) *Notice of Filing.* A party who files the deposition must promptly notify all other parties of the filing.

(g) Failure to Attend a Deposition or Serve a Subpoena; Expenses. A party who, expecting a deposition to be taken, attends in person or by an attorney may recover reasonable expenses for attending, including attorney's fees, if the noticing party failed to:

(1) attend and proceed with the deposition; or

(2) serve a subpoena on a nonparty deponent, who consequently did not attend.

Rule 31. Depositions by Written Questions

(a) When a Deposition may be Taken.

(1) *Without Leave.* A party may, by written questions, depose any person, including a party, without leave of court except as provided in Rule 31(a)(2). The deponent's attendance may be compelled by subpoena under Rule 45.

(2) *With Leave.* A party must obtain leave of court, and the court must grant leave to the extent consistent with Rule 26(b)(1) and (2):

    (A) if the parties have not stipulated to the deposition and:

        (i)   the deposition would result in more than 10 depositions being taken under this rule or Rule 30 by the plaintiffs, or by the defendants, or by the third-party defendants;

        (ii) the deponent has already been deposed in the case; or

        (iii) the party seeks to take a deposition before the time specified in Rule 26(d); or

    (B) if the deponent is confined in prison.

(3) *Service; Required Notice.* A party who wants to depose a person by written questions must serve them on every other party, with a notice stating, if known, the deponent's name and address. If the name is unknown, the notice must provide a general description sufficient to identify the person or the particular class or group to which the person belongs. The notice must also state the name or descriptive title and the address of the officer before whom the deposition will be taken.

(4) *Questions Directed to an Organization.* A public or private corporation, a partnership, an association, or a governmental agency may be deposed by written questions in accordance with Rule 30(b)(6).

(5) *Questions from Other Parties.* Any questions to the deponent from other parties must be served on all parties as follows: cross-questions, within 14 days after being served with the notice and direct questions; redirect questions, within 7 days after being served with cross-questions; and recross-questions, within 7 days after being served with redirect questions. The court may, for good cause, extend or shorten these times.

(b) Delivery to the Officer; Officer's Duties. The party who noticed the deposition must deliver to the officer a copy of all the questions served and of the notice. The officer must promptly proceed in the manner provided in Rule 30(c), (e), and (f) to:

(1) take the deponent's testimony in response to the questions;

(2) prepare and certify the deposition; and

(3) send it to the party, attaching a copy of the questions and of the notice.

(c) Notice of Completion or Filing.

(1) *Completion.* The party who noticed the deposition must notify all other parties when it is completed.

(2) *Filing.* A party who files the deposition must promptly notify all other parties of the filing.

Rule 32. Using Depositions in Court Proceedings

(a) Using Depositions.

(1) *In General.* At a hearing or trial, all or part of a deposition may be used against a party on these conditions:

(A) the party was present or represented at the taking of the deposition or had reasonable notice of it;

(B) it is used to the extent it would be admissible under the Federal Rules of Evidence if the deponent were present and testifying; and

(C) the use is allowed by Rule 32(a)(2) through (8).

(2) *Impeachment and Other Uses.* Any party may use a deposition to contradict or impeach the testimony given by the deponent as a witness, or for any other purpose allowed by the Federal Rules of Evidence.

(3) *Deposition of Party, Agent, or Designee.* An adverse party may use for any purpose the deposition of a party or anyone who, when deposed, was the party's officer, director, managing agent, or designee under Rule 30(b)(6) or 31(a)(4).

(4) *Unavailable Witness.* A party may use for any purpose the deposition of a witness, whether or not a party, if the court finds:

(A) that the witness is dead;

(B) that the witness is more than 100 miles from the place of hearing or trial or is outside the United States, unless it appears that the witness's absence was procured by the party offering the deposition;

(C) that the witness cannot attend or testify because of age, illness, infirmity, or imprisonment;

(D) that the party offering the deposition could not procure the witness's attendance by subpoena; or

(E) on motion and notice, that exceptional circumstances make it desirable—in the interest of justice and with due regard to the importance of live testimony in open court—to permit the deposition to be used.

(5) *Limitations on Use.*

(A) *Deposition Taken on Short Notice.* A deposition must not be used against a party who, having received less than 14 days' notice of the deposition, promptly moved for a protective order under Rule 26(c)(1)(B) requesting that it not be taken or be taken at a different time or place—and this motion was still pending when the deposition was taken.

(B) *Unavailable Deponent; Party Could Not Obtain an Attorney.* A deposition taken without leave of court under the unavailability provision of Rule 30(a)(2)(A)(iii) must not be used against a party who shows that, when served with the notice, it could not, despite diligent efforts, obtain an attorney to represent it at the deposition.

(6) *Using Part of a Deposition.* If a party offers in evidence only part of a deposition, an adverse party may require the offeror to introduce other parts that in fairness should be considered with the part introduced, and any party may itself introduce any other parts.

(7) *Substituting a Party.* Substituting a party under Rule 25 does not affect the right to use a deposition previously taken.

(8) *Deposition Taken in an Earlier Action.* A deposition lawfully taken and, if required, filed in any federal- or state-court action may be used in a later action involving the same subject matter between the same parties, or their representatives or successors in interest, to the same extent as if taken in the later action. A deposition previously taken may also be used as allowed by the Federal Rules of Evidence.

(b) Objections to Admissibility. Subject to Rules 28(b) and 32(d)(3), an objection may be made at a hearing or trial to the admission of any deposition testimony that would be inadmissible if the witness were present and testifying.

(c) Form of Presentation. Unless the court orders otherwise, a party must provide a transcript of any deposition testimony the party offers, but may provide the court with the testimony in non-transcript form as well. On any party's request, deposition testimony offered in a jury trial for any purpose other than impeachment must be presented in nontranscript form, if available, unless the court for good cause orders otherwise.

(d) Waiver of Objections.

(1) *To the Notice.* An objection to an error or irregularity in a deposition notice is waived unless promptly served in writing on the party giving the notice.

(2) *To the Officer's Qualification.* An objection based on disqualification of the officer before whom a deposition is to be taken is waived if not made:

(A) before the deposition begins; or

(B) promptly after the basis for disqualification becomes known or, with reasonable diligence, could have been known.

(3) *To the Taking of the Deposition.*

(A) *Objection to Competence, Relevance, or Materiality.* An objection to a deponent's competence—or to the competence, relevance, or materiality of testimony—is not waived by a failure to make the objection before or during the deposition, unless the ground for it might have been corrected at that time.

(B) *Objection to an Error or Irregularity.* An objection to an error or irregularity at an oral examination is waived if:

(i)   it relates to the manner of taking the deposition, the form of a question or answer, the oath or affirmation, a party's conduct, or other matters that might have been corrected at that time; and

(ii)   it is not timely made during the deposition.

(C) *Objection to a Written Question.* An objection to the form of a written question under Rule 31 is waived if not served in writing on the party submitting the question within the time for serving responsive questions or, if the question is a recross-question, within 7 days after being served with it.

(4) *To Completing and Returning the Deposition.* An objection to how the officer transcribed the testimony—or prepared, signed, certified, sealed, endorsed, sent, or otherwise dealt with the deposition—is waived unless a motion to suppress is made promptly after the error or irregularity becomes known or, with reasonable diligence, could have been known.

Rule 33. Interrogatories to Parties

(a) In General.

(1) *Number.* Unless otherwise stipulated or ordered by the court, a party may serve on any other party no more than 25 written interrogatories, including all discrete subparts. Leave to serve additional interrogatories may be granted to the extent consistent with Rule 26(b)(1) and (2).

(2) *Scope.* An interrogatory may relate to any matter that may be inquired into under Rule 26(b). An interrogatory is not objectionable merely because it asks for an opinion or contention that relates to fact or the application of law to fact, but the court may order that the interrogatory need not be answered until designated discovery is complete, or until a pretrial conference or some other time.

(b) Answers and Objections.

(1) *Responding Party.* The interrogatories must be answered:

(A) by the party to whom they are directed; or

(B) if that party is a public or private corporation, a partnership, an association, or a governmental agency, by any officer or agent, who must furnish the information available to the party.

(2) *Time to Respond.* The responding party must serve its answers and any objections within 30 days after being served with the interrogatories. A shorter or longer time may be stipulated to under Rule 29 or be ordered by the court.

(3) *Answering Each Interrogatory.* Each interrogatory must, to the extent it is not objected to, be answered separately and fully in writing under oath.

(4) *Objections.* The grounds for objecting to an interrogatory must be stated with specificity. Any ground not stated in a timely objection is waived unless the court, for good cause, excuses the failure.

(5) *Signature.* The person who makes the answers must sign them, and the attorney who objects must sign any objections.

(c) Use. An answer to an interrogatory may be used to the extent allowed by the Federal Rules of Evidence.

(d) Option to Produce Business Records. If the answer to an interrogatory may be determined by examining, auditing, compiling, abstracting, or summarizing a party's business records (including electronically stored information), and if the burden of deriving or ascertaining the answer will be substantially the same for either party, the responding party may answer by:

(1) specifying the records that must be reviewed, in sufficient detail to enable the interrogating party to locate and identify them as readily as the responding party could; and

(2) giving the interrogating party a reasonable opportunity to examine and audit the records and to make copies, compilations, abstracts, or summaries.

Rule 34. Producing Documents, Electronically Stored Information, and Tangible Things, or Entering onto Land, for Inspection and Other Purpose

(a) In General. A party may serve on any other party a request within the scope of Rule 26(b):

(1) to produce and permit the requesting party or its representative to inspect, copy, test, or sample the following items in the responding party's possession, custody, or control:

(A) any designated documents or electronically stored information—including writings, drawings, graphs, charts, photographs, sound recordings, images, and other data or data compilations—stored in any medium from which information can be obtained either directly or, if necessary, after translation by the responding party into a reasonably usable form; or

(B) any designated tangible things; or

(2) to permit entry onto designated land or other property possessed or controlled by the responding party, so that the requesting party may inspect, measure, survey, photograph, test, or sample the property or any designated object or operation on it.

(b) Procedure.

(1) *Contents of the Request.* The request:

(A) must describe with reasonable particularity each item or category of items to be inspected;

(B) must specify a reasonable time, place, and manner for the inspection and for performing the related acts; and

(C) may specify the form or forms in which electronically stored information is to be produced.

(2) *Responses and Objections.*

(A) *Time to Respond.* The party to whom the request is directed must respond in writing within 30 days after being served or – if the request was delivered under Rule 26(d)(2) – within 30 days after the parties' first Rule 26(f) conference. A shorter or longer time may be stipulated to under Rule 29 or be ordered by the court.

(B) *Responding to Each Item.* For each item or category, the response must either state that inspection and related activities will be permitted as requested or state with specificity the grounds for objecting to the request, including the reasons. The responding party may state that it will produce copies of documents or of electronically stored information instead of permitting inspection. The production must then be completed no later than the time for inspection specified in the request or another reasonable time specified in the response.

(C) *Objections.* An objection must state whether any responsive materials are being withheld on the basis of that objection. An objection to part of a request must specify the part and permit inspection of the rest.

(D) *Responding to a Request for Production of Electronically Stored Information.* The response may state an objection to a requested form for producing electronically stored information. If the responding party objects to a requested form—or if no form was specified in the request—the party must state the form or forms it intends to use.

(E) *Producing the Documents or Electronically Stored Information.* Unless otherwise stipulated or ordered by the court, these procedures apply to producing documents or electronically stored information:

(i) A party must produce documents as they are kept in the usual course of business or must organize and label them to correspond to the categories in the request;

(ii) If a request does not specify a form for producing electronically stored information, a party must produce it in a form or forms in which it is ordinarily maintained or in a reasonably usable form or forms; and

(iii) A party need not produce the same electronically stored information in more than one form.

(c) **Nonparties.** As provided in Rule 45, a nonparty may be compelled to produce documents and tangible things or to permit an inspection.

Rule 35. Physical and Mental Examinations

(a) Order for an Examination.

(1) *In General.* The court where the action is pending may order a party whose mental or physical condition—including blood group—is in controversy to submit to a physical or mental examination by a suitably licensed or certified examiner. The court has the same authority to order a party to produce for examination a person who is in its custody or under its legal control.

(2) *Motion and Notice; Contents of the Order.* The order:

(A) may be made only on motion for good cause and on notice to all parties and the person to be examined; and

(B) must specify the time, place, manner, conditions, and scope of the examination, as well as the person or persons who will perform it.

(b) Examiner's Report.

(1) *Request by the Party or Person Examined.* The party who moved for the examination must, on request, deliver to the requester a copy of the examiner's report, together with like reports of all earlier examinations of the same condition. The request may be made by the party against whom the examination order was issued or by the person examined.

(2) *Contents.* The examiner's report must be in writing and must set out in detail the examiner's findings, including diagnoses, conclusions, and the results of any tests.

(3) *Request by the Moving Party.* After delivering the reports, the party who moved for the examination may request—and is entitled to receive—from the party against whom the examination order was issued like reports of all earlier or later examinations of the same condition. But those reports need not be delivered by the party with custody or control of the person examined if the party shows that it could not obtain them.

(4) *Waiver of Privilege.* By requesting and obtaining the examiner's report, or by deposing the examiner, the party examined waives any privilege it may have—in that action or any other action involving the same controversy—concerning testimony about all examinations of the same condition.

(5) *Failure to Deliver a Report.* The court on motion may order—on just terms—that a party deliver the report of an examination. If the report is not provided, the court may exclude the examiner's testimony at trial.

(6) *Scope.* This subdivision (b) applies also to an examination made by the parties' agreement, unless the agreement states otherwise. This subdivision does not preclude obtaining an examiner's report or deposing an examiner under other rules.

Rule 36. Requests for Admission

(a) Scope and Procedure.

(1) *Scope.* A party may serve on any other party a written re quest to admit, for purposes of the pending action only, the truth of any matters within the scope of Rule 26(b)(1) relating to:

(A) facts, the application of law to fact, or opinions about either; and

(B) the genuineness of any described documents.

(2) *Form; Copy of a Document.* Each matter must be separately stated. A request to admit the genuineness of a document must be accompanied by a copy of the document unless it is, or has been, otherwise furnished or made available for inspection and copying.

(3) *Time to Respond; Effect of Not Responding.* A matter is admitted unless, within 30 days after being served, the party to whom the request is directed serves on the requesting party a written answer or objection addressed to the matter and signed by the party or its attorney. A shorter or longer time for responding may be stipulated to under Rule 29 or be ordered by the court.

(4) *Answer.* If a matter is not admitted, the answer must specifically deny it or state in detail why the answering party cannot truthfully admit or deny it. A denial must fairly respond to the substance of the matter; and when good faith requires that a party qualify an answer or deny only a part of a matter, the answer must specify the part admitted and qualify or deny the rest. The answering party may assert lack of knowledge or information as a reason for failing to admit or deny only if the party states that it has made reasonable inquiry and that the information it knows or can readily obtain is insufficient to enable it to admit or deny.

(5) *Objections.* The grounds for objecting to a request must be stated. A party must not object solely on the ground that the request presents a genuine issue for trial.

(6) *Motion Regarding the Sufficiency of an Answer or Objection.* The requesting party may move to determine the sufficiency of an answer or objection. Unless the court finds an objection justified, it must order that an answer be served. On finding that an answer does not comply with this rule, the court may order either that the matter is admitted or that an amended answer be served. The court may defer its final decision until a pretrial conference or a specified time before trial. Rule 37(a)(5) applies to an award of expenses.

(b) Effect of an Admission; Withdrawing or Amending It. A matter admitted under this rule is conclusively established unless the court, on motion, permits the admission to be withdrawn or amended. Subject to Rule 16(e), the court may permit withdrawal or amendment if it would promote the presentation of the merits of the action and if the court is not persuaded that it would prejudice the requesting party in maintaining or defending the action on the merits. An admission under this rule is not an admission for any other purpose and cannot be used against the party in any other proceeding.

Rule 37. Failure to Make Disclosures or to Cooperate in Discovery; Sanctions

(a) Motion for an Order Compelling Disclosure or Discovery.

(1) *In General.* On notice to other parties and all affected persons, a party may move for an order compelling disclosure or discovery. The motion must include a certification that the movant has in good faith conferred or attempted to confer with the person or party failing to make disclosure or discovery in an effort to obtain it without court action.

(2) *Appropriate Court.* A motion for an order to a party must be made in the court where the action is pending. A motion for an order to a nonparty must be made in the court where the discovery is or will be taken.

(3) *Specific Motions.*

(A) *To Compel Disclosure.* If a party fails to make a disclosure required by Rule 26(a), any other party may move to compel disclosure and for appropriate sanctions.

(B) *To Compel a Discovery Response.* A party seeking discovery may move for an order compelling an answer, designation, production, or inspection. This motion may be made if:

(i) a deponent fails to answer a question asked under Rule 30 or 31;

(ii) a corporation or other entity fails to make a designation under Rule 30(b)(6) or 31(a)(4);

(iii) a party fails to answer an interrogatory submitted under Rule 33; or

(iv) a party fails to produce documents or fails to respond that inspection will be permitted—or fails to permit inspection—as requested under Rule 34.

(C) *Related to a Deposition.* When taking an oral deposition, the party asking a question may complete or adjourn the examination before moving for an order.

(4) *Evasive or Incomplete Disclosure, Answer, or Response.* For purposes of this subdivision (a), an evasive or incomplete disclosure, answer, or response must be treated as a failure to disclose, answer, or respond.

(5) *Payment of Expenses; Protective Orders.*

(A) *If the Motion Is Granted (or Disclosure or Discovery Is Provided After Filing).* If the motion is granted—or if the disclosure or requested discovery is provided after the motion was filed—the court must, after giving an opportunity to be heard, require the party or deponent whose conduct necessitated the motion, the party or attorney advising that conduct, or both to pay the movant's reasonable expenses incurred in making the motion, including attorney's fees. But the court must not order this payment if:

(i) the movant filed the motion before attempting in good faith to obtain the disclosure or discovery without court action;

(ii) the opposing party's nondisclosure, response, or objection was substantially justified; or

(iii) other circumstances make an award of expenses unjust.

(B) *If the Motion Is Denied.* If the motion is denied, the court may issue any protective order authorized under Rule 26(c) and must, after giving an opportunity to be heard, require the movant, the attorney filing the motion, or both to pay the party or deponent who opposed the motion its reasonable expenses incurred in opposing the motion, including attorney's fees. But the court must not order this payment if the motion was substantially justified or other circumstances make an award of expenses unjust.

(C) *If the Motion Is Granted in Part and Denied in Part.* If the motion is granted in part and denied in part, the court may issue any protective order authorized under Rule 26(c) and may, after giving an opportunity to be heard, apportion the reasonable expenses for the motion.

(b) Failure to Comply With a Court Order.

(1) *Sanctions Sought in the District Where the Deposition Is Taken.* If the court where the discovery is taken orders a deponent to be sworn or to answer a question and the deponent fails to obey, the failure may be treated as contempt of court. If a deposition-related motion is transferred to the court where the action is pending, and that court orders a deponent to be sworn or to answer a question and the deponent fails to obey, the failure may be treated as contempt of either the court where the discovery is taken or the court where the action is pending.

(2) *Sanctions Sought in the District Where the Action Is Pending.*

(A) *For Not Obeying a Discovery Order.* If a party or a party's officer, director, or managing agent—or a witness designated under Rule 30(b)(6) or 31(a)(4)—fails to obey an order to provide or permit discovery, including an order under Rule 26(f), 35, or 37(a), the court where the action is pending may issue further just orders. They may include the following:

(i) directing that the matters embraced in the order or other designated facts be taken as established for purposes of the action, as the prevailing party claims;

(ii) prohibiting the disobedient party from supporting or opposing designated claims or defenses, or from introducing designated matters in evidence;

(iii) striking pleadings in whole or in part;

(iv) staying further proceedings until the order is obeyed;

(v) dismissing the action or proceeding in whole or in part;

(vi) rendering a default judgment against the disobedient party; or

(vii) treating as contempt of court the failure to obey any order except an order to submit to a physical or mental examination.

(B) *For Not Producing a Person for Examination.* If a party fails to comply with an order under Rule 35(a) requiring it to produce another person for examination, the court may issue any of the orders listed in Rule 37(b)(2)(A)(i)-(vi), unless the disobedient party shows that it cannot produce the other person.

(C) *Payment of Expenses.* Instead of or in addition to the orders above, the court must order the disobedient party, the attorney advising that party, or both to pay the reasonable expenses, including attorney's fees, caused by the failure, unless the failure was substantially justified or other circumstances make an award of expenses unjust.

(c) Failure to Disclose, to Supplement an Earlier Response, or to Admit.

(1) *Failure to Disclose or Supplement.* If a party fails to provide information or identify a witness as required by Rule 26(a) or (e), the party is not allowed to use that information or witness to supply evidence on a motion, at a hearing, or at a trial, unless the failure was substantially justified or is harmless. In addition to or instead of this sanction, the court, on motion and after giving an opportunity to be heard:

    (A) may order payment of the reasonable expenses, including attorney's fees, caused by the failure;

    (B) may inform the jury of the party's failure; and

    (C) may impose other appropriate sanctions, including any of the orders listed in Rule 37(b)(2)(A)(i)-(vi).

(2) *Failure to Admit.* If a party fails to admit what is requested under Rule 36 and if the requesting party later proves a document to be genuine or the matter true, the requesting party may move that the party who failed to admit pay the reasonable expenses, including attorney's fees, incurred in making that proof. The court must so order unless:

    (A) the request was held objectionable under Rule 36(a);

    (B) the admission sought was of no substantial importance;

    (C) the party failing to admit had a reasonable ground to believe that it might prevail on the matter; or

    (D) there was other good reason for the failure to admit.

(d) Party's Failure to Attend Its Own Deposition, Serve Answers to Interrogatories, or Respond to a Request for Inspection.

(1) *In General.*

    (A) *Motion; Grounds for Sanctions.* The court where the action is pending may, on motion, order sanctions if:

        (i) a party or a party's officer, director, or managing agent—or a person designated under Rule 30(b)(6) or 31(a)(4)—fails, after being served with proper notice, to appear for that person's deposition; or

        (ii) a party, after being properly served with interrogatories under Rule 33 or a request for inspection under Rule 34, fails to serve its answers, objections, or written response.

    (B) *Certification.* A motion for sanctions for failing to answer or respond must include a certification that the movant has in good faith conferred or attempted to confer with the party failing to act in an effort to obtain the answer or response without court action.

(2) *Unacceptable Excuse for Failing to Act.* A failure described in Rule 37(d)(1)(A) is not excused on the ground that the discovery sought was objectionable, unless the party failing to act has a pending motion for a protective order under Rule 26(c).

(3) *Types of Sanctions.* Sanctions may include any of the orders listed in Rule 37(b)(2)(A)(i)-(vi). Instead of or in addition to these sanctions, the court must require the party failing to act, the attorney advising that party, or both to pay the reasonable expenses, including attorney's fees, caused by the failure, unless the failure was substantially justified or other circumstances make an award of expenses unjust.

(e) Failure to Preserve Electronically Stored Information. If electronically stored information that should have been preserved in the anticipation or conduct of litigation is lost because a party failed to take reasonable steps to preserve it, and it cannot be restored or replaced through additional discovery, the court:

    (1) upon finding prejudice to another party from loss of the information, may order measures no greater than necessary to cure the prejudice; or

    (2) only upon finding that the party acted with the intent to deprive another party of the information's use in the litigation may:

        (A) presume that the lost information was unfavorable to the party;

        (B) instruct the jury that it may or must presume the information was unfavorable to the party; or

        (C) dismiss the action or enter a default judgment.

(f) Failure to Participate in Framing a Discovery Plan. If a party or its attorney fails to participate in good faith in developing and submitting a proposed discovery plan as required by Rule 26(f), the court may, after giving an opportunity to be heard, require that party or attorney to pay to any other party the reasonable expenses, including attorney's fees, caused by the failure.

TITLE VI. TRIALS

Rule 38. Right to a Jury Trial; Demand

(a) Right Preserved. The right of trial by jury as declared by the Seventh Amendment to the Constitution—or as provided by a federal statute—is preserved to the parties inviolate.

(b) Demand. On any issue triable of right by a jury, a party may demand a jury trial by:

    (1) serving the other parties with a written demand—which may be included in a pleading—no later than 14 days after the last pleading directed to the issue is served; and

    (2) filing the demand in accordance with Rule 5(d).

(c) Specifying Issues. In its demand, a party may specify the issues that it wishes to have tried by a jury; otherwise, it is considered to have demanded a jury trial on all the issues so triable. If the party has demanded a jury trial on only some issues, any other party may—within 14 days after being served with the demand or within a shorter time ordered by the court—serve a demand for a jury trial on any other or all factual issues triable by jury.

(d) Waiver; Withdrawal. A party waives a jury trial unless its demand is properly served and filed. A proper demand may be withdrawn only if the parties consent.

(e) Admiralty and Maritime Claims. These rules do not create a right to a jury trial on issues in a claim that is an admiralty or maritime claim under Rule 9(h).

Rule 39. Trial by Jury or by the Court

(a) When a Demand Is Made. When a jury trial has been demanded under Rule 38, the action must be designated on the docket as a jury action. The trial on all issues so demanded must be by jury unless:

    (1) the parties or their attorneys file a stipulation to a nonjury trial or so stipulate on the record; or

(2) the court, on motion or on its own, finds that on some or all of those issues there is no federal right to a jury trial.

(b) When No Demand Is Made. Issues on which a jury trial is not properly demanded are to be tried by the court. But the court may, on motion, order a jury trial on any issue for which a jury might have been demanded.

(c) Advisory Jury; Jury Trial by Consent. In an action not triable of right by a jury, the court, on motion or on its own:

(1) may try any issue with an advisory jury; or

(2) may, with the parties' consent, try any issue by a jury whose verdict has the same effect as if a jury trial had been a matter of right, unless the action is against the United States and a federal statute provides for a nonjury trial.

Rule 40. Scheduling Cases for Trial

Each court must provide by rule for scheduling trials. The court must give priority to actions entitled to priority by a federal statute.

Rule 41. Dismissal of Actions

(a) Voluntary Dismissal.

(1) *By the Plaintiff.*

(A) *Without a Court Order.* Subject to Rules 23(e), 23.1(c), 23.2, and 66 and any applicable federal statute, the plaintiff may dismiss an action without a court order by filing:

(i) a notice of dismissal before the opposing party serves either an answer or a motion for summary judgment; or

(ii) a stipulation of dismissal signed by all parties who have appeared.

(B) *Effect.* Unless the notice or stipulation states otherwise, the dismissal is without prejudice. But if the plaintiff previously dismissed any federal- or state-court action based on or including the same claim, a notice of dismissal operates as an adjudication on the merits.

(2) *By Court Order; Effect.* Except as provided in Rule 41(a)(1), an action may be dismissed at the plaintiff's request only by court order, on terms that the court considers proper. If a defendant has pleaded a counterclaim before being served with the plaintiff's motion to dismiss, the action may be dismissed over the defendant's objection only if the counterclaim can remain pending for independent adjudication. Unless the order states otherwise, a dismissal under this paragraph (2) is without prejudice.

(b) Involuntary Dismissal; Effect. If the plaintiff fails to prosecute or to comply with these rules or a court order, a defendant may move to dismiss the action or any claim against it. Unless the dismissal order states otherwise, a dismissal under this subdivision (b) and any dismissal not under this rule—except one for lack of jurisdiction, improper venue, or failure to join a party under Rule 19—operates as an adjudication on the merits.

(c) Dismissing a Counterclaim, Crossclaim, or Third-Party Claim. This rule applies to a dismissal of any counterclaim, crossclaim, or third-party claim. A claimant's voluntary dismissal under Rule 41(a)(1)(A)(i) must be made:

    (1) before a responsive pleading is served; or

    (2) if there is no responsive pleading, before evidence is introduced at a hearing or trial.

(d) Costs of a Previously Dismissed Action. If a plaintiff who previously dismissed an action in any court files an action based on or including the same claim against the same defendant, the court:

    (1) may order the plaintiff to pay all or part of the costs of that previous action; and

    (2) may stay the proceedings until the plaintiff has complied.

Rule 42. Consolidation; Separate Trials

(a) Consolidation. If actions before the court involve a common question of law or fact, the court may:

    (1) join for hearing or trial any or all matters at issue in the actions;

    (2) consolidate the actions; or

    (3) issue any other orders to avoid unnecessary cost or delay.

(b) Separate Trials. For convenience, to avoid prejudice, or to expedite and economize, the court may order a separate trial of one or more separate issues, claims, crossclaims, counterclaims, or third-party claims. When ordering a separate trial, the court must preserve any federal right to a jury trial.

Rule 43. Taking Testimony

(a) In Open Court. At trial, the witnesses' testimony must be taken in open court unless a federal statute, the Federal Rules of Evidence, these rules, or other rules adopted by the Supreme Court provide otherwise. For good cause in compelling circumstances and with appropriate safeguards, the court may permit testimony in open court by contemporaneous transmission from a different location.

(b) Affirmation Instead of an Oath. When these rules require an oath, a solemn affirmation suffices.

(c) Evidence on a Motion. When a motion relies on facts outside the record, the court may hear the matter on affidavits or may hear it wholly or partly on oral testimony or on depositions.

(d) Interpreter. The court may appoint an interpreter of its choosing; fix reasonable compensation to be paid from funds provided by law or by one or more parties; and tax the compensation as costs.

Rule 45. Subpoena

(a) In General.

    (1) *Form and Contents.*

        (A) *Requirements—In General.* Every subpoena must:

            (i) state the court from which it issued;

            (ii) state the title of the action and its civil-action number;

(iii)   command each person to whom it is directed to do the following at a specified time and place: attend and testify; produce designated documents, electronically stored information, or tangible things in that person's possession, custody, or control; or permit the inspection of premises; and

(iv)   set out the text of Rule 45(d) and (e).

(B) *Command to Attend a Deposition—Notice of the Recording Method.* A subpoena commanding attendance at a deposition must state the method for recording the testimony.

(C) *Combining or Separating a Command to Produce or to Permit Inspection; Specifying the Form for Electronically Stored Information.* A command to produce documents, electronically stored information, or tangible things or to permit the inspection of premises may be included in a subpoena commanding attendance at a deposition, hearing, or trial, or may be set out in a separate subpoena. A subpoena may specify the form or forms in which electronically stored information is to be produced.

(D) *Command to Produce; Included Obligations.* A command in a subpoena to produce documents, electronically stored information, or tangible things requires the responding person to permit inspection, copying, testing, or sampling of the materials.

(2) *Issuing Court.* A subpoena must issue from the court where the action is pending.

(3) *Issued by Whom.* The clerk must issue a subpoena, signed but otherwise in blank, to a party who requests it. That party must complete it before service. An attorney also may issue and sign a subpoena if the attorney is authorized to practice in the issuing court.

(4) *Notice to Other Parties Before Service.* If the subpoena commands the production of documents, electronically stored information, or tangible things or the inspection of premises before trial, then before it is served on the person to whom it is directed, a notice and a copy of the subpoena must be served on each party.

(b) Service.

(1) *By Whom and How; Tendering Fees.* Any person who is at least 18 years old and not a party may serve a subpoena. Serving a subpoena requires delivering a copy to the named person and, if the subpoena requires that person's attendance, tendering the fees for 1 day's attendance and the mileage allowed by law. Fees and mileage need not be tendered when the subpoena issues on behalf of the United States or any of its officers or agencies.

(2) *Service in the United States.* A subpoena may be served at any place within the United States.

(3) *Service in a Foreign Country.* 28 U.S.C. §1783 governs issuing and serving a subpoena directed to a United States national or resident who is in a foreign country.

(4) *Proof of Service.* Proving service, when necessary, requires filing with the issuing court a statement showing the date and manner of service and the names of the persons served. The statement must be certified by the server.

(c) Place of Compliance.

(1) *For a Trial, Hearing, or Deposition.* A subpoena may command a person to attend a trial, hearing, or deposition only as follows:

(A)   within 100 miles of where the person resides, is employed, or regularly transacts business in person; or

(B) within the state where the person resides, is employed, or regularly transacts business in person, if the person

> (i)   is a party or a party's officer; or
>
> (ii)   is commanded to attend a trial and would not incur substantial expense.

(2) *For Other Discovery.* A subpoena may command:

(A) production of documents, electronically stored information, or tangible things at a place within 100 miles of where the person resides, is employed, or regularly transacts business in person; and

(B) inspection of premises at the premises to be inspected.

(d) Protecting a Person Subject to a Subpoena; Enforcement.

(1) *Avoiding Undue Burden or Expense; Sanctions.* A party or attorney responsible for issuing and serving a subpoena must take reasonable steps to avoid imposing undue burden or expense on a person subject to the subpoena. The court for the district where compliance is required must enforce this duty and impose an appropriate sanction—which may include lost earnings and reasonable attorney's fees—on a party or attorney who fails to comply.

(2) *Command to Produce Materials or Permit Inspection.*

(A) *Appearance Not Required.* A person commanded to produce documents, electronically stored information, or tangible things, or to permit the inspection of premises, need not appear in person at the place of production or inspection unless also commanded to appear for a deposition, hearing, or trial.

(B) *Objections.* A person commanded to produce documents or tangible things or to permit inspection may serve on the party or attorney designated in the subpoena a written objection to inspecting, copying, testing or sampling any or all of the materials or to inspecting the premises—or to producing electronically stored information in the form or forms requested. The objection must be served before the earlier of the time specified for compliance or 14 days after the subpoena is served. If an objection is made, the following rules apply:

> (i)   At any time, on notice to the commanded person, the serving party may move the court for the district where compliance is required for an order compelling production or inspection.
>
> (ii)   These acts may be required only as directed in the order, and the order must protect a person who is neither a party nor a party's officer from significant expense resulting from compliance.

(3) *Quashing or Modifying a Subpoena.*

(A) *When Required.* On timely motion, the court for the district where compliance is required must quash or modify a subpoena that:

> (i)   fails to allow a reasonable time to comply;
>
> (ii)   requires a person to comply beyond the geographical limits specified in Rule 45(c);
>
> (iii)   requires disclosure of privileged or other protected matter, if no exception or waiver applies; or
>
> (iv)   subjects a person to undue burden.

(B) *When Permitted.* To protect a person subject to or affected by a subpoena, the court for the district where compliance is required may, on motion, quash or modify the subpoena if it requires:

(i)   disclosing a trade secret or other confidential research, development, or commercial information; or

(ii)   disclosing an unretained expert's opinion or information that does not describe specific occurrences in dispute and results from the expert's study that was not requested by a party.

(C) *Specifying Conditions as an Alternative.* In the circumstances described in Rule 45(d)(3)(B), the court may, instead of quashing or modifying a subpoena, order appearance or production under specified conditions if the serving party:

(i)   shows a substantial need for the testimony or material that cannot be otherwise met without undue hardship; and

(ii)   ensures that the subpoenaed person will be reasonably compensated.

(e) Duties in Responding to a Subpoena.

(1) *Producing Documents or Electronically Stored Information.* These procedures apply to producing documents or electronically stored information:

(A) *Documents.* A person responding to a subpoena to produce documents must produce them as they are kept in the ordinary course of business or must organize and label them to correspond to the categories in the demand.

(B) *Form for Producing Electronically Stored Information Not Specified.* If a subpoena does not specify a form for producing electronically stored information, the person responding must produce it in a form or forms in which it is ordinarily maintained or in a reasonably usable form or forms.

(C) *Electronically Stored Information Produced in Only One Form.* The person responding need not produce the same electronically stored information in more than one form.

(D) *Inaccessible Electronically Stored Information.* The person responding need not provide discovery of electronically stored information from sources that the person identifies as not reasonably accessible because of undue burden or cost. On motion to compel discovery or for a protective order, the person responding must show that the information is not reasonably accessible because of undue burden or cost. If that showing is made, the court may nonetheless order discovery from such sources if the requesting party shows good cause, considering the limitations of Rule 26(b)(2)(C). The court may specify conditions for the discovery.

(2) *Claiming Privilege or Protection.*

(A) *Information Withheld.* A person withholding subpoenaed information under a claim that it is privileged or subject to protection as trial-preparation material must:

(i)   expressly make the claim; and

(ii)   describe the nature of the withheld documents, communications, or tangible things in a manner that, without revealing information itself privileged or protected, will enable the parties to assess the claim.

(B) *Information Produced.* If information produced in response to a subpoena is subject to a claim of privilege or of protection as trial-preparation material, the person making the claim may notify any party that received the information of the claim and the basis for it. After being notified, a party must promptly return, sequester, or destroy the specified information and any copies it has; must not use or disclose the information until the claim is resolved; must take reasonable steps to retrieve the information if the party disclosed it before being notified; and may promptly present the information under seal to the court for the district where compliance is required for a determination of the claim. The person who produced the information must preserve the information until the claim is resolved.

(f) Transferring a Subpoena-Related Motion. When the court where compliance is required did not issue the subpoena, it may transfer a motion under this rule to the issuing court if the person subject to the subpoena consents or if the court finds exceptional circumstances. Then, if the attorney for a person subject to a subpoena is authorized to practice in the court where the motion was made, the attorney may file papers and appear on the motion as an officer of the issuing court. To enforce its order, the issuing court may transfer the order to the court where the motion was made.

(g) Contempt. The court for the district where compliance is required — and also, after a motion is transferred, the issuing court — may hold in contempt a person who, having been served, fails without adequate excuse to obey the subpoena or an order related to it.

Rule 46. Objecting to a Ruling or Order

A formal exception to a ruling or order is unnecessary. When the ruling or order is requested or made, a party need only state the action that it wants the court to take or objects to, along with the grounds for the request or objection. Failing to object does not prejudice a party who had no opportunity to do so when the ruling or order was made.

TITLE VII. JUDGMENT

Rule 54. Judgment; Costs

(a) Definition; Form. "Judgment" as used in these rules includes a decree and any order from which an appeal lies. A judgment should not include recitals of pleadings, a master's report, or a record of prior proceedings.

(b) Judgment on Multiple Claims or Involving Multiple Parties. When an action presents more than one claim for relief— whether as a claim, counterclaim, crossclaim, or third-party claim—or when multiple parties are involved, the court may direct entry of a final judgment as to one or more, but fewer than all, claims or parties only if the court expressly determines that there is no just reason for delay. Otherwise, any order or other decision, however designated, that adjudicates fewer than all the claims or the rights and liabilities of fewer than all the parties does not end the action as to any of the claims or parties and may be revised at any time before the entry of a judgment adjudicating all the claims and all the parties' rights and liabilities.

(c) Demand for Judgment; Relief to Be Granted. A default judgment must not differ in kind from, or exceed in amount, what is demanded in the pleadings. Every other final judgment should grant the relief to which each party is entitled, even if the party has not demanded that relief in its pleadings.

(d) Costs; Attorney's Fees.

(1) *Costs Other Than Attorney's Fees.* Unless a federal statute, these rules, or a court order provides otherwise, costs—other than attorney's fees—should be allowed to the prevailing

party. But costs against the United States, its officers, and its agencies may be imposed only to the extent allowed by law. The clerk may tax costs on 14 days' notice. On motion served within the next 7 days, the court may review the clerk's action.

(2) *Attorney's Fees.*

(A) *Claim to Be by Motion.* A claim for attorney's fees and related nontaxable expenses must be made by motion unless the substantive law requires those fees to be proved at trial as an element of damages.

(B) *Timing and Contents of the Motion.* Unless a statute or a court order provides otherwise, the motion must:

(i)   be filed no later than 14 days after the entry of judgment;

(ii)   specify the judgment and the statute, rule, or other grounds entitling the movant to the award;

(iii) state the amount sought or provide a fair estimate of it; and

(iv)   disclose, if the court so orders, the terms of any agreement about fees for the services for which the claim is made.

(C) *Proceedings.* Subject to Rule 23(h), the court must, on a party's request, give an opportunity for adversary submissions on the motion in accordance with Rule 43(c) or 78. The court may decide issues of liability for fees before receiving submissions on the value of services. The court must find the facts and state its conclusions of law as provided in Rule 52(a).

(D) *Special Procedures by Local Rule; Reference to a Master or a Magistrate Judge.* By local rule, the court may establish special procedures to resolve fee-related issues without extensive evidentiary hearings. Also, the court may refer issues concerning the value of services to a special master under Rule 53 without regard to the limitations of Rule 53(a)(1), and may refer a motion for attorney's fees to a magistrate judge under Rule 72(b) as if it were a dispositive pretrial matter.

(E) *Exceptions.* Subparagraphs (A)–(D) do not apply to claims for fees and expenses as sanctions for violating these rules or as sanctions under 28 U.S.C. § 1927.

Rule 55. Default; Default Judgment

(a) Entering a Default. When a party against whom a judgment for affirmative relief is sought has failed to plead or otherwise defend, and that failure is shown by affidavit or otherwise, the clerk must enter the party's default.

(b) Entering a Default Judgment.

(1) *By the Clerk.* If the plaintiff's claim is for a sum certain or a sum that can be made certain by computation, the clerk—on the plaintiff's request, with an affidavit showing the amount due—must enter judgment for that amount and costs against a defendant who has been defaulted for not appearing and who is neither a minor nor an incompetent person.

(2) *By the Court.* In all other cases, the party must apply to the court for a default judgment. A default judgment may be entered against a minor or incompetent person only if represented by a general guardian, conservator, or other like fiduciary who has appeared. If the party against whom a default judgment is sought has appeared personally or by a representative, that party or its representative must be served with written notice of the application at least

7 days before the hearing. The court may conduct hearings or make referrals—preserving any federal statutory right to a jury trial—when, to enter or effectuate judgment, it needs to:

> (A) conduct an accounting;
>
> (B) determine the amount of damages;
>
> (C) establish the truth of any allegation by evidence; or
>
> (D) investigate any other matter.

(c) Setting Aside a Default or a Default Judgment. The court may set aside an entry of default for good cause, and it may set aside a final default judgment under Rule 60(b).

(d) Judgment Against the United States. A default judgment may be entered against the United States, its officers, or its agencies only if the claimant establishes a claim or right to relief by evidence that satisfies the court.

Rule 56. Summary Judgment

(a) Motion for Summary Judgment or Partial Summary Judgment. A party may move for summary judgment, identifying each claim or defense—or the part of each claim or defense—on which summary judgment is sought. The court shall grant summary judgment if the movant shows that there is no genuine dispute as to any material fact and the movant is entitled to judgment as a matter of law. The court should state on the record the reasons for granting or denying the motion.

(b) Time to File a Motion. Unless a different time is set by local rule or the court orders otherwise, a party may file a motion for summary judgment at any time until 30 days after the close of all discovery.

(c) Procedures.

> (1) *Supporting Factual Positions.* A party asserting that a fact cannot be or is genuinely disputed must support the assertion by:
>
> > (A) citing to particular parts of materials in the record, including depositions, documents, electronically stored information, affidavits or declarations, stipulations (including those made for purposes of the motion only), admissions, interrogatory answers, or other materials; or
> >
> > (B) showing that the materials cited do not establish the absence or presence of a genuine dispute, or that an adverse party cannot produce admissible evidence to support the fact.
>
> (2) *Objection That a Fact Is Not Supported by Admissible Evidence.* A party may object that the material cited to support or dispute a fact cannot be presented in a form that would be admissible in evidence.
>
> (3) *Materials Not Cited.* The court need consider only the cited materials, but it may consider other materials in the record.
>
> (4) *Affidavits or Declarations.* An affidavit or declaration used to support or oppose a motion must be made on personal knowledge, set out facts that would be admissible in evidence, and show that the affiant or declarant is competent to testify on the matters stated.

(d) When Facts Are Unavailable to the Nonmovant. If a nonmovant shows by affidavit or declaration that, for specified reasons, it cannot present facts essential to justify its opposition, the court may:

> (1) defer considering the motion or deny it;

(2) allow time to obtain affidavits or declarations or to take discovery; or

(3) issue any other appropriate order.

(e) Failing to Properly Support or Address a Fact. If a party fails to properly support an assertion of fact or fails to properly address another party's assertion of fact as required by Rule 56(c), the court may:

(1) give an opportunity to properly support or address the fact;

(2) consider the fact undisputed for purposes of the motion;

(3) grant summary judgment if the motion and supporting materials—including the facts considered undisputed—show that the movant is entitled to it; or

(4) issue any other appropriate order.

(f) Judgment Independent of the Motion. After giving notice and a reasonable time to respond, the court may:

(1) grant summary judgment for a nonmovant;

(2) grant the motion on grounds not raised by a party; or

(3) consider summary judgment on its own after identifying for the parties material facts that may not be genuinely in dispute.

(g) Failing to Grant All the Requested Relief. If the court does not grant all the relief requested by the motion, it may enter an order stating any material fact—including an item of damages or other relief—that is not genuinely in dispute and treating the fact as established in the case.

(h) Affidavit or Declaration Submitted In Bad Faith. If satisfied that an affidavit or declaration under this rule is submitted in bad faith or solely for delay, the court—after notice and a reasonable time to respond—may order the submitting party to pay the other party the reasonable expenses, including attorney's fees, it incurred as a result. An offending party or attorney may also be held in contempt or subjected to other appropriate sanctions.

Rule 57. Declaratory Judgment

These rules govern the procedure for obtaining a declaratory judgment under 28 U.S.C. § 2201. Rules 38 and 39 govern a demand for a jury trial. The existence of another adequate remedy does not preclude a declaratory judgment that is otherwise appropriate. The court may order a speedy hearing of a declaratory-judgment action.

TITLE VIII. PROVISIONAL AND FINAL REMEDIES

Rule 64. Seizing a Person or Property

(a) Remedies Under State Law—In General. At the commencement of and throughout an action, every remedy is available that, under the law of the state where the court is located, provides for seizing a person or property to secure satisfaction of the potential judgment. But a federal statute governs to the extent it applies.

(b) Specific Kinds of Remedies. The remedies available under this rule include the following—however designated and regardless of whether state procedure requires an independent action:

- arrest;
- attachment;

- garnishment;
- replevin;
- sequestration; and
- other corresponding or equivalent remedies.

Rule 65. Injunctions and Restraining Orders

(a) Preliminary Injunction.

(1) *Notice.* The court may issue a preliminary injunction only on notice to the adverse party.

(2) *Consolidating the Hearing with the Trial on the Merits.* Before or after beginning the hearing on a motion for a preliminary injunction, the court may advance the trial on the merits and consolidate it with the hearing. Even when consolidation is not ordered, evidence that is received on the motion and that would be admissible at trial becomes part of the trial record and need not be repeated at trial. But the court must preserve any party's right to a jury trial.

(b) Temporary Restraining Order.

(1) *Issuing Without Notice.* The court may issue a temporary restraining order without written or oral notice to the adverse party or its attorney only if:

(A) specific facts in an affidavit or a verified complaint clearly show that immediate and irreparable injury, loss, or damage will result to the movant before the adverse party can be heard in opposition; and

(B) the movant's attorney certifies in writing any efforts made to give notice and the reasons why it should not be required.

(2) *Contents; Expiration.* Every temporary restraining order issued without notice must state the date and hour it was issued; describe the injury and state why it is irreparable; state why the order was issued without notice; and be promptly filed in the clerk's office and entered in the record. The order expires at the time after entry—not to exceed 14 days—that the court sets, unless before that time the court, for good cause, extends it for a like period or the adverse party consents to a longer extension. The reasons for an extension must be entered in the record.

(3) *Expediting the Preliminary-Injunction Hearing.* If the order is issued without notice, the motion for a preliminary injunction must be set for hearing at the earliest possible time, taking precedence over all other matters except hearings on older matters of the same character. At the hearing, the party who obtained the order must proceed with the motion; if the party does not, the court must dissolve the order.

(4) *Motion to Dissolve.* On 2 days' notice to the party who obtained the order without notice—or on shorter notice set by the court—the adverse party may appear and move to dissolve or modify the order. The court must then hear and decide the motion as promptly as justice requires.

(c) Security. The court may issue a preliminary injunction or a temporary restraining order only if the movant gives security in an amount that the court considers proper to pay the costs and damages sustained by any party found to have been wrongfully enjoined or restrained. The United States, its officers, and its agencies are not required to give security.

(d) Contents and Scope of Every Injunction and Restraining Order.

(1) *Contents.* Every order granting an injunction and every restraining order must:

(A) state the reasons why it issued;

(B) state its terms specifically; and

(C) describe in reasonable detail—and not by referring to the complaint or other document—the act or acts restrained or required.

(2) *Persons Bound.* The order binds only the following who receive actual notice of it by personal service or otherwise:

(A) the parties;

(B) the parties' officers, agents, servants, employees, and attorneys; and

(C) other persons who are in active concert or participation with anyone described in Rule 65(d)(2)(A) or (B).

(e) Other Laws Not Modified. These rules do not modify the following:

(1) any federal statute relating to temporary restraining orders or preliminary injunctions in actions affecting employer and employee;

(2) 28 U.S.C. § 2361, which relates to preliminary injunctions in actions of interpleader or in the nature of interpleader; or

(3) 28 U.S.C. § 2284, which relates to actions that must be heard and decided by a three-judge district court.

(f) Copyright Impoundment. This rule applies to copyright-impoundment proceedings.

Rule 68. Offer of Judgment

(a) Making An Offer; Judgment On An Accepted Offer. At least 14 days before the date set for trial, a party defending against a claim may serve on an opposing party an offer to allow judgment on specified terms, with the costs then accrued. If, within 14 days after being served, the opposing party serves written notice accepting the offer, either party may then file the offer and notice of acceptance, plus proof of service. The clerk must then enter judgment.

(b) Unaccepted Offer. An unaccepted offer is considered withdrawn, but it does not preclude a later offer. Evidence of an unaccepted offer is not admissible except in a proceeding to determine costs.

(c) Offer After Liability Is Determined. When one party's liability to another has been determined but the extent of liability remains to be determined by further proceedings, the party held liable may make an offer of judgment. It must be served within a reasonable time—but at least 14 days—before the date set for a hearing to determine the extent of liability.

(d) Paying Costs After An Unaccepted Offer. If the judgment that the offeree finally obtains is not more favorable than the unaccepted offer, the offeree must pay the costs incurred after the offer was made.

TITLE IX. SPECIAL PROCEEDINGS

Rule 72. Magistrate Judges: Pretrial Order

(a) Nondispositive Matters. When a pretrial matter not dispositive of a party's claim or defense is referred to a magistrate judge to hear and decide, the magistrate judge must promptly conduct the required proceedings and, when appropriate, issue a written order stating the decision. A party may serve and file objections to the order within 14 days after being served with a copy. A party may not assign as error a defect in the order not timely objected to. The district judge in the case must consider timely objections and modify or set aside any part of the order that is clearly erroneous or is contrary to law.

(b) Dispositive Motions and Prisoner Petitions.

(1) *Findings and Recommendations.* A magistrate judge must promptly conduct the required proceedings when assigned, without the parties' consent, to hear a pretrial matter dispositive of a claim or defense or a prisoner petition challenging the conditions of confinement. A record must be made of all evidentiary proceedings and may, at the magistrate judge's discretion, be made of any other proceedings. The magistrate judge must enter a recommended disposition, including, if appropriate, proposed findings of fact. The clerk must promptly mail a copy to each party.

(2) *Objections.* Within 14 days after being served with a copy of the recommended disposition, a party may serve and file specific written objections to the proposed findings and recommendations. A party may respond to another party's objections within 14 days after being served with a copy. Unless the district judge orders otherwise, the objecting party must promptly arrange for transcribing the record, or whatever portions of it the parties agree to or the magistrate judge considers sufficient.

(3) *Resolving Objections.* The district judge must determine de novo any part of the magistrate judge's disposition that has been properly objected to. The district judge may accept, reject, or modify the recommended disposition; receive further evidence; or return the matter to the magistrate judge with instructions.

TITLE X. DISTRICT COURTS AND CLERKS: CONDUCTING BUSINESS; ISSUING ORDERS

Rule 77. Conducting Business; Clerk's Authority; Notice of an Order or Judgment

(a) When Court Is Open. Every district court is considered always open for filing any paper, issuing and returning process, making a motion, or entering an order.

(b) Place for Trial and Other Proceedings. Every trial on the merits must be conducted in open court and, so far as convenient, in a regular courtroom. Any other act or proceeding may be done or conducted by a judge in chambers, without the attendance of the clerk or other court official, and anywhere inside or outside the district. But no hearing—other than one ex parte—may be conducted outside the district unless all the affected parties consent.

(c) Clerk's Office Hours; Clerk's Orders.

(1) *Hours.* The clerk's office—with a clerk or deputy on duty—must be open during business hours every day except Saturdays, Sundays, and legal holidays. But a court may, by local rule or order, require that the office be open for specified hours on Saturday or a particular legal holiday other than one listed in Rule 6(a)(6)(A).

(2) *Orders.* Subject to the court's power to suspend, alter, or rescind the clerk's action for good cause, the clerk may:

(A) issue process;

(B) enter a default;

(C) enter a default judgment under Rule 55(b)(1); and

(D) act on any other matter that does not require the court's action.

(d) SERVING NOTICE OF AN ORDER OR JUDGMENT.

(1) *Service.* Immediately after entering an order or judgment, the clerk must serve notice of the entry, as provided in Rule 5(b), on each party who is not in default for failing to appear. The clerk must record the service on the docket. A party also may serve notice of the entry as provided in Rule 5(b).

(2) *Time to Appeal Not Affected by Lack of Notice.* Lack of notice of the entry does not affect the time for appeal or relieve—or authorize the court to relieve—a party for failing to appeal within the time allowed, except as allowed by Federal Rule of Appellate Procedure (4)(a).

Rule 78. Hearing Motions; Submission on Briefs

(a) **Providing a Regular Schedule for Oral Hearings.** A court may establish regular times and places for oral hearings on motions.

(b) **Providing For Submission on Briefs.** By rule or order, the court may provide for submitting and determining motions on briefs, without oral hearings.

Rule 79. Records Kept by the Clerk

(a) **Civil Docket.**

(1) *In General.* The clerk must keep a record known as the "civil docket" in the form and manner prescribed by the Director of the Administrative Office of the United States Courts with the approval of the Judicial Conference of the United States. The clerk must enter each civil action in the docket. Actions must be assigned consecutive file numbers, which must be noted in the docket where the first entry of the action is made.

(2) *Items to be Entered.* The following items must be marked with the file number and entered chronologically in the docket:

(A) papers filed with the clerk;

(B) process issued, and proofs of service or other returns showing execution; and

(C) appearances, orders, verdicts, and judgments.

(3) *Contents of Entries; Jury Trial Demanded.* Each entry must briefly show the nature of the paper filed or writ issued, the substance of each proof of service or other return, and the substance and date of entry of each order and judgment. When a jury trial has been properly demanded or ordered, the clerk must enter the word "jury" in the docket.

(b) **Civil Judgments and Orders.** The clerk must keep a copy of every final judgment and appealable order; of every order affecting title to or a lien on real or personal property; and of any other order that the court directs to be kept. The clerk must keep these in the form and manner prescribed by the Director of the Administrative Office of the United States Courts with the approval of the Judicial Conference of the United States.

(c) **Indexes; Calendars.** Under the court's direction, the clerk must:

(1) keep indexes of the docket and of the judgments and orders described in Rule 79(b); and

(2) prepare calendars of all actions ready for trial, distinguishing jury trials from nonjury trials.

(d) Other Records. The clerk must keep any other records required by the Director of the Administrative Office of the United States Courts with the approval of the Judicial Conference of the United States.

Rule 80. Stenographic Transcript as Evidence

If stenographically reported testimony at a hearing or trial is admissible in evidence at a later trial, the testimony may be proved by a transcript certified by the person who reported it.

Rule 84. Forms

[Abrogated Apr. 29, 2015, eff. Dec. 1, 2015.]

FEDERAL RULES OF CIVIL PROCEDURE
APPENDIX OF FORMS

(Note: As of December 1, 2015, the Appendix of Forms is no longer an official part of the Federal Rules of Civil Procedure. We have retained the Appendix in this Document Supplement because it remains useful to illustrate documents that are filed in the course of a lawsuit.)

Civil Forms 1 and 2 (combined). Caption, Date, Signature, Address, E-mail Address, and Telephone Number.

UNITED STATES DISTRICT COURT
for the
<_____> DISTRICT OF <_____>

<Name(s) of plaintiff(s)>,	)
	)
Plaintiff(s)	)
	)
v.	)
	) Civil Action No. <Number>
	)
<Name(s) of defendant(s)>,	)
	)
Defendant(s)	)
	)
v. <Use if needed>	)
	)
<Name(s) of third-party defendant(s)>,	)
	)
Third-Party Defendant(s)	)
	)

<NAME OF DOCUMENT>

Date: <Date>   <Signature of the attorney or unrepresented party>

_____

<Printed name>
<Address>
<E-mail address>
<Telephone number>

Civil Form 3. Summons.

UNITED STATES DISTRICT COURT
for the
<_____> DISTRICT OF <_____>

<Name(s) of plaintiff(s)>,	)	
	)	
Plaintiff(s)	)	
	)	
v.	)	
	)	Civil Action No. <Number>
<Name(s) of defendant(s)>,	)	
	)	
Defendant(s)	)	
	)	

SUMMONS

To: <Name of the defendant>

A lawsuit has been filed against you.

Within 20 days <Use 60 days if the defendant is the United States or a United States agency, or is an officer or employee of the United States allowed 60 days by Rule 12(a)(3)> after service of this summons on you (not counting the day you received it), you must serve on the plaintiff an answer to the attached complaint or a motion under Rule 12 of the Federal Rules of Civil Procedure. The answer or motion must be served on the plaintiff's attorney, <Name of Plaintiff's Attorney>, whose address is <Address of Plaintiff's Attorney>. If you fail to do so, judgment by default will be entered against you for the relief demanded in the complaint. You also must file your answer or motion with the court.

Date: <Date>   <Signature of Clerk of Court>

_____

Clerk of Court

(Court Seal)

Civil Form 4. Summons on a Third-Party Complaint.

UNITED STATES DISTRICT COURT
for the
<_____> DISTRICT OF <_____>

\<Name(s) of plaintiff(s)\>,	)	
	)	
Plaintiff(s)	)	
	)	
v.	)	
	)	Case No. \<Number\>
\<Name(s) of defendant(s)\>,	)	
	)	
Defendant(s)	)	
	)	
v.	)	
	)	
\<Name(s) of third-party defendant(s)\>,	)	
	)	
Third-Party Defendant(s)	)	
	)	

SUMMONS ON A THIRD PARTY COMPLAINT

To: \<Name of the third-party defendant\>

A lawsuit has been filed against defendant \<Name of the defendant\>, who as third-party plaintiff is making this claim against you to pay part or all of what the defendant may owe to the plaintiff \<Name of the plaintiff\>.

Within 20 days after service of this summons on you (not counting the day you received it), you must serve on the plaintiff and on the defendant an answer to the attached third-party complaint or a motion under Rule 12 of the Federal Rules of Civil Procedure. The answer or motion must be served on the defendant's attorney, \<Name of defendant's attorney\>, whose address is \<Address of defendant's attorney\>, and also on the plaintiff's attorney, \<Name of plaintiff's attorney\>, whose address is \<Address of plaintiff's attorney\>. If you fail to do so, judgment by default will be entered against you for the relief demanded in the third-party complaint. You also must file the answer or motion with the court and serve it on any other parties.

A copy of the plaintiff's complaint is also attached. You may — but are not required to — respond to it.

Date: \<Date\>   \<Signature of Clerk of Court\>

_____

Clerk of Court

(Court Seal)

Civil Form 7. Statement of Jurisdiction.

\<Statement of Jurisdiction (choose applicable paragraph).\>

    \<a.   For diversity-of-citizenship jurisdiction.\> The plaintiff is [a citizen of State A] [a corporation incorporated under the laws of State A with its principal place of business in State A]. The defendant is [a citizen of State B] [a corporation incorporated under the laws of State B with its principal place of business in State B]. The amount in controversy, without interest and costs, exceeds the sum or value specified by 28 U.S.C. § 1332.

    \<b.   For federal-question jurisdiction.\> This action arises under [the United States Constitution; specify the article or amendment and the section] [a United States treaty; specify] [a federal statute, _____U.S.C. § _____].

    \<c.   For a claim in the admiralty or maritime jurisdiction.\> This is a case of admiralty or maritime jurisdiction. **\<To invoke admiralty status under Rule 9(h) use the following**: This is an admiralty or maritime claim within the meaning of Rule 9(h).\>

Civil Form 8. Statement of Reasons for Omitting a Party

\<Statement of Reasons for Omitting a Party.
_If a person who ought to be made a party under Rule 19(a) is not named, include this statement in accordance with Rule 19(c)._\>

    This complaint does not join as a party \<Name\> who [is not subject to this court's personal jurisdiction] [cannot be made a party without depriving this court of subject-matter jurisdiction] because \<state the reason\>.

Civil Form 11. Complaint for Negligence.

UNITED STATES DISTRICT COURT
for the
<_____> DISTRICT OF <_____>

<Name(s) of plaintiff(s)>,	)	
	)	
Plaintiff(s)	)	
	)	
v.	)	
	)	Civil Action No. <Number>
<Name(s) of defendant(s)>,	)	
	)	
Defendant(s)	)	
	)	

COMPLAINT FOR NEGLIGENCE

1.   **<Statement of Jurisdiction. See Form 7.>**
    <a. For diversity-of-citizenship jurisdiction.> The plaintiff is [a citizen of State A] [a corporation incorporated under the laws of State A with its principal place of business in State A]. The defendant is [a citizen of State B] [a corporation incorporated under the laws of State B with its principal place of business in State B]. The amount in controversy, without interest and costs, exceeds the sum or value specified by 28 U.S.C. § 1332.
    <b. For federal-question jurisdiction.> This action arises under [the United States Constitution; specify the article or amendment and the section] [a United States treaty; specify] [a federal statute, _____U.S.C. § _____].
    <c. For a claim in the admiralty or maritime jurisdiction.> This is a case of admiralty or maritime jurisdiction. *<To invoke admiralty status under Rule 9(h) use the following*: This is an admiralty or maritime claim within the meaning of Rule 9(h).>

2.   On <Date>, at <Place>, the defendant negligently drove a motor vehicle against the plaintiff.

3.   As a result, the plaintiff was physically injured, lost wages or income, suffered physical and mental pain, and incurred medical expenses of $ <_____>.

    Therefore, the plaintiff demands judgment against the defendant for $ <_____>, plus costs.

Date: <Date>   <Signature of the attorney or unrepresented party>

                                          _____
                                          <Printed name>
                                          <Address>
                                          <E-mail address>
                                          <Telephone number>

Civil Form 12. Complaint for Negligence When the Plaintiff Does Not Know Who Is Responsible.

UNITED STATES DISTRICT COURT
for the
<_____> DISTRICT OF <_____>

<Name(s) of plaintiff(s)>,	)	
	)	
Plaintiff(s)	)	
	)	
v.	)	
	)	Civil Action No. <Number>
<Name(s) of defendant(s)>,	)	
	)	
Defendant(s)	)	
	)	

COMPLAINT FOR NEGLIGENCE WHEN THE PLAINTIFF DOES NOT KNOW WHO IS RESPONSIBLE

1. **<Statement of Jurisdiction. See Form 7.>**
    <a. For diversity-of-citizenship jurisdiction.> The plaintiff is [a citizen of State A] [a corporation incorporated under the laws of State A with its principal place of business in State A]. The defendant is [a citizen of State B] [a corporation incorporated under the laws of State B with its principal place of business in State B]. The amount in controversy, without interest and costs, exceeds the sum or value specified by 28 U.S.C. § 1332.
    <b. For federal-question jurisdiction.> This action arises under [the United States Constitution; specify the article or amendment and the section] [a United States treaty; specify] [a federal statute, _____ U.S.C. § _____].
    <c. For a claim in the admiralty or maritime jurisdiction.> This is a case of admiralty or maritime jurisdiction. *<To invoke admiralty status under Rule 9(h) use the following*: This is an admiralty or maritime claim within the meaning of Rule 9(h).>

2. On <Date>, at <Place>, defendant <Name of first defendant> or defendant <Name of second defendant> or both of them willfully or recklessly or negligently drove, or caused to be driven, a motor vehicle against the plaintiff.

3. As a result, the plaintiff was physically injured, lost wages or income, suffered mental and physical pain, and incurred medical expenses of $ <_____>.

    Therefore, the plaintiff demands judgment against one or both defendants for $ <_____>, plus costs.

Date: <Date>   <Signature of the attorney or unrepresented party>

                                          _____
                                          <Printed name>
                                          <Address>
                                          <E-mail address>
                                          <Telephone number>

**Civil Form 13. Complaint for Negligence
Under the Federal Employers' Liability Act.**

UNITED STATES DISTRICT COURT
for the
<_____> DISTRICT OF <_____>

<Name(s) of plaintiff(s)>,	)	
	)	
Plaintiff(s)	)	
	)	
v.	)	
	)	Civil Action No. <Number>
<Name(s) of defendant(s)>,	)	
	)	
Defendant(s)	)	
	)	

COMPLAINT FOR NEGLIGENCE UNDER THE FEDERAL EMPLOYERS' LIABILITY ACT

1. <Statement of Jurisdiction. See Form 7.>

   <*a. For diversity-of-citizenship jurisdiction.*> The plaintiff is [a citizen of State A] [a corporation incorporated under the laws of State A with its principal place of business in State A]. The defendant is [a citizen of State B] [a corporation incorporated under the laws of State B with its principal place of business in State B]. The amount in controversy, without interest and costs, exceeds the sum or value specified by 28 U.S.C. § 1332.

   <*b. For federal-question jurisdiction.*> This action arises under [the United States Constitution; specify the article or amendment and the section] [a United States treaty; specify] [a federal statute, _____U.S.C. § _____].

   <*c. For a claim in the admiralty or maritime jurisdiction.*> This is a case of admiralty or maritime jurisdiction. <*To invoke admiralty status under Rule 9(h) use the following*: This is an admiralty or maritime claim within the meaning of Rule 9(h).>

2. <At the times below, the defendant owned and operated in interstate commerce a railroad line that passed through a tunnel located at _____.>

3. <On _____(Date), the plaintiff was working to repair and enlarge the tunnel to make it convenient and safe for use in interstate commerce.>

4. <During this work, the defendant, as the employer, negligently put the plaintiff to work in a section of the tunnel that the defendant had left unprotected and unsupported.>

5. <The defendant's negligence caused the plaintiff to be injured by a rock that fell from an unsupported portion of the tunnel.>

6. <As a result, the plaintiff was physically injured, lost wages or income, suffered mental and physical pain, and incurred medical expenses of $ _____.>

   Therefore, the plaintiff demands judgment against the defendant for $ <_____>, and costs.

82

Date: \<Date\>   \<Signature of the attorney or unrepresented party\>

\<Printed name\>
\<Address\>
\<E-mail address\>
\<Telephone number\>

Civil Form 16. Third-Party Complaint.

UNITED STATES DISTRICT COURT
for the
<_____> DISTRICT OF <_____>

<Name(s) of plaintiff(s)>,	)	
	)	
Plaintiff(s)	)	
	)	
v.	)	
	)	Civil Action No. <Number>
<Name(s) of defendant(s)>,	)	
	)	
Defendant(s)	)	
	)	
v.	)	
	)	
<Name(s) of third-party defendant(s)>,	)	
	)	
Third-Party Defendant(s)	)	
	)	

THIRD-PARTY COMPLAINT

1.   Plaintiff <Name of plaintiff> has filed against defendant <Name of defendant> a complaint, a copy of which is attached.

2.   <State grounds entitling (defendant's name) to recover from (third-party defendant's name) for (all or an identified share) of any judgment for (plaintiff's name) against (defendant's name).>

   Therefore, the defendant demands judgment against <third-party defendant's name> for <all or an identified share> of sums that may be adjudged against the defendant in the plaintiff's favor.

Date: <Date>   <Signature of the attorney or unrepresented party>

                                            _____
                                            <Printed name>
                                            <Address>
                                            <E-mail address>
                                            <Telephone number>

Civil Form 30. Answer Presenting Defenses Under Rule 12(b).

UNITED STATES DISTRICT COURT
for the
<_____> DISTRICT OF <_____>

<Name(s) of plaintiff(s)>,
 	
          Plaintiff(s)
 	
       v.
 	
<Name(s) of defendant(s)>,
 	
          Defendant(s)
	)
	)
	)
	)
	)
	)
	)
	)
	)
	) Civil Action No. <Number>

ANSWER PRESENTING DEFENSES UNDER RULE 12(B)

Responding to Allegations in the Complaint

1. Defendant admits the allegations in paragraphs <_____>.

2. Defendant lacks knowledge or information sufficient to form a belief about the truth of the allegations in paragraphs <_____>.

3. Defendant admits <identify part of the allegation> in paragraph <_____> and denies or lacks knowledge or information sufficient to form a belief about the truth of the rest of the paragraph.

Failure to State a Claim

4. The complaint fails to state a claim upon which relief can be granted.

Failure to Join a Required Party

5. If there is a debt, it is owed jointly by the defendant and <Name>, who is a citizen of <_____>. This person can be made a party without depriving this court of jurisdiction over the existing parties.

Affirmative Defense – Statute of Limitations

6. The plaintiff's claim is barred by the statute of limitations because it arose more than <_____> years before this action was commenced.

Counterclaim

7. <Set forth any counterclaim in the same way a claim is pleaded in a complaint. Include a further statement of jurisdiction if needed.>

Crossclaim

8. <Set forth a crossclaim against a coparty in the same way a claim is pleaded in a complaint. Include a further statement of jurisdiction if needed.>

<Signature block, see Form 2>

Civil Form 40. Motion to Dismiss Under Rule 12(b) for Lack of Jurisdiction, Improper Venue, Insufficient Service of Process, or Failure to State a Claim.

UNITED STATES DISTRICT COURT
for the
<_____> DISTRICT OF <_____>

<Name(s) of plaintiff(s)>,	)	
	)	
Plaintiff(s)	)	
	)	
v.	)	
	)	Civil Action No. <Number>
<Name(s) of defendant(s)>,	)	
	)	
Defendant(s)	)	
	)	

MOTION TO DISMISS UNDER RULE 12(b) FOR LACK OF JURISDICTION, IMPROPER VENUE, INSUFFICIENT SERVICE OF PROCESS, OR FAILURE TO STATE A CLAIM

The defendant moves to dismiss the action because:

1. the amount in controversy is less than the sum or value specified by 28 U.S.C. § 1332;

2. the defendant is not subject to the personal jurisdiction of this court;

3. venue is improper (this defendant does not reside in this district and no part of the events or omissions giving rise to the claim occurred in the district);

4. the defendant has not been properly served, as shown by the attached affidavits of <_____>; or

5. the complaint fails to state a claim upon which relief can be granted.

Date: <Date>

<Signature of the attorney or unrepresented party>

<Printed name>
<Address>
<E-mail address>
<Telephone number>

Civil Form 41. Motion to Bring in a Third-Party Defendant.

UNITED STATES DISTRICT COURT
for the
<_____> DISTRICT OF <_____>

<Name(s) of plaintiff(s)>,	)	
	)	
Plaintiff(s)	)	
	)	
v.	)	
	)	Civil Action No. <Number>
<Name(s) of defendant(s)>,	)	
	)	
Defendant(s)	)	
	)	

MOTION TO BRING IN A THIRD-PARTY DEFENDANT

The defendant, as third-party plaintiff, moves for leave to serve on <Name> a summons and third-party complaint, copies of which are attached.

Date: <Date>   <Signature of the attorney or unrepresented party>

_____

<Printed name>
<Address>
<E-mail address>
<Telephone number>

Civil Form 42. Motion to Intervene as a Defendant Under Rule 24.

UNITED STATES DISTRICT COURT
for the
<_____> DISTRICT OF <_____>

<Name(s) of plaintiff(s)>,	)	
	)	
Plaintiff(s)	)	
	)	
v.	)	
	)	Civil Action No. <Number>
<Name(s) of defendant(s)>,	)	
	)	
Defendant(s)	)	
	)	

MOTION TO INTERVENE AS A DEFENDANT UNDER RULE 24

1. <Name> moves for leave to intervene as a defendant in this action and to file the attached answer.

    <State grounds under Rule 24(a) or (b).>

2. The plaintiff alleges patent infringement. We manufacture and sell to the defendant the articles involved, and we have a defense to the plaintiff's claim.

3. Our defense presents questions of law and fact that are common to this action.

Date: <Date>   <Signature of the attorney or unrepresented party>

                                                _____
                                                <Printed name>
                                                <Address>
                                                <E-mail address>
                                                <Telephone number>

<An Intervener's Answer must be attached. See Form 30.>

Civil Form 50. Request to Produce Documents and Tangible Things, or to Enter onto Land Under Rule 34.

UNITED STATES DISTRICT COURT
for the
<_____> DISTRICT OF <_____>

<Name(s) of plaintiff(s)>,	)	
	)	
Plaintiff(s)	)	
	)	
v.	)	
	)	Civil Action No. <Number>
<Name(s) of defendant(s)>,	)	
	)	
Defendant(s)	)	
	)	

REQUEST TO PRODUCE DOCUMENTS AND TANGIBLE THINGS, OR TO ENTER ONTO LAND UNDER RULE 34

The plaintiff <Name> requests that the defendant <Name> respond within <_____> days to the following requests:

1. To produce and permit the plaintiff to inspect and copy and to test or sample the following documents, including electronically stored information:

   <Describe each document and the electronically stored information, either individually or by category.>

   <State the time, place, and manner of the inspection and any related acts.>

2. To produce and permit the plaintiff to inspect and copy — and to test or sample — the following tangible things:

   <Describe each thing, either individually or by category.>

   <State the time, place, and manner of the inspection and any related acts.>

3. To permit the plaintiff to enter onto the following land to inspect, photograph, test, or sample the property or an object or operation on the property.

   <Describe the property and each object or operation.>

   <State the time and manner of the inspection and any related acts.>

Date: <Date>   <Signature of the attorney or unrepresented party>

_____

<Printed name>
<Address>
<E-mail address>
<Telephone number>

Civil Form 51. Request for Admissions Under Rule 36.

UNITED STATES DISTRICT COURT
for the
<_____> DISTRICT OF <_____>

<Name(s) of plaintiff(s)>,	)	
	)	
Plaintiff(s)	)	
	)	
v.	)	
	)	Civil Action No. <Number>
<Name(s) of defendant(s)>,	)	
	)	
Defendant(s)	)	
	)	

REQUEST FOR ADMISSIONS UNDER RULE 36

The plaintiff <Name> asks the defendant <Name> to respond within 30 days to these requests by admitting, for purposes of this action only and subject to objections to admissibility at trial:

1. The genuineness of the following documents, copies of which [are attached] [are or have been furnished or made available for inspection and copying].

   <List each document.>

2. The truth of each of the following statements:

   <List each statement.>

Date: <Date>   <Signature of the attorney or unrepresented party>

                                          _____
                                          <Printed name>
                                          <Address>
                                          <E-mail address>
                                          <Telephone number>

Civil Form 52. Report of the Parties' Planning Meeting.

UNITED STATES DISTRICT COURT
for the
<————> DISTRICT OF <————>

<Name(s) of plaintiff(s)>,   )
)
    Plaintiff(s))
)
    v.   )
)
<Name(s) of defendant(s)>,)
)
    Defendant(s))
)
	Civil Action No. <Number>

REPORT OF THE PARTIES' PLANNING MEETING

1. The following persons participated in a Rule 26(f) conference on <Date> by <State the method of conferring>:

   <Name>, representing the <plaintiff>
   <Name>, representing the <defendant>

2. Initial Disclosures. The parties [have completed] [will complete by <Date>] the initial disclosures required by Rule 26(a)(1).

3. Discovery Plan. The parties propose this discovery plan:

   <Use separate paragraphs or subparagraphs if the parties disagree.>

   (a) Discovery will be needed on these subjects: <Describe>.

   (b) Disclosure or discovery of electronically stored information should be handled as follows: <briefly describe the parties' proposals, including the form or forms for production.>

   (c) The parties have agreed to an order regarding claims of privilege or protection as trial preparation material asserted after production, as follows: <briefly describe the provisions of the proposed order.>

   (d) <Dates for commencing and completing discovery, including discovery to be commenced or completed before other discovery.>

   (e) <Maximum number of interrogatories by each party to another party, along with the dates the answers are due.>

   (f) <Maximum number of requests for admission, along with the dates responses are due.>

   (g) <Maximum number of depositions by each party.>

   (h) <Limits on the length of depositions, in hours.>

   (i) <Dates for exchanging reports of expert witnesses.>

   (j) <Dates for supplementations under Rule 26(e).>

4. **Other Items:**

    (a) \<A date if the parties ask to meet with the court before a scheduling order.\>

    (b) \<Requested dates for pretrial conferences.\>

    (c) \<Final dates for the plaintiff to amend pleadings or to join parties.\>

    (d) \<Final dates for the defendant to amend pleadings or to join parties.\>

    (e) \<Final dates to file dispositive motions.\>

    (f) \<State the prospects for settlement.\>

    (g) \<Identify any alternative dispute resolution procedure that may enhance settlement prospects.\>

    (h) \<Final dates for submitting Rule 26(a)(3) witness lists, designations of witnesses whose testimony will be presented by deposition, and exhibit lists.\>

    (i) \<Final dates to file objections under Rule 26(a)(3).\>

    (j) \<Suggested trial date and estimate of trial length.\>

    (k) \<Other matters.\>

Date: \<Date\>   \<Signature of the attorney or unrepresented party\>

\<Printed name\>
\<Address\>
\<E-mail address\>
\<Telephone number\>

Date: \<Date\>   \<Signature of the attorney or unrepresented party\>

\<Printed name\>
\<Address\>
\<E-mail address\>
\<Telephone number\>

APPEARANCE FORM

(AO 458 rev 06/09)

UNITED STATES DISTRICT COURT
for the
<_____> DISTRICT OF <_____>

<Name(s) of plaintiff(s)>,	)	
	)	
Plaintiff(s)	)	
	)	
v.	)	
	)	Civil Action No. <Number>
<Name(s) of defendant(s)>,	)	
	)	
Defendant(s)	)	
	)	

APPEARANCE OF COUNSEL

To: The clerk of court and all parties of record

   I am admitted or otherwise authorized to practice in this court, and I appear in this case as counsel
for: _____.

Date: <Date>   <Signature of the attorney or unrepresented party>

                    _____
                    <Printed name>
                    <Address>
                    <E-mail address>
                    <Telephone number>
                    <FAX number>

CIVIL COVER SHEET

JS 44 (Rev. 09/11)

The JS 44 civil cover sheet and the information contained herein neither replace nor supplement the filing and service of pleadings or other papers as required by law, except as provided by local rules of court. This form, approved by the Judicial Conference of the United States in September 1974, is required for the use of the Clerk of Court for the purpose of initiating the civil docket sheet. *(SEE INSTRUCTIONS ON NEXT PAGE OF THIS FORM.)*

I. (a) PLAINTIFFS	DEFENDANTS
(b) County of Residence of First Listed Plaintiff _____ *(EXCEPT IN U.S. PLAINTIFF CASES)*	County of Residence of First Listed Defendant _____ *(IN U.S. PLAINTIFF CASES ONLY)* NOTE: IN LAND CONDEMNATION CASES, USE THE LOCATION OF THE TRACT OF LAND INVOLVED.
(c) Attorneys *(Firm Name, Address, and Telephone Number)*	Attorneys *(If Known)*

II. BASIS OF JURISDICTION *(Place an "X" in One Box Only)*

❏ 1 U.S. Government
Plaintiff

❏ 3 Federal Question
(U.S. Government Not a Party)

❏ 2 U.S. Government
Defendant

❏ 4 Diversity
(Indicate Citizenship of Parties in Item III)

III. CITIZENSHIP OF PRINCIPAL PARTIES *(Place an "X" in One Box for Plaintiff)*
(For Diversity Cases Only) and One Box for Defendant)

	PTF	DEF		PTF	DEF
Citizen of This State	❏ 1	❏ 1	Incorporated *or* Principal Place of Business in This State	❏ 4	❏ 4
Citizen of Another State	❏ 2	❏ 2	Incorporated *and* Principal Place of Business In Another State	❏ 5	❏ 5
Citizen or Subject of a Foreign Country	❏ 3	❏ 3	Foreign Nation	❏ 6	❏ 6

IV. NATURE OF SUIT *(Place an "X" in One Box Only)*

CONTRACT	TORTS		FORFEITURE/PENALTY	BANKRUPTCY	OTHER STATUTES
❏ 110 Insurance ❏ 120 Marine ❏ 130 Miller Act ❏ 140 Negotiable Instrument ❏ 150 Recovery of Overpayment & Enforcement of Judgment ❏ 151 Medicare Act ❏ 152 Recovery of Defaulted Student Loans (Excl. Veterans) ❏ 153 Recovery of Overpayment of Veteran's Benefits ❏ 160 Stockholders' Suits ❏ 190 Other Contract ❏ 195 Contract Product Liability ❏ 196 Franchise	**PERSONAL INJURY** ❏ 310 Airplane ❏ 315 Airplane Product Liability ❏ 320 Assault, Libel & Slander ❏ 330 Federal Employers' Liability ❏ 340 Marine ❏ 345 Marine Product Liability ❏ 350 Motor Vehicle ❏ 355 Motor Vehicle Product Liability ❏ 360 Other Personal Injury ❏ 362 Personal Injury - Med. Malpractice	**PERSONAL INJURY** ❏ 365 Personal Injury - Product Liability ❏ 367 Health Care/ Pharmaceutical Personal Injury Product Liability ❏ 368 Asbestos Personal Injury Product Liability **PERSONAL PROPERTY** ❏ 370 Other Fraud ❏ 371 Truth in Lending ❏ 380 Other Personal Property Damage ❏ 385 Property Damage Product Liability	❏ 625 Drug Related Seizure of Property 21 USC 881 ❏ 690 Other **LABOR** ❏ 710 Fair Labor Standards Act ❏ 720 Labor/Mgmt. Relations ❏ 740 Railway Labor Act ❏ 751 Family and Medical Leave Act ❏ 790 Other Labor Litigation ❏ 791 Empl. Ret. Inc. Security Act	❏ 422 Appeal 28 USC 158 ❏ 423 Withdrawal 28 USC 157 **PROPERTY RIGHTS** ❏ 820 Copyrights ❏ 830 Patent ❏ 840 Trademark **SOCIAL SECURITY** ❏ 861 HIA (1395ff) ❏ 862 Black Lung (923) ❏ 863 DIWC/DIWW (405(g)) ❏ 864 SSID Title XVI ❏ 865 RSI (405(g))	❏ 375 False Claims Act ❏ 400 State Reapportionment ❏ 410 Antitrust ❏ 430 Banks and Banking ❏ 450 Commerce ❏ 460 Deportation ❏ 470 Racketeer Influenced and Corrupt Organizations ❏ 480 Consumer Credit ❏ 490 Cable/Sat TV ❏ 850 Securities/Commodities/ Exchange ❏ 890 Other Statutory Actions ❏ 891 Agricultural Acts ❏ 893 Environmental Matters ❏ 895 Freedom of Information Act ❏ 896 Arbitration ❏ 899 Administrative Procedure Act/Review or Appeal of Agency Decision ❏ 950 Constitutionality of State Statutes
REAL PROPERTY ❏ 210 Land Condemnation ❏ 220 Foreclosure ❏ 230 Rent Lease & Ejectment ❏ 240 Torts to Land ❏ 245 Tort Product Liability ❏ 290 All Other Real Property	**CIVIL RIGHTS** ❏ 440 Other Civil Rights ❏ 441 Voting ❏ 442 Employment ❏ 443 Housing/ Accommodations ❏ 445 Amer. w/Disabilities - Employment ❏ 446 Amer. w/Disabilities - Other ❏ 448 Education	**PRISONER PETITIONS** ❏ 510 Motions to Vacate Sentence **Habeas Corpus:** ❏ 530 General ❏ 535 Death Penalty ❏ 540 Mandamus & Other ❏ 550 Civil Rights ❏ 555 Prison Condition ❏ 560 Civil Detainee - Conditions of Confinement	**IMMIGRATION** ❏ 462 Naturalization Application ❏ 463 Habeas Corpus - Alien Detainee (Prisoner Petition) ❏ 465 Other Immigration Actions	**FEDERAL TAX SUITS** ❏ 870 Taxes (U.S. Plaintiff or Defendant) ❏ 871 IRS—Third Party 26 USC 7609	

V. ORIGIN *(Place an "X" in One Box Only)*

❏ 1 Original Proceeding   ❏ 2 Removed from State Court   ❏ 3 Remanded from Appellate Court   ❏ 4 Reinstated or Reopened   ❏ 5 Transferred from another district *(specify)*   ❏ 6 Multidistrict Litigation

VI. CAUSE OF ACTION

Cite the U.S. Civil Statute under which you are filing *(Do not cite jurisdictional statutes unless diversity)*:

Brief description of cause:

VII. REQUESTED IN COMPLAINT:

❏ CHECK IF THIS IS A CLASS ACTION UNDER F.R.C.P. 23

DEMAND $

CHECK YES only if demanded in complaint:
JURY DEMAND: ❏ Yes   ❏ No

VIII. RELATED CASE(S) IF ANY

(See instructions):   JUDGE _____   DOCKET NUMBER _____

DATE _____   SIGNATURE OF ATTORNEY OF RECORD _____

FOR OFFICE USE ONLY

RECEIPT # _____   AMOUNT _____   APPLYING IFP _____   JUDGE _____   MAG. JUDGE _____

JS 44 Reverse (Rev. 09/11)

INSTRUCTIONS FOR ATTORNEYS COMPLETING CIVIL COVER SHEET FORM JS 44

Authority For Civil Cover Sheet

The JS 44 civil cover sheet and the information contained herein neither replaces nor supplements the filings and service of pleading or other papers as required by law, except as provided by local rules of court. This form, approved by the Judicial Conference of the United States in September 1974, is required for the use of the Clerk of Court for the purpose of initiating the civil docket sheet. Consequently, a civil cover sheet is submitted to the Clerk of Court for each civil complaint filed. The attorney filing a case should complete the form as follows:

I. **(a) Plaintiffs-Defendants.** Enter names (last, first, middle initial) of plaintiff and defendant. If the plaintiff or defendant is a government agency, use only the full name or standard abbreviations. If the plaintiff or defendant is an official within a government agency, identify first the agency and then the official, giving both name and title.

(b) County of Residence. For each civil case filed, except U.S. plaintiff cases, enter the name of the county where the first listed plaintiff resides at the time of filing. In U.S. plaintiff cases, enter the name of the county in which the first listed defendant resides at the time of filing. (NOTE: In land condemnation cases, the county of residence of the "defendant" is the location of the tract of land involved.)

(c) Attorneys. Enter the firm name, address, telephone number, and attorney of record. If there are several attorneys, list them on an attachment, noting in this section "(see attachment)".

II. **Jurisdiction.** The basis of jurisdiction is set forth under Rule 8(a), F.R.C.P., which requires that jurisdictions be shown in pleadings. Place an "X" in one of the boxes. If there is more than one basis of jurisdiction, precedence is given in the order shown below.

United States plaintiff. (1) Jurisdiction based on 28 U.S.C. 1345 and 1348. Suits by agencies and officers of the United States are included here.

United States defendant. (2) When the plaintiff is suing the United States, its officers or agencies, place an "X" in this box.

Federal question. (3) This refers to suits under 28 U.S.C. 1331, where jurisdiction arises under the Constitution of the United States, an amendment to the Constitution, an act of Congress or a treaty of the United States. In cases where the U.S. is a party, the U.S. plaintiff or defendant code takes precedence, and box 1 or 2 should be marked.

Diversity of citizenship. (4) This refers to suits under 28 U.S.C. 1332, where parties are citizens of different states. When Box 4 is checked, the citizenship of the different parties must be checked. (See Section III below; federal question actions take precedence over diversity cases.)

III. **Residence (citizenship) of Principal Parties.** This section of the JS 44 is to be completed if diversity of citizenship was indicated above. Mark this section for each principal party.

IV. **Nature of Suit.** Place an "X" in the appropriate box. If the nature of suit cannot be determined, be sure the cause of action, in Section VI below, is sufficient to enable the deputy clerk or the statistical clerks in the Administrative Office to determine the nature of suit. If the cause fits more than one nature of suit, select the most definitive.

V. **Origin.** Place an "X" in one of the seven boxes.

Original Proceedings. (1) Cases which originate in the United States district courts.

Removed from State Court. (2) Proceedings initiated in state courts may be removed to the district courts under Title 28 U.S.C., Section 1441. When the petition for removal is granted, check this box.

Remanded from Appellate Court. (3) Check this box for cases remanded to the district court for further action. Use the date of remand as the filing date.

Reinstated or Reopened. (4) Check this box for cases reinstated or reopened in the district court. Use the reopening date as the filing date.

Transferred from Another District. (5) For cases transferred under Title 28 U.S.C. Section 1404(a). Do not use this for within district transfers or multidistrict litigation transfers.

Multidistrict Litigation. (6) Check this box when a multidistrict case is transferred into the district under authority of Title 28 U.S.C. Section 1407. When this box is checked, do not check (5) above.

Appeal to District Judge from Magistrate Judgment. (7) Check this box for an appeal from a magistrate judge's decision.

VI. **Cause of Action.** Report the civil statute directly related to the cause of action and give a brief description of the cause. **Do not cite jurisdictional statutes unless diversity.** Example: U.S. Civil Statute: 47 USC 553
Brief Description: Unauthorized reception of cable service

VII. **Requested in Complaint.** Class Action. Place an "X" in this box if you are filing a class action under Rule 23, F.R.Cv.P.

Demand. In this space enter the dollar amount (in thousands of dollars) being demanded or indicate other demand such as a preliminary injunction.

Jury Demand. Check the appropriate box to indicate whether or not a jury is being demanded.

VIII. **Related Cases.** This section of the JS 44 is used to reference related pending cases if any. If there are related pending cases, insert the docket numbers and the corresponding judge names for such cases.

Date and Attorney Signature. Date and sign the civil cover sheet.

Subpoena to Testify in a Deposition

UNITED STATES DISTRICT COURT
for the
<_____> DISTRICT OF <_____>

<Name(s) of plaintiff(s)>,	)	
	)	
Plaintiff(s)	)	
	)	
v.	)	
	)	Civil Action No. <Number>
<Name(s) of defendant(s)>,	)	
	)	
Defendant(s)	)	

SUBPOENA TO TESTIFY AT A DEPOSITION IN A CIVIL ACTION

To:

____ *Testimony.* YOU ARE COMMANDED to appear at the time, date, and place set forth below to testify at a deposition to be taken in this civil action. If you are an organization that is *not* a party in this case, you must designate one or more officers, directors, or managing agents, or designate other persons who consent to testify on your behalf about the matters set forth in an attachment:

Place: Date and time:

The deposition will be recorded by this method:_____.

____ *Production.* You, or your representatives, must also bring with you to the deposition the following documents, electronically stored information, or objects, and permit their inspection, copying, testing, or sampling of the material:

The provisions of Fed. R. Civ. P. 45(c), relating to your protection as a person subject to a subpoena, and Rule 45(d) and (e), relating to your duty to respond to this subpoena and the potential consequences of not doing so, are attached:

Date: _____   _____ or _____
                                   Signature of clerk of court   Attorney's signature

The name, address, e-mail and telephone number of the attorney representing _____ (name of party), who issues this subpoena are:

Attach Rule 45 (c)(d)(e).

UNITED STATES DISTRICT COURT
SAMPLE CASE MANAGEMENT PLAN

[INSERT CASE CAPTION]

CASE MANAGEMENT PLAN

I.   **Parties and Representatives**

     A.   [Insert correct name of each party]

     B.   [Insert full name, address, telephone, fax number, and e-mail address of all counsel]

     Counsel shall promptly file a notice with the Clerk if there is any change in this information.

II.   **Synopsis of Case**

     A.   [Insert a one paragraph statement of plaintiff's claims, including basis for subject matter jurisdiction.

     B.   [Insert a one paragraph responsive statement of defendant's claims, including subject matter jurisdiction.]

III.   **Pretrial Pleadings and Disclosures**

     A.   The parties shall serve their Fed. R. Civ. P. 26 initial disclosures on or before _____. [Note: Fed. R. Civ. P. 26(a)(1)(E) permits the parties to object to making initial disclosures or to stipulate to a different deadline for making such disclosures based upon the circumstances of the action. If any objection and/or stipulation is made to initial disclosures in the CMP, the parties shall briefly state the circumstances justifying their respective positions].

     B.   Plaintiff(s) shall file preliminary witness and exhibit lists on or before _____.

     C.   Defendant(s) shall file preliminary witness and exhibit lists on or before _____.

     D.   All motions for leave to amend the pleadings and/or to join additional parties shall be filed on or before _____.

     E.   Plaintiff(s) shall serve on Defendant(s) a statement of special damages, if any, and make a settlement demand, on or before _____. Defendant(s) shall serve on the Plaintiff(s) a response thereto within _____ days after receipt of the demand.

     F.   Plaintiff(s) shall disclose the name, address, and vita of any expert witness, and shall serve the report required by Fed. R. Civ. P. 26(a)(2) on or before _____. Defendant(s) shall disclose the name, address, and vita of any expert witness, and shall serve the report required by Fed. R. Civ. P. 26(a)(2) on or before _____.

     G.   Any party who wishes to limit or preclude expert testimony at trial shall file any such objections no later than _____. Any party who wishes to preclude expert witness testimony at the summary judgment stage shall file any such objections with their responsive brief within the briefing schedule established by Local Rule 56-1.

     H.   All parties shall file and serve their final witness and exhibit lists on or before _____.

     I.   Any party who believes that bifurcation of discovery and/or trial is appropriate with respect to any issue or claim shall notify the Court as soon as practicable.

J. The parties have discussed preservation and disclosure of electronically stored discovery information, including a timetable for making the materials available to the opposing party. [Include brief description addressing such other matters as cost allocation, treatment of "embedded data" or "metadata"; and any protocols agreed upon to facilitate discovery without waiving any claims of privilege, such as "quick peek" or "clawback" agreements."]

IV. Discovery[1] and Dispositive Motions

Due to the time and expense involved in conducting expert witness depositions and other discovery, as well as preparing and resolving dispositive motions, the Court requires counsel to use the CMP as an opportunity to seriously explore whether this case is appropriate for such motions (including specifically motions for summary judgment), whether expert witnesses will be needed, and how long discovery should continue. To this end, counsel must select the track set forth below that they believe best suits this case. If the parties are unable to agree on a track, the parties must: (1) state this fact in the CMP where indicated below; (2) indicate which track each counsel believes is most appropriate; and (3) provide a brief statement supporting the reasons for the track each counsel believes is most appropriate. If the parties are unable to agree on a track, the Court will pick the track it finds most appropriate, based upon the contents of the CMP or, if necessary, after receiving additional input at an initial pretrial conference.

A. Does any party believe that this case may be appropriate for summary judgment or other dispositive motion? If yes, the party(ies) that expect to file such a motion must provide a brief statement of the factual and/or legal basis for such a motion. [Note: A statement such as, "Defendant will seek summary judgment because no material facts are in dispute," is insufficient. Such a statement does not indicate to the Court that the parties used the CMP as an opportunity to seriously explore whether this case is appropriate for summary judgment or other dispositive motion. However, the failure to set forth a basis for a dispositive motion in the CMP will not bar a party from raising this argument at the motions stage.]

B. Select the track that best suits this case:

_____ Track 1: No dispositive motions are anticipated and the discovery issues are not complicated. All discovery shall be completed by _____ (date within 4 months of anchor date). The parties will be ready for trial on _____ (date within 12 months of anchor date).

_____ Track 2: Dispositive motions are expected. Discovery needed prior to the filing of dispositive motions shall be completed by _____ (date within 4 months of anchor date). Dispositive motions shall be filed by _____ (date within 6 months of anchor date). If dispositive motions are denied, the parties shall within 30 days supplement the CMP with dates by which non-expert witness discovery and discovery relating to liability issues shall be completed, by which expert witness discovery and discovery relating to damages shall be completed, and by which they will be ready for trial.

Absent leave of court, and for good cause shown, all issues raised on summary judgment under Fed. R. Civ. P. 56 must be raised by a party in a single motion.

V. Pre-Trial/Settlement Conferences

Indicate here whether any of the parties deem it helpful to hold an initial conference with the Magistrate Judge or District Judge, to discuss the possibility of settlement or for other reasons, and if so, the suggested timing and forum (i.e., in person or by telephone) of such a conference. At any time, any party may call the Judge's Staff to request a conference, or the Court may sua sponte schedule a conference at any time.

---

[1] The term "completed," as used in Section IV.B, means that counsel must serve their discovery requests in sufficient time to receive responses before this deadline. Counsel may not serve discovery requests within the 30-day period before this deadline unless they seek leave of Court to serve a belated request and show good cause for the same. In such event, the proposed belated discovery request shall be filed with the motion, and the opposing party will receive it with service of the motion but need not respond to the same until such time as the Court grants the motion.

VI. Trial

The parties request trial by _____ (court or jury) and is anticipated to take _____ hours/days. If the parties disagree, summarize the position of each.

VII. Referral to Magistrate Judge

At this time, all parties _____ [do/do not] consent to refer this matter to the currently assigned Magistrate Judge pursuant to 28 U.S.C. 636(b) and Federal Rules of Civil Procedure 73 for all further proceedings including trial. [Indicating the parties' consent in this paragraph may result in this matter being referred to the currently assigned Magistrate Judge for all further proceedings, including trial. It is not necessary to file a separate consent. Should this case be reassigned to another Magistrate Judge, any attorney or party of record may object within 30 days of such reassignment. If no objection is filed, the consent will remain in effect.]

VIII. Required Pre-Trial Preparation

A. TWO WEEKS BEFORE THE FINAL PRETRIAL CONFERENCE, the parties shall:

1. File a list of witnesses who are expected to be called to testify at trial.

2. Number in sequential order all exhibits, including graphs, charts and the like, that will be used during the trial. Provide the Court with a list of these exhibits, including a description of each exhibit and the identifying designation. Make the original exhibits available for inspection by opposing counsel. Stipulations as to the authenticity and admissibility of exhibits are encouraged to the greatest extent possible.

3. Submit all stipulations of facts in writing to the Court. Stipulations are always encouraged so that at trial, counsel can concentrate on relevant contested facts.

4. A party who intends to offer any depositions into evidence during the party's case in chief shall prepare and file with the Court and copy to all opposing parties either:

   a. brief written summaries of the relevant facts in the depositions that will be offered. (Because such a summary will be used in lieu of the actual deposition testimony to eliminate time reading depositions in a question and answer format, this is strongly encouraged.); or

   b. if a summary is inappropriate, a document which lists the portions of the deposition(s), including the specific page and line numbers, that will be read, or, in the event of a video-taped deposition, the portions of the deposition that will be played, designated specifically by counter-numbers.

5. Provide all other parties and the Court with any trial briefs and motions in limine, along with all proposed jury instructions, voir dire questions, and areas of inquiry for voir dire (or, if the trial is to the Court, with proposed findings of fact and conclusions of law).

6. Notify the Court and opposing counsel of the anticipated use of any evidence presentation equipment.

B. ONE WEEK BEFORE THE FINAL PRETRIAL CONFERENCE, the parties shall:

1. Notify opposing counsel in writing of any objections to the proposed exhibits. If the parties desire a ruling on the objection prior to trial, a motion should be filed noting the objection and a description and designation of the exhibit, the basis of the objection, and the legal authorities supporting the objection.

2. If a party has an objection to the deposition summary or to a designated portion of a deposition that will be offered at trial, or if a party intends to offer additional portions at trial in response to the opponent's designation, and the parties desire a ruling on the objection prior to trial, the party shall submit the objections and counter summaries or designations to the Court in writing. Any objections shall be made in the same manner as for proposed exhibits. However, in the case of objections to video-taped depositions, the objections shall be brought to the Court's immediate attention to allow adequate time for editing of the deposition prior to trial.

3. File objections to any motions in limine, proposed instructions, and voir dire questions submitted by the opposing parties.

4. Notify the Court and opposing counsel of requests for separation of witnesses at trial.

IX. Other Matters

[Insert any other matters any party believes should be brought to the Court's attention]

[INSERT SIGNATURE BLOCKS FOR ALL COUNSEL TO SIGN THE CMP HERE]

****

_____ PARTIES APPEARED IN PERSON/BY COUNSEL ON _____ FOR A PRETRIAL/STATUS CONFERENCE.

_____ APPROVED AS SUBMITTED.

_____ APPROVED AS AMENDED.

_____ APPROVED AS AMENDED PER SEPARATE ORDER.

_____ APPROVED, BUT ALL OF THE FOREGOING DEADLINES ARE SHORTENED/ LENGTHENED BY _____ MONTHS.

_____ APPROVED, BUT THE DEADLINES SET IN SECTION(S)_____ OF THE PLAN IS/ARE SHORTENED/LENGTHENED BY _____ MONTHS.

_____ THIS MATTER IS SET FOR TRIAL BY _____ ON _____. FINAL PRETRIAL CONFERENCE IS SCHEDULED FOR _____ AT .M., ROOM _____.

_____ A SETTLEMENT/STATUS CONFERENCE IS SET IN THIS CASE FOR _____ AT.M. COUNSEL SHALL APPEAR:

_____ IN PERSON IN ROOM _____; OR

_____BY TELEPHONE, WITH COUNSEL FOR INITIATING THE CALL TO ALL OTHER PARTIES AND ADDING THE COURT JUDGE AT (____) _____; OR

_____BY TELEPHONE, WITH COUNSEL CALLING THE JUDGE'S
STAFF AT (____) _____; OR

_____DISPOSITIVE MOTIONS SHALL BE FILED NO LATER THAN

Upon approval, this Plan constitutes an Order of the Court. Failure to comply with an Order of the Court may result in sanctions for contempt, or as provided under Rule 16(f), to and including dismissal or default.

Approved and So Ordered.

_____

Date

_____

U. S. District Court

SAMPLE LOCAL RULES OF THE
UNITED STATES DISTRICT COURT

[Adapted from the Local Rules for various U.S. District Courts]

Local Rule 1.1 Scope of the Rules

(a)   These Rules shall govern all proceedings in civil actions.

(b)   The court may, on its own motion or at the request of a party, suspend or modify any rule in a particular case in the interest of justice.

(c)   Each judge of the district may suspend, modify, or supplement these Rules with a Standing Order, which is to be served on every attorney who enters an appearance.

Local Rule 1.2 Appearance and Withdrawal of Appearance

(a)   Any attorney representing a party shall file his/her formal written appearance for such party prior to, or at the same time as, the filing of any papers with the court. If more than one attorney from the same firm shall appear on behalf of a client, the firm should file only a single notice of appearance, which shall designate one of the attorneys in the firm as counsel of record to receive service.

(b)   The appearance shall designate an email address to which pleadings and other filings may be served, and shall either state consent to receive service by electronic means or request an exemption for good cause if the receiving of service by electronic means imposes a hardship.

(c)   Counsel desiring to withdraw his/her appearance in any action shall file a petition requesting leave to do so. Such petition shall fix a date for such withdrawal, and petitioning counsel shall file with the Court satisfactory evidence of written notice to his/her client at least five (5) days in advance of such withdrawal date.

(d)   A withdrawal of appearance when accompanied by the appearance of other counsel shall constitute a waiver of the provisions of paragraph (c) of this Rule.

Local Rule 5.1. Filing of Papers

All papers must be filed with the Clerk unless the court orders a filing to be made directly to the Judge. A filing is not timely unless received by the clerk on the date due. If the clerk's office is closed, mark the date and time of the filing in the upper right corner and place the materials in the drop box located in the courthouse.

Local Rule 5.2. Service by Electronic Means

Unless otherwise provided by court order, all papers shall be served on all counsel who have entered an appearance as email attachments in Word or .pdf format, or in such other format as may be agreed upon among the parties.

Local Rule 5.3 General Format of Papers Presented for Filing

(a)   *Rule applies to all filings.* This rule applies to all papers filed in this court by hand or electronically.

(b) *Electronic filing.* Electronic filing is subject to additional rules and procedures as set out in the Local Rules for Electronic Filing.

(c) *Form, Style and Size of Papers.* All filings shall be on white paper of good quality, 8 1/2" x 11" in size, and shall be plainly printed, or prepared by a clearly legible duplication process, and double spaced, except for quoted material. Printed material must be in Times Roman or other standard font of at least 12 pt. size. All papers shall have margins of at least 1" on all sides. papers filed by hand shall be either stapled in the top left corner or bound in a manner which permits the document to lie reasonably flat when open (*e.g.*, spiral bound). The title of each filing must be set out on the first page with the filing party clearly designated. Each page shall be numbered consecutively. Any filing containing four or more exhibits shall include a separate index identifying and briefly describing each exhibit.

(d) *Signature.* Every pleading, motion, or other paper shall clearly identify the name, address, telephone number and email address of the *pro se* litigant or attorney. Any pleading, motion, or other paper not signed by at least one attorney appearing of record as required by Rule 11, *Federal Rules of Civil Procedure* shall, upon discovery of such omission, be stricken from the record unless such omission is promptly corrected upon notice to said attorney. A rubber stamp or facsimile signature on the original copy of such document shall not be used. Papers filed electronically shall be signed in accordance with the rules governing electronic filing.

(e) *Number of Copies; Return of File-Stamped Copies.* One copy of all pleadings, motions, and other papers shall be submitted for filing unless ordered otherwise.

(f) *Form of Orders.* The filing of a motion or petition requiring the entry of a routine or uncontested order by the Judge shall be accompanied by a suitable tendered form of order together with sufficient copies thereof for service upon all parties or their counsel whose names and addresses shall be typed in the lower left-hand corner of the tendered order.

Local Rule 6.1 Extensions of Time

The clerk is authorized to grant extensions of time of up to 3 days upon the request of any attorney. Such requests must be made before the time for filing has expired. Requests for extensions of time beyond three days shall not be granted except upon ex parte order of the presiding judge. Requests to the clerk may be made orally or in writing; requests to the judge must be made in writing and be accompanied by a detailed explanation of the reason for the request.

Local Rule 7.1 Motion Practice; Length, Form, and Schedule of Briefs; Attorneys'

Conference; Notification of Settlement/Resolution of Pending Motions

(a) *Dispositive motions.* A motion to dismiss, for summary judgment, for judgment on the pleadings, or other dispositive motion shall be accompanied by a separate supporting brief. Unless the Court otherwise directs, an adverse party shall have fourteen (14) days after service of the initial brief in which to serve and file an answer brief. No reply brief is permitted without leave of court.

(b) *Other motions.* All other motions shall be accompanied by a memorandum in support that may not exceed ten pages in length. Unless the Court otherwise directs, an adverse party shall have ten (10) days after service of the initial motion in which to serve and file a responsive memorandum.

(c) *Factual basis.* Motions shall be accompanied where appropriate by affidavits based on personal knowledge, and other evidence.

(d) *Proposed order.* Routine motions shall be accompanied by a proposed order that complies with Local Rule 5.2(d).

(e) *Length.* Except by permission of the Court, no brief shall exceed 15 pages in length (excluding table of contents, table of authorities, and appendices). Ordinarily, copies of cited authorities need not be appended to court filings. However, a party citing a decision, statute, or regulation that is not available on Westlaw or Lexis/Nexis shall furnish a copy to the Court and other parties.

(f) *Settlement.* The parties shall immediately notify the Court of any reasonably anticipated settlement of a case or the resolution of any pending motion.

Local Rule 7.2. Certificate of Conference

Counsel are expected to hold informal conferences in person or by phone to resolve any disputes involving non-dispositive issues that may otherwise require submission of a motion to the Court. Therefore, prior to filing any non-dispositive motion except a motion for sanctions, the moving party must contact opposing counsel to determine whether there is an objection to the motion. The motion must contain a statement by the movant certifying that she or he sought consent from the opposing party, and shall state whether consent was given or refused. This statement shall recite, in addition, the date, time, and place of such conference and the names of all parties participating therein. If after a reasonable effort, opposing counsel cannot be reached, the moving party shall recite in the motion the dates and times that messages were left for opposing counsel. If counsel for any party advises the Court in writing that opposing counsel has refused or delayed meeting and discussing the matters covered in this Rule, the Court may take such action as is appropriate to avoid unreasonable delay.

Local Rule 7.3 Requests for Oral Arguments and Hearings

(a) A request for oral argument on a motion shall be made by separate paragraph clearly designated as such appearing on the first page of the motion. The request for oral argument shall set forth specifically the purpose of the request and an estimate of the time reasonably required for the Court to devote to the argument. An oral argument shall be confined to argument and shall not include the presentation of additional evidence. The granting of a motion for oral argument shall be wholly discretionary with the Court. The Court, upon its own initiative, may also direct that oral argument be held.

(b) A request for an evidentiary hearing on a motion or petition may be made by any party after a motion or petition has been filed. The request for hearing shall set forth specifically the purpose of the hearing and an estimate of the time reasonably required for the Court to devote to the hearing. Dates of hearing shall not be specified in a notice of a motion or petition unless prior authorization is obtained from the Court or Deputy Court Clerk. The Court upon its own initiative may also direct that a hearing be held.

Local Rule 15.1 Form of a Motion to Amend and Its Supporting Documentation

A party who moves to amend a pleading shall attach the proposed amended pleading as an exhibit. Any amendment to a pleading, whether filed as a matter of course or upon a motion to amend, must, except by leave of Court, reproduce the entire pleading as amended, and may not incorporate any prior pleading by reference.

Local Rule 16.1 Pretrial Procedures

(a) *Purpose.* The fundamental purpose of pretrial procedure as provided in Rule 16 of the FED. R. CIV. P. is to eliminate issues not genuinely in contest and to facilitate the trial of issues that must be tried. The normal pretrial requirements are set forth in Rule 16. It is anticipated that the requirements will be followed in all respects unless any Judge of this Court shall vary the requirements and shall so advise counsel.

(b) *Notice.* In any civil case, the assigned or presiding Judge may direct the Clerk to issue notice of a pretrial conference, directing the parties to prepare and to appear before the Court.

(c) *Initial pretrial conference.* In all cases the Court shall order the parties to appear for an initial pretrial conference promptly following the appearance of counsel for all defendants.

(d) *Contents of case management plan.* In every case, as soon as all parties have entered an appearance, the parties shall meet and prepare a joint case management plan. A sample CMP can be found at the end of these rules.

    (1)   The case management plan shall address the following matters:

        (A) *Trial date.* The plan shall set a date at which the parties will be ready for trial. The plan shall also state the estimated time required for trial.

        (B) *Discovery schedule.* The plan shall provide for the timely and efficient completion of discovery, taking into account the desirability of staged discovery where discovery in stages might materially advance the resolution of the case. The plan should include a schedule for the exchange of initial disclosures and expert witness disclosures.

        (C) *Limits on depositions, interrogatories, and admissions.* The plan shall discuss whether the limits on the number or length of depositions imposed by FED. R. CIV. P. 30, the number of interrogatories imposed by FED. R. CIV. P. 33, or the number of admissions should be varied by stipulation.

        (D) *Omnibus motion date.* The parties shall agree upon a date by which all motions are due.

        (K) *Settlement.* The plan shall address the possibility of settlement both presently and at future stages of the case, and should contain a statement as to the reasonable possibility of settlement. Counsel should anticipate that the subject of settlement will be discussed at any pretrial conference. Accordingly, counsel should be prepared to state his or her client's present position on settlement. In particular, prior to any conference, counsel should have ascertained his or her settlement authority and be prepared to enter into negotiations in good faith. The Court may require the parties or their agents or insurers to appear in person or by telephone for settlement negotiations.

Local Rule 16.3 Continuances in Civil Cases

Continuances shall be granted only upon showing of extraordinary cause.

Local Rule 26.1 Form of Certain Discovery Documents

The party propounding written interrogatories pursuant to Rule 33 of the FED. R. CIV. P., requests for production of documents or things pursuant to Rule 34, or requests for admission pursuant to Rule 36, shall number each such interrogatory or request sequentially. The party answering, responding or objecting to such interrogatories or requests shall quote each such interrogatory or request in full immediately preceding the statement of any answer, response or objection thereto, and shall number each such response to correspond with the number assigned to the request. Counsel serving discovery requests shall supply a copy of his or her requests in Word or WordPerfect text.

Local Rule 26.2 Filing of Discovery Materials

Because of the considerable cost to the parties of furnishing discovery materials, and the serious problems encountered with storage, this Court adopts the following procedure for filing of discovery materials with the Court:

(a) If relief is sought under Rules 26(c) or 37 concerning any disclosures, interrogatories, or requests for production or inspection, answers to interrogatories or responses to requests for production or inspection, copies of the portions of the disclosures, interrogatories, requests, answers or responses in dispute shall be filed with the Court contemporaneously with any motion filed under these Rules.

(b) If disclosures, interrogatories, requests, answers, responses or depositions are to be used at trial or are necessary to a pretrial motion which might result in a final order on any issue, the portions to be used shall be filed with the Clerk at the outset of the trial or at the filing of the motion insofar as their use can be reasonably anticipated. Such filing may be accomplished by attaching the discovery to such motion in the form of an appendix.

(c) When documentation of discovery not previously in the record is needed for appeal purposes, upon an application and order of the Court, or by stipulation of counsel, the necessary discovery papers shall be filed with the Clerk.

Local Rule 30.1 Conduct of Depositions

(a) If a claim of privilege has been asserted as a basis for an instruction not to answer, the attorney seeking disclosure shall have reasonable latitude during the deposition to question the deponent to establish relevant information concerning the legal appropriateness of the assertion of the privilege, including (i) the applicability of the privilege being asserted, (ii) circumstances that may result in the privilege having been waived, and (iii) circumstances that may overcome a claim of qualified privilege.

(b) An attorney for a deponent shall not initiate a private conference with the deponent regarding a pending question except for the purpose of determining whether a claim of privilege should be asserted.

(c) Counsel are expected to conduct a deposition in a civil manner and to resolve disputes among themselves. If a dispute cannot be resolved, the Court may resolve the matter in accordance with Local Rule 37.3. The Court in its discretion may assess costs against any attorney who causes unnecessary disruptions of a deposition or brings unnecessary motions to the court concerning the deposition, which may include a reasonable attorney's fee.

Local Rule 36.1 Requests for Admissions

No party shall serve on any other party more than 25 requests for admission without leave of Court. Requests relating to the authenticity or genuineness of documents are not subject to this limitation. Any party desiring to serve additional requests for admission shall file a written motion setting forth the proposed additional requests for admission and the reason(s) for their use.

Local Rule 37.1 Informal Conference to Settle Discovery Disputes

The Court may deny any discovery motion unless counsel for the moving party files with the Court, at the time of filing the motion, a separate statement showing that the attorney making the motion has made a reasonable effort to reach agreement with opposing attorney(s) on the matter(s) set forth in the motion. This statement shall recite, in addition, the date, time, and place of such conference and the names of all parties participating therein. If counsel for any party advises the Court in writing that opposing counsel has refused or delayed meeting and discussing the problems covered in this Rule, the Court may take such action as is appropriate to avoid unreasonable delay.

Local Rule 37.3 Mode of Raising Discovery Disputes with the Court

Where an objection is raised during the taking of a deposition which threatens to prevent the completion of the deposition and which is susceptible to resolution by the Court without the submission of written materials, any party may recess the deposition for the purpose of submitting the objection by telephone to the Magistrate Judge assigned to supervise discovery for a ruling *instanter*.

Local Rule 56.1 Summary Judgment Procedure

(a) *Requirements for Moving Party.* A party filing a motion for summary judgment pursuant to FED. R. CIV. P. 56 must also serve and file the following:

(1) A Statement of Material Facts (separately submitted or included in the brief) as to which the moving party contends there is no genuine issue and that entitles the moving party to a judgment as a matter of law;

(2) To the extent not previously filed, any affidavits and other admissible evidence the moving party relies upon to support the facts material to the motion, including, but not limited to, portions of depositions and discovery responses; and

(3) A supporting brief.

(b) *Requirements for Non-Movant.* A party opposing a motion filed pursuant to FED. R.CIV. P. 56 must serve and file the following:

(1) A Response to Statement of Material Facts (either as a section of the brief or as a separate document) that contains a response to each material factual assertion in the moving party's Statement of Material Facts, and if applicable, a separate Statement of Additional Material Facts that warrant denial of summary judgment;

(2) To the extent not previously filed, any additional affidavits and other admissible evidence to support material facts the opposing party relies upon, including, but not limited to, portions of depositions and discovery responses; and

(3) An answer brief.

(c) *Requirements for Factual Statements and Responses Thereto.*

(1) Format and Numbering. The Statement of Material Facts shall consist of numbered sentences. The Response to Statement of Material Facts must be numbered to correspond with the sentence numbers of the Statement of Material Facts.

(2) Format of Factual Assertions. Each material fact set forth in a Statement of Material Facts or Response to Statement of Material Facts must consist of concise, numbered sentences with the contents of each sentence limited as far as practicable to a single factual proposition.

(3) Format of Objections to Asserted Material Facts or Cited Evidence. Objections to material facts and/or cited evidence shall (to the extent practicable) set forth the grounds for the objection in a concise, single sentence, with citation to appropriate authorities.

Local Rule 79.1 Custody of Files and Exhibits

After being marked for identification, models, diagrams, exhibits and material offered or admitted in evidence in any cause pending or tried in this Court shall be placed in the custody of the Clerk, unless otherwise ordered by the Court, and shall not be withdrawn until after the time for appeal has run or the case is disposed of otherwise. Such items shall not be withdrawn until the final mandate of the reviewing Court is filed in the office of the Clerk and until the case is disposed of as to all issues, unless otherwise ordered.

LOCAL RULES FOR ELECTRONIC FILING
UNITED STATES DISTRICT COURT

[Adapted from the Electronic Filing Rules of Various District Courts]

Local Rule E-1. ECF Registration.

(a) Registration Required. Unless excused for cause, an attorney must register as an ECF user within 14 days of the date the attorney appears in a case.

(b) Registration Procedures. To register to use the ECF system, an attorney must complete the registration form adopted by the clerk. The form must require:

1. the attorney's name, address, and telephone number;

2. the attorney's e-mail address; and

3. a declaration that the attorney is admitted to this court's bar.

(c) Change in Information; Compromise of Password. An attorney who has registered to use the ECF system must notify the clerk:

1. in writing within 30 days after the attorney's address, telephone number, or e-mail address changes; and

2. immediately upon learning that the attorney's password for the ECF system has been compromised.

(d) Consent to Electronic Service. By registering to use the ECF system, attorneys consent to electronic service of papers filed in cases maintained on the ECF system.

Local Rule E-2. Filing by Electronic Means.

(a) Filing Complaint by Electronic Means. A plaintiff may file a complaint by electronic means by following the procedures set forth in the ECF Administrative Procedures Manual. The complaint must be accompanied by:

1. a civil cover sheet;

2. the required filing fee or the appropriate application to proceed without prepayment of fees; and

3. a separately signed certificate of interested persons—in a form approved by the clerk—that contains—in addition to the information required by Fed. R. Civ. P. 7.1(a)—a complete list of all persons, associations of persons, firms, partnerships, corporations, guarantors, insurers, affiliates, parent or subsidiary corporations, or other legal entities that are financially interested in the outcome of the case. If a large group of persons or firms can be specified by a generic description, individual listing is not necessary.

(b) Filing Other Documents by Electronic Means.

1. **Electronic Filing Required.** All civil cases (other than those cases the court specifically exempts) must be maintained in the court's electronic case filing (ECF) system. Accordingly, as allowed by Fed. R. Civ. P. 5(d)(3), every paper filed in this court (including exhibits) must be transmitted to the clerk's office via the ECF system except:

A. complaints or other case-initiating documents;

B. papers filed by *pro se* litigants;

C. transcripts in cases filed by claimants under the Social Security Act (and related statutes);

D. exhibits in a format that does not readily permit electronic filing (such as videos and large maps and charts);

E. papers that are illegible when scanned into .pdf format;

F. papers filed in cases not maintained on the ECF system; and

G. any other papers that the court or these rules specifically allow to be filed directly with the clerk.

2. **Format.** Any paper submitted via the court's electronic case filing (ECF) system must be:

A. in text-searchable .pdf format;

B. converted to a .pdf file directly from a word processing program, unless it exists only in paper format (in which case it may be scanned to create a .pdf document); and

C. submitted as one or more .pdf files that do not exceed 5 megabytes each.

3. **Paper Filing by Non-Exempt Party.** When a party who is not exempt from the electronic filing requirement files a paper directly with the clerk, the party must:

A. electronically file a notice of manual filing that explains why the paper cannot be filed electronically;

B. present the paper to the clerk within 1 business day after filing the notice of manual filing; and

C. present the clerk with a copy of the notice of manual filing when the party files the paper with the clerk.

Local Rule E-3. Timing and Consequences of Electronic Filing.

(a) Deadlines. A paper due on a particular day must be filed before midnight local time of the division where the case is pending.

(b) When Electronic Filing Is Completed. Electronic transmission of a paper to the Electronic Case Filing System consistent with these rules, together with the transmission of a notice of Electronic Filing from the court, constitutes filing of the paper for all purposes of the Federal Rules of Civil Procedure and the court's local rules.

(c) Consequences of Electronic Filing. When a paper has been filed electronically:

1. it is deemed entered on the clerk's docket under Fed. R. Civ. P. 58 and 79;

2. the paper's electronic recording stored by the court is the official record of the paper;

3. the paper, as filed, binds the filing party;

4. the notice of electronic filing for the paper serves as the court's date-stamp and proof of filing; and

5. transmission of the notice of electronic filing generated by the ECF system to an attorney's e-mail address constitutes service of the paper on that attorney.

(d) Service on Exempt Parties. A filer must serve a copy of the paper consistent with Fed. R. Civ. P. 5 on any pro se party as well as any other party or attorney who is exempt from participating in the CM/ECF system.

Local Rule E-4. Attachments and Exhibits to Electronic Filings.

(a) General Requirements. Each electronically filed exhibit to a main paper must be:

1. created as a separate .pdf file;

2. submitted as an attachment to the main paper and given a title which describes its content; and

3. limited to excerpts that are directly germane to the main paper's subject matter.

(b) Excerpts. A party filing an exhibit that consists of excerpts from a larger document must clearly and prominently identify the exhibit as containing excerpted material. Either party will have the right to timely file additional excerpts or the complete document to the extent they are or become directly germane to the main paper's subject matter.

Local Rule E-5. Signatures in Electronic Filings.

(a) Filing Certain Papers Signed by an Attorney. A pleading, motion, brief, or notice filed electronically under an attorney's ECF log-in and password must be signed by that attorney.

(b) Form of Electronic Signature. If a paper is converted directly from a word processing application to .pdf (as opposed to scanning), the name of the Filing User under whose log-in and password the paper is submitted must be preceded by a "s/" and typed on the signature line where the Filing User's handwritten signature would otherwise appear.

(c) Other Papers. A signature on a paper other than a paper filed as provided under subdivision (a) must be an original handwritten signature and must be scanned into .pdf format for electronic filing.

(d) Effect of Electronic Signature. Filing an electronically signed paper under an attorney's ECF log-in and password constitutes the attorney's signature on the paper under the Federal Rules of Civil Procedure, under these local rules, and for any other reason a signature is required in connection with the court's activities.

(e) Papers with Multiple Attorneys' Signatures. A paper signed by more than one attorney and electronically filed must:

1. include a representation on the signature lines where the handwritten signatures of the non-filing attorneys would otherwise appear that the non-filing attorneys consent to the paper;

2. identify in the signature block the non-filing attorneys whose signatures are required and be followed by notices of endorsement filed by the other attorneys within three business days after the original paper is filed; or

3. include a scanned paper containing all necessary signatures.

Local Rule E-6. Retention of Papers in Cases Filed Electronically.

A person who electronically files a paper that requires an original signature must maintain the original signed paper for two years after all deadlines for appeals in the case expire. On request of the court, the Filing User must provide original papers for review.

Local Rule E-7. Filing Papers Under Seal.

(a) General Rule. The clerk may not maintain a paper under seal unless authorized to do so by statute, court rule, or court order. But once a paper is sealed, the clerk may not, without a court order, allow anyone to see it other than:

1. the court and its staff;
2. the clerk's staff; and
3. the attorneys who have appeared in the case that the paper pertains to.

(b) Filing Papers Under Seal. To seal a paper, a party must either file it electronically or file the paper with a cover sheet containing:

1. the case caption;
2. the name of the paper or (if the name can't be disclosed publicly) an appropriate title to identify it on the public docket;
3. the name, address, and telephone number of the person filing the paper; and
4. information identifying the statute, rule, or court order authorizing the paper to be sealed, if a motion requesting that it be sealed does not accompany the paper.

(c) Serving Sealed Papers Filed Electronically. The ECF System does not automatically serve electronically filed papers that have been filed under seal. A party who files a sealed paper electronically must serve it consistent with Fed. R. Civ. P. 5.

Local Rule E-8. Service of Documents by Electronic Means.

(a) Notice of Electronic Case Filing. When an ECF Filing User electronically files a pleading or other document using the ECF system, a Notice of Electronic Case Filing shall automatically be generated by the system, and shall be sent automatically to all parties entitled to service who have consented to electronic service. Electronic service of the Notice of Electronic Case Filing constitutes service of the filed document to all such parties and shall be deemed to satisfy the requirements of Rule 5(b)(2)(D) of the Federal Rules of Civil Procedure.

(b) Certificate of Service. All documents filed using the ECF system shall contain a Certificate of Service stating that the document has been filed electronically and is available for viewing and downloading from the ECF system. The Certificate of Service must identify the manner in which service on each party was accomplished, including any party who has not consented to electronic service.

(c) Service on Non-Consenting Parties. Parties who have not consented to electronic service are entitled to receive a paper copy of any electronically filed pleading or other document. Service of such paper copy must be made according to the Federal Rules of Civil Procedure.

(d) Timing of Service. Service by electronic means is complete on transmission, but service by electronic means is not effective if the party making service learns that the attempted service did not reach the person to be served.

(e) Calculation of Response Deadlines. If the recipient of notice or service is a registered participant in the CM/ECF System, service by electronic means of the Notice of Electronic Filing shall be the equivalent of service by hand delivery for the purposes of calculating deadlines triggered by such service.

ATTORNEY'S HANDBOOK FOR PRACTICE IN THE DISTRICT COURT

[Modified version of the Handbook for the
U.S. District Court for the Southern District of Indiana]

This *Handbook* is provided as a supplement to the Local Rules of the District Court to assist attorneys and litigants in dealing with the administrative requirements of the Court and the Clerk's Office. Its scope is limited to civil matters. Every effort has been made to be accurate, but for definitive guidance on procedural matters you should refer to the applicable *Rules of Civil Procedure* and/or the *Local Rules*. If any information in this handbook conflicts with the Rules, the Rules take precedence.

I. THE CLERK'S OFFICE

Office Structure and Informational Requests

The Clerk's Office is staffed by both operational and administrative staff. We are dedicated to serving the Judges, the Bar and the public in every appropriate manner to assist in the creation and maintenance of records and information pertinent to litigation in this District. Reliable and accessible records are the backbone of the courts. The majority of the Clerk's staff with whom attorneys and members of the public most often come into contact are "operational" personnel, in the sense that these deputy clerks maintain extensive "hands-on" contact with the case files. Inquiries regarding hearings, scheduling matters or the status of pending cases should be directed first to the clerk's office. **Inquiries should not be directed to the chambers of a judge unless the judge has authorized or requested it.**

Filing of Documents Outside Normal Office Hours

The Clerk's Office is open to the public between 9:00 a.m. and 4:45 p.m. daily except for Saturdays, Sundays and legal holidays.

In the event counsel needs to file papers outside of normal working hours, advance contact should be made with the Clerk's Office during regular business hours. A drop box is available outside the clerk's office in the courthouse for after-hours filing, but items should not be left there unless the clerk's office is first notified.

II. FILING

Local Rule 5.1 contains information on general aspects of filing, which is worth repeating here:

All papers presented to the Clerk or Judge for filing shall be flat and unfolded. All filings shall be on white paper of good quality, 8-1/2" x 11" in size, and shall be plainly typewritten, printed, or prepared by a clearly legible duplication process, and double spaced, except for quoted material. The filings shall have no covers or backs and shall be fastened together at the top left cover and at no other place. The title of each pleading must be set out on the first page. Each page shall be numbered consecutively. Any paper presented to the Clerk for filing which contains four or more exhibits shall include a separate index identifying and briefly describing each exhibit.

Documents not conforming to these requirements will not be rejected by the Clerk, but the Court may disregard them, order them stricken or order any defect corrected. Under no circumstances are pleadings to be delivered to chambers. A delivery to chambers is not deemed filing with the Clerk.

A motion or petition requiring the entry of a routine or uncontested order by the Judge or Clerk shall be accompanied by a suitable tendered form of order together with sufficient copies thereof for service upon all parties or their counsel whose names and addresses shall be typed in the lower left-hand corner of the tendered form of order.

Requirements for Filing a Civil Lawsuit

Five (5) items are necessary for the filing of a civil lawsuit:

1. Complaint.

2. Summons

3. Filing fee of $350.00 or a request that the filing fee be waived.

4. Notice of appearance by counsel

5. Civil cover sheet

The preferred method of demanding a jury trial is to set forth the demand on a separate document. However, it may also be noted in a *prominent* place on the document setting forth the claim for relief. Such notation shall be placed on the front page of the pleading, immediately following the title of the pleading, stating 'Demand For Jury Trial' or an equivalent statement. In addition, the attorney must check the designated box on the Civil Cover Sheet.

When papers are presented for filing, the Clerk retains only the original of each pleading or document. Each such pleading or document must be signed by the attorney(s) of record. An unsigned document or one containing only a rubber stamp or facsimile signature tendered for filing will not be refused, but the attorney who should have signed it will be contacted and expected to promptly cure the defect, pursuant to the requirements of *Fed. R. Civ. P.* 11.

Service of Process

The party asserting a claim for relief, whether through a complaint, a counter-claim or a cross-claim, bears the responsibility for properly notifying any adverse parties of the existence and nature of that claim. The traditional method by which this notice has been delivered is via a summons, although other methods are available in some circumstances.

At the time an action is commenced, the filing party may submit an original summons with the required number of copies needed for service. Alternatively, the party may utilize the notice and waiver provisions provided for in *Fed. R. Civ. P.* 4(d). Regardless of which method is selected, the party on whom the burden rests has 120 days from the filing of the complaint (or cross-claim or counterclaim) in which to serve process on the adverse parties. *See Fed. R. Civ. P.* 4(m).

a. Service by summons

The original and all copies of the summons are signed by a deputy clerk. The deputy clerk places one *copy* in the Court's file and returns the original and remaining copies to the attorney or pro se initiating party for service.

Under the present *Federal Rules of Civil Procedure*, a single summons may be prepared and issued for multiple defendants in the same case. Utilizing this procedure can result in considerable savings of time and paper.

A copy of the complaint (or other pleading in which a claim for relief is asserted) must be included with each summons being served.

Entry and Withdrawal of Appearance
Consent to Electronic Service

The appearance and withdrawal of counsel are governed by Local Rule 1.2. The Clerk will accept a notice of appearance in any form that contains the necessary information.

A lawyer's appearance, when filed, places his or her name on the distribution list and constitutes consent to receive notice of rulings and other actions by the court in electronic form. Where there are multiple attorneys appearing in the same case *from the same firm,* the firm should file only a single notice of appearance which must designate one attorney as "counsel of record." All mailings from the court will be sent addressed to counsel of record. If the designated "NOTICE" counsel changes, please inform the Clerk's Office to allow designation of another attorney.

Any change of name or address should be communicated to the Court in writing and to all the parties.

Amended Complaints and Amendment of Other Pleadings

When an amended complaint (or other amended pleading) is submitted but not filed as of right under *Fed. R. Civ. P.* 15(a) or pursuant to court order, the following procedures should be observed:

1. A motion for leave to file an amended complaint is filed, accompanied by an original of the proposed amended complaint and one extra copy. A proposed Order granting the motion with sufficient copies for all parties must also be submitted.

2. If an order granting the motion is entered, the **original** of the amended complaint (offered with the motion) will be filed and docketed and the extra copy will be filed-stamped and returned to the moving party for service on the other parties.

Pretrial Procedures

The Court has adopted specific pretrial procedures to conform to the requirements of the Civil Justice Reform Act of 1990 (CJRA). Counsel should refer to the Local Rules 1 for the details regarding pretrial procedures and the filing of case management plans. Questions concerning any specifics can be referred to the chambers of the assigned judge.

Very often the Court, in consonance with the case management plan in a particular case, will set a case for trial *only one time*. This deadline places significant responsibilities on counsel to adhere diligently to pretrial schedules.

The case management plan requires counsel to confer (preferably in person) and give thoughtful consideration to the merits and the amount of damages at issue in a case at the initial stages, rather than waiting until immediately before trial. The parties are then able to consider a realistic time frame and mechanisms for resolution of the dispute, whether through alternative dispute resolution or by the Court. The purposes of the plan **CANNOT** be fulfilled by merely exchanging a document in which the parties simply supply deadlines without any reasoned consideration of the difficulty of the issues in the case and the schedules of the parties.

Discovery

Because of the considerable cost to the parties in furnishing additional copies of discovery materials and the serious problems encountered with storage, the Court has directed, through Local Rule 26.2, that most discovery materials not be filed with the Clerk.

Even as to the written discovery and depositions counsel anticipate utilizing at trial or in support of a dispositive motion, only the portions directly relevant to the resolution of the issues presented should be filed. For example, if only four pages of a deposition are necessary to support a motion for summary judgment, only those pages, excerpted from the whole, should be included as an exhibit supporting the motion.

Motions to publish depositions are not required under the Federal Rules of Civil Procedure or the court's local rules.

In furtherance of the policy of the court that discovery matters be conducted without the unnecessary intervention of the Court, counsel are required in most circumstances, before filing a motion pursuant to Rule 26(c) or Rule 37 of the Federal Rules of Civil Procedure to meet and confer with a goal of reaching agreement on the matter(s) set forth in the motion.

III. JUDGMENT

When tendering proposed forms of judgment, either following trial or settlement, counsel should take care to comply in every respect with the separate document requirement of *Fed. R. Civ. P.* 58, specifying precisely what relief is awarded or not granted and as to which parties. A partial final judgment may be entered pursuant to *Fed. R. Civ. P.* 54(b) only when the specific criteria of that Rule are present and where the Court expressly directs the entry of a partial final judgment. Otherwise, a ruling which resolves less than all the claims against all the parties remains interlocutory.

IV. COURT PROCEDURES

Emergency Matters; Motions Judge

a. Requests for Temporary Restraining Order or Preliminary Injunction

Motions for preliminary injunctions and temporary restraining orders are governed by *Fed. R. Civ. P.* 65.1. In particular, such motions must be verified, must be submitted on a separate document and must be supported by a brief.

Such motions are to be presented to the Court immediately upon filing. The Court, however, expects that every reasonable effort has been made to reach an accord with opposing counsel on the issues advanced in the motions before relief in the form of these extraordinary remedies is sought. Once such a request is made counsel should coordinate the scheduling and other aspects of a hearing or conference with the assigned Judge's staff.

b. Emergency Matters and Motions Judge

Jurisdiction over any specific action is vested in the Court, not in individual judges. Nonetheless, civil, criminal and miscellaneous cases are assigned to particular judicial officers to facilitate their orderly process and resolution. When the assigned judge is not available to act on a matter requiring an immediate ruling, a Motions Judge is available in each Division for that purpose. The calendar reflecting assignments of Motions Judge duties is available from the Clerk in each Division.

Motions Practice

a. In General

When a party filing a motion has contacted the opposing parties, a practice which is required except for dispositive motions, and there is no objection to the relief sought in the motion, that fact should be recited in the motion, and the motion should be appropriately titled as an "uncontested" motion.

With the advent of electronic docketing, the clear identification in the title of motions and supporting documents is essential for accurate docketing. Several aspects of motions practice are particularly crucial and thus should be carefully observed:

1. **Each motion, unless submitted in the alternative, must be on a separate document.**

2. **Supporting briefs must be designated as supporting or opposing a specific (named) motion or petition, and should describe the party filing.**

3. **Notwithstanding the precision of labeling shown below, brevity and clarity in labeling and composing documents for filing are highly valued.**

For example, a motion and supporting brief could be entitled:

DEFENDANT SMITH'S MEMORANDUM IN OPPOSITION
TO PLAINTIFF'S MOTION FOR JUDGMENT ON THE PLEADINGS

PLAINTIFF TURNER'S REPLY
IN SUPPORT OF PLAINTIFF'S MOTION FOR JUDGMENT ON THE PLEADINGS

b. Ripeness of Motions for Ruling and Requests for Oral Arguments

A motion will be deemed ripe for ruling upon the passage of the applicable time for response and reply. Those periods are subject to modification upon application by a party.

A request for oral argument or an evidentiary hearing on a motion should be submitted separate from the motion itself. Any such request should include a statement of the specific purpose or reason for the request and an estimate of the time reasonably required for the Court to devote to the argument or hearing. Oral arguments on motions other than dispositive motions are generally not held.

c. Motions for Summary Judgment

The requirements and operation of Local Rule 56.1 are of vital importance to both the Court and counsel. Although Local Rule 7.1 establishes the presumptive briefing period for a summary judgment motion–an adverse party has fourteen (14) days after service of the initial brief in which to serve and file an answer brief – Rule 56.1 prescribes specific additional steps which are to be followed. These steps:

- First, "[i]n the text of the supporting brief or an appendix thereto . . . there shall be a 'Statement of Material Facts,' supported by appropriate citations to discovery responses, depositions, affidavits, and other admissible evidence, as to which the moving party contends there is no genuine issue."

- Second, any party opposing the motion has until the time in which a response is due in which to "serve and file any affidavits or other documentary material controverting the movant's position, together with an answer brief that shall include in its text or appendix thereto a 'Statement of Genuine Issues' setting forth, with appropriate citations to discovery responses, affidavits, depositions, or other admissible evidence, all material facts as to which it is contended there exists a genuine issue necessary to be litigated."

The importance of the moving party complying with this Rule is that the burden rests on it to go forward. The importance of complying with this Rule for any party opposing a properly supported motion is illustrated by the Rule's further provision that "the Court will assume that the facts as claimed and supported by admissible evidence by the moving party are admitted to exist without controversy, except to the extent that such facts are controverted in the [record]." In other words, if a non-moving party does not both *identify* factual issues created by the evidentiary record and **specify** what specific portions of the record create such issues, the Court will not comb the record in search of issues, but will instead follow Local Rule 56.1 by assuming that the factual averments of the moving party with respect to properly supported facts "exist without controversy." Conversely, if a moving party fails to specifically demonstrate where in the record the basis for such averments exist, the Court is not compelled to comb the record searching for them.

Exhibits

Non-trial exhibits. Exhibits attached to a pleading should be marked. *Exhibits offered in support of or in opposition to a particular motion should be attached to the motion and numbered and indexed consistent with Local Rule 5.1(a)* ("Any paper presented to the Clerk for filing which contains four or more exhibits shall include a separate index identifying and briefly describing each exhibit.") Exhibits too large or numerous to be attached to a motion should be presented separately in an appendix with a cover page bearing the caption of the action and identifying the material.

Trial exhibits. Unless the Court directs otherwise, after an item is offered for identification as an exhibit or demonstrative evidence, it remains with the Clerk until the action is closed, whether or not it actually becomes a trial exhibit. A case is closed on the date the final judgment or the mandate from the Court of Appeals (in the case of an affirmance) is docketed, whichever occurs later.

Unless other arrangements are made, the party who offered an exhibit has ninety (90) days after the case is closed to retrieve it from the Clerk. An appropriate receipt is given to the Clerk and filed at the time of retrieval. If an exhibit is not retrieved in accordance with this procedure, the Clerk will issue notice to the offering party. If the exhibit remains unclaimed for another thirty (30) days, it may be sold or otherwise disposed of as the Court orders. The proceeds from any such sale are deposited with the registry of the Court.

Weapons and exhibits consisting of contraband are not retained by the Clerk. Items of this nature are released to the investigating agency at the conclusion of trial or otherwise handled as the Court directs.

In Court

Each judicial officer has specific, individual requirements of decorum and procedure in the courtroom. In general, all Judges require the following:

1. Punctuality;

2. Premarked exhibits (exhibit and witness lists should be provided to court and court reporter);

3. Witnesses present and ready to testify;

4. Your own presentation devices, such as video players, projectors and screens, easels, x-ray viewers, etc.;

5. Advance formulation, if possible, of all objections to witnesses, exhibits, etc.

Please confer with the assigned judge's staff before the scheduled proceeding to ensure that your presentation will be handled in the most efficient, effective, and productive manner. Any specific questions concerning the handling of exhibits, witnesses, jury, etc., may be answered by the judge's staff.

The Official Record

Prior to the commencement of protracted and/or technical trials, attorneys should supply the court reporter with copies of witness and exhibit lists and a glossary of technical terms which may be utilized during the course of the proceeding.

When delivering oral arguments which include case or statutory cites, complete and full citations should be provided, including case name, source, volume, and page number.

VII. MISCELLANEOUS

Filing by Mail

Papers must be filed with the clerk, and are deemed filed only when actually received by the clerk. Filing is *not* completed upon mailing unless specific permission is given by the clerk or assigned judge.

HANDBOOK ON CIVIL DISCOVERY PRACTICE

(Adapted from the U.S. District Court, Middle District of Florida)

INTRODUCTION

The Federal Rules of Civil Procedure, the Local Rules, and existing case law cover only some aspects of civil discovery practice. Many of the gaps have been filled by the actual practice of trial lawyers and, over the years, a custom and usage has developed in frequently recurring discovery situations. Originally developed by a group of trial lawyers, this handbook on civil discovery practice, updated in 2001, attempts to supplement the rules and decisions by capturing this custom and practice. The revised handbook also incorporates portions of the American Bar Association's 1999 Civil Discovery Standards. This handbook is neither substantive law nor inflexible rule; it is an expression of generally acceptable discovery practice in the district. Judges and lawyers practicing in the district should regard the handbook as highly persuasive in addressing discovery issues.

I.   DISCOVERY IN GENERAL

A.   Courtesy and Cooperation Among Counsel

1 - Courtesy. Discovery in this district should be practiced with a spirit of cooperation and civility. The district's lawyers and the Court are justifiably proud of the courteous practice that is traditional in the District. Courtesy suggests that good faith consultation is appropriate before commencing action that might result in disagreement among counsel.

2 - Scheduling. A lawyer shall reasonably attempt to accommodate the schedules of opposing lawyers, parties, and witnesses in scheduling discovery.

3 - Stipulations. Unless contrary to Rule 29, Federal Rules of Civil Procedure, the parties may stipulate in writing to alter, amend, or modify any practice with respect to discovery. However, any such stipulations do not relieve the parties from compliance with court orders, absent approval of the Court.

4 - Withdrawal of Motions. If counsel resolve their differences and render a pending discovery motion moot, the moving party should immediately file a notice of withdrawal of the motion in order to avoid unnecessary judicial labor.

B.   Duty of Disclosure

Attorneys are responsible for complying with the provisions of Rule 26(a)(1), Federal Rules of Civil Procedure . . . regarding required initial disclosures.

C.   Filing of Discovery Materials and Other Discovery Considerations

1 - General Rule Governing Filing of Discovery Materials. Copies of written interrogatories, answers and objections to interrogatories, notices of oral depositions, transcripts of oral depositions, requests for the production of documents and other things, responses to requests for production, matters disclosed pursuant to Rule 26(a)(1), Federal Rules of Civil Procedure, requests for admissions, and responses to requests for admissions shall not be filed with the Court as a matter of course. Discovery materials are filed only in limited circumstances, including if ordered by the Court, if necessary to the presentation or defense of a motion, or if required by Rule 26(a)(3). Correspondence

exchanged during the course of litigation either between opposing counsel or between counsel for one party and an unrepresented party should be filed with the Court only to comply with an order of the Court or when necessary to the presentation and consideration of a motion and only when the filing of traditional discovery material will clearly not suffice for the purpose. Counsel should carefully redact correspondence to exclude irrelevant and prejudicial material, e.g., settlement discussions.

2 - <u>Filing Discovery or Other Papers Under Seal.</u> In certain rare circumstances involving trade secrets or other confidential information, the Court may order the filing under seal of discovery in order to preserve the integrity of the information. However, the Court wishes to minimize the number of documents filed under seal. Applicable precedent allows the Court to file documents under seal only in certain limited circumstances. Therefore, no paper may be filed under seal without prior approval by the Court upon the demonstration of a sufficient legal and factual basis.

3 - <u>Tailoring Discovery Requests to the Needs of the Case.</u> A party should tailor discovery requests to the needs of each case. The content of the requests should apply to the particular case, and the form of discovery requested should be the one best suited to obtain the information sought. In each case a party should carefully determine which discovery methods will achieve the discovery goal of obtaining useful information as efficiently and inexpensively as possible for everyone concerned.

4 - <u>Responding to Discovery Requests.</u> A party responding to a discovery request should make diligent effort to provide a response that (i) fairly meets and complies with the discovery request and (ii) imposes no unnecessary burden or expense on the requesting party.

D. Supplementing Answers

Rule 26(e), Federal Rules of Civil Procedure, expressly provides that in many instances a party is under a duty to supplement or correct prior disclosures pursuant to Rule 26(a) or in discovery responses. Fairness and professionalism suggest a broader range of circumstances requiring supplementation. However, a party may not vary the provisions of the Federal Rules of Civil Procedure by placing supplementation language in a discovery request.

E. Timeliness and Sanctions

1 - <u>Timeliness of Discovery Responses.</u> The Federal Rules of Civil Procedure set forth explicit time limits for responding to discovery requests. If unable to answer timely, a lawyer should first seek an informal extension of time from counsel propounding the discovery. Counsel in this district typically accommodate reasonable requests for additional time. If unable to informally resolve the matter, counsel should move for an extension of time to respond. Remember that you may not move for additional time unless you have first conferred with opposing counsel.

2 - <u>Motions for Extensions of Time.</u> Motions for extension of time within which to respond to discovery should be filed sparingly and only when counsel are unable to informally resolve their disputes. Counsel should be aware that the mere filing of a motion for an extension of time in which to respond does not, absent an order of the Court, extend the deadline for responding to discovery requests.

3 - <u>Sanctions.</u> Rule 37, Federal Rules of Civil Procedure, provides that if a party must seek relief from the Court to compel a recalcitrant party to respond, the moving party may be awarded reasonable expenses including attorney's fees incurred in compelling the responses. Rule 37 is enforced in this district. Further, if a Court order is obtained compelling discovery, unexcused failure to comply with such an order is treated by the Court with special gravity and disfavor.

4 - <u>Stays of Discovery.</u> Normally, the pendency of a motion to dismiss or a motion for summary judgment will not justify a unilateral motion to stay discovery pending resolution of the dispositive

motion. Such motions for stay are rarely granted. However, unusual circumstances may justify a stay of discovery in a particular case upon a specific showing of prejudice or undue burden. This policy also applies to cases referred to arbitration or mediation under the Local Rules.

F. Completion of Discovery

1 - Deadline for Discovery Completion. The Court ordinarily sets a discovery completion date through its Case Management and Scheduling Order (although a Judge may have another method of setting and extending that deadline). The Court follows the rule that the completion date means that *all discovery must be completed by that date.* For example, interrogatories must be served more than thirty days prior to the completion date to permit the opposing party to respond before the discovery deadline. Untimely discovery requests are subject to objection on that basis. Counsel, by agreement, may conduct discovery after the formal completion date but should not expect the Court to resolve discovery disputes arising after the discovery completion date.

2 - Extension of Time for Discovery Completion. Occasionally, the Court will allow additional discovery time upon motion, but it is a serious mistake to assume that an extension of the discovery completion date will be granted. When allowed, the discovery completion date is normally extended only upon a written motion showing good cause (including due diligence in the pursuit of discovery before the completion date) and stating both the specific additional discovery needed and its purpose. Motions for extension of discovery time are treated with special disfavor if filed after the discovery completion date and will normally be granted only if it clearly appears that an extension will not necessitate the continuance of a scheduled trial.

II.   DEPOSITIONS

A. General Policy and Practice

1 - Scheduling. A courteous lawyer is normally expected to accommodate the schedules of opposing lawyers. In doing so, the attorney should normally pre-arrange a deposition with opposing counsel before serving the notice. If this is not possible, counsel may unilaterally notice the deposition while at the same time indicating a willingness to be reasonable about any necessary rescheduling. Rule 30(a)(2)(A), Federal Rules of Civil Procedure limits each *side* to no more than ten depositions unless otherwise ordered by the Court. Additionally, the party noticing the deposition is to give a minimum (absent agreement or an order based upon some exigent circumstance) of ten days written notice to every other party and the deponent, if not a party, although giving substantially more than ten days notice is strongly encouraged. Customarily parties provide at least thirty days notice of a deposition. Rule 30(d)(2) limits a deposition to one day of seven hours, unless otherwise authorized by the Court or stipulated by the parties. This is generally interpreted to mean seven hours of actual testimony, with appropriate adjournments for meals, rest, or refreshment.

2 - Persons Who May Attend Depositions. Each lawyer may ordinarily be accompanied at the deposition by one representative of each client and, in technical depositions, one or more experts. Business necessity may require substitution for the representative of a party, but this privilege should not be abused. Lawyers may also be accompanied by records custodians, paralegals, secretaries, and the like, even though they may be called as technical witnesses on such questions as chain of custody, the foundation for the business record rule, or other technical matters. While more than one lawyer for each party may attend, only one should question the witness or make objections, absent an agreement to the contrary. Those in attendance should conduct themselves in the manner expected during courtroom proceedings in the presence of a judge.

3 - Place Where Deposition May Be Taken. A non-resident plaintiff may reasonably expect to be deposed at least once in this district during the discovery stages of the case and that a non-resident

defendant who intends to be present in person at trial may be deposed at least once in this district either during discovery in the case or within a week before trial, as the circumstances suggest. A non-resident is defined by Local Rule 3.04(b) as a person residing outside the state.

4 - <u>Designations by an Organization of Someone to Testify on Its Behalf.</u> In issuing or responding to a properly drawn notice of deposition pursuant to Rule 30(b)(6), Federal Rules of Civil Procedure, counsel should adhere to the following guidelines:

    (a) <u>Requested Areas of Testimony.</u> A notice or subpoena to an entity, association, or other organization should accurately and concisely identify the designated area(s) of requested testimony, giving due regard to the nature, business, size, and complexity of the entity being asked to testify.

    (b) <u>Designating the Best Person to Testify for the Organization.</u> An entity, association, or other organization responding to a deposition notice or subpoena should make a diligent inquiry to determine the individual(s) best suited to testify.

    (c) <u>Reasonable Interpretation Is Required.</u> Both in preparing and in responding to a notice or subpoena to an entity, association, or other organization, a party or witness is expected to interpret the designated area(s) of inquiry in a reasonable manner consistent with the entity's business and operations.

    (d) <u>If in Doubt, Clarification Is Appropriate.</u> A responding party or witness, who is unclear about the meaning and intent of any designated area of inquiry, should communicate in a timely manner with the requesting party to clarify the matter so that the deposition may proceed as scheduled. The requesting party is obligated to provide clarification sufficient to permit informed, practical, and efficient identification of the proper witness.

    (e) <u>Duty to Prepare Witness.</u> Counsel for the entity should prepare the designated witness so that the witness can provide meaningful information about the designated area(s) of inquiry.

5 - <u>If an Officer Lacks Knowledge.</u> Whenever an officer, director, or managing agent of an entity is served with a deposition notice or subpoena that contemplates testimony on a subject about which the witness lacks knowledge or information, that individual may submit to the noticing party, reasonably before the date noticed for the deposition, an affidavit or declaration under penalty of perjury so stating and identifying a person within the entity, if any, having knowledge of the subject matter. The noticing party should then proceed with the deposition of the officer, director, or managing agent initially noticed or subpoenaed only after careful consideration and for a specific reason, provided to the deponent in writing in advance of the deposition.

6 - <u>Consideration for an Organization's Senior Management.</u> If information is sought from an organization, counsel ordinarily should not seek in the first instance to take the deposition of the organization's senior management if someone else in the organization can be expected to have more direct and firsthand knowledge or information. Depositions are not properly used as a mechanism to inconvenience or distract senior management who may not be immediately involved in the dispute.

B. Objections

1 - <u>Objection to the Form of the Question.</u> Rule 32(d)(3)(B), Federal Rules of Civil Procedure, provides that an objection to the form of the question is waived unless asserted during the deposition. Many lawyers object by simply stating "I object to the form of the question." This normally suffices because it is usually apparent that the objection is, for example, "leading" or based upon an insufficient or inaccurate foundation. The interrogating lawyer has a right to ask the objecting party to state a sufficiently specific objection so that any problem with the question can be understood and, if

possible, cured. If the interrogating lawyer chooses not to ask for clarification, the objecting lawyer should stand on the objection without further elaboration; the objection is preserved.

2 - <u>Instruction That a Witness Not Answer.</u> Occasionally during a deposition, a lawyer may instruct a deponent not to answer a question. Rule 30(d), Federal Rules of Civil Procedure, expressly provides that a lawyer may instruct a deponent not to answer only when necessary to preserve a privilege, to enforce a limitation established by the Court, or to present a motion to show that the examination is being conducted in bad faith or in such a manner as unreasonably to annoy, embarrass, or oppress the deponent or party.

The use of the instruction not to answer, absent the limited circumstances set forth in Rule 30(d)(1), Federal Rules of Civil Procedure, is disfavored by the Court. A party or a lawyer who improperly instructs a deponent not to answer is subject to the expense and sanction provisions of Rule 37(a)(4).

3 - <u>Attorney-Deponent Conference During Deposition.</u> Except during routine recesses and for purposes of determining the existence of a privilege, an attorney and a deponent should not normally confer during a deposition. Likewise, attorneys should not attempt to prompt a deponent by suggestive or unnecessarily narrative objections.

4 - <u>Attorney-Deponent Communication During a Recess.</u> During a recess, an attorney for a deponent may communicate with the deponent; this communication should be deemed subject to the rules governing the attorney-client privilege. If, as a result of a communication between the deponent and his or her attorney, a decision is made to clarify or correct testimony previously given by the deponent, the deponent or the attorney for the deponent should, promptly upon the resumption of the deposition, bring the clarification or correction to the attention of the examining attorney. The examining attorney should not attempt to inquire into communications between the deponent and the attorney for the deponent that are protected by the attorney-client privilege. The examining attorney may inquire as to the circumstances that led to any clarification or correction, including inquiry into any matter that was used to refresh the deponent's recollection.

5 - <u>Telephone Hearing to Resolve Disputes During Deposition.</u> In unusual circumstances with material and adverse consequences, the parties involved in a deposition may telephone the chambers of the assigned Magistrate Judge for resolution of an intractable dispute that has arisen during the deposition. The Magistrate Judge, if available, will entertain such a request only if all parties are present. This procedure should be employed rarely (and only after counsel have made every effort to resolve the dispute).

C. Production of Documents at Depositions

1 - <u>Scheduling.</u> Consistent with the requirements of Rules 30 and 34, Federal Rules of Civil Procedure, a party seeking production of documents and other matters from another party in connection with a deposition should schedule the deposition to allow for the production in advance of the deposition.

2 - <u>Option to Adjourn or Proceed.</u> If requested documents that are discoverable are not timely produced prior to the deposition, the party noticing the deposition may either adjourn the deposition until after such documents are produced or, without waiving the right to have access to the documents and to subsequently examine the deponent regarding the documents, proceed with the deposition.

D. Non-Stenographic Recording of Depositions

Rule 30(b), Federal Rules of Civil Procedure, provides that parties are authorized to record deposition testimony by non-stenographic means without first obtaining permission of the Court or agreement from other counsel. Rule 30(b)(2) states that the party taking the deposition shall state in the notice the method by which the testimony shall be recorded. Unless the Court orders otherwise, the testimony may be recorded by sound, sound and visual, or stenographic means, and the party taking the deposition shall bear the costs of recording. Rule 30(b)(3) allows any party to designate an additional method to record the deponent's testimony so long as prior notice is provided to the deponent and other parties. The additional record or transcript shall be made at that party's expense unless the Court otherwise orders.

A party choosing to record a deposition only by videotape or audiotape should understand that a transcript will be required by Rules 26(a)(3)(B) and 32(c), Federal Rules of Civil Procedure, if the deposition is later to be offered as evidence at trial or in conjunction with a Rule 56 motion. Objections to the non-stenographic recording of a deposition may be presented to the Court under the provisions of Rule 26(c).

Parties using non-stenographic means to record deposition testimony shall refer to Rule 30(b)(4), Federal Rules of Civil Procedure, for specific procedures to ensure proper recording.

E. Experts

1 - *Disclosure of Expert Witnesses.* Each party should disclose the identity of prospective retained expert witnesses and provide a complete expert report under Rule 26(a)(2), Federal Rules of Civil Procedure, within the time provided in the Court's Case Management and Scheduling Order (which often adopts the schedule proposed by the parties in the Case Management Report). This includes any expert witness retained by another party (such as a co-defendant's expert) who may be used by the disclosing party. The expert report is not required of a "hybrid" witness, such as a treating physician, who was not specifically retained for the litigation and will provide both fact and expert testimony (though non-retained experts must still be disclosed and are subject to regular document and deposition discovery). The parties are encouraged to communicate openly about all opinions that a treating physician is expected to render in support of a party's case.

2 - *Scheduling the Deposition.* Pursuant to Rule 26(b)(4)(A), Federal Rules of Civil Procedure, a party may depose any person who has been identified as an expert whose opinions may be presented at trial. If a report from the expert is required under Rule 26(a)(2)(B), the deposition shall not be conducted until after the report is provided.

III.   PRODUCTION OF DOCUMENTS

A. Preparation and Interpretation of Requests for Documents

1 - *Formulating Requests for Documents.* In addition to complying with the provisions of Rules 34 and 45, Federal Rules of Civil Procedure, a request for documents, whether a request for production or a subpoena *duces tecum*, should be clear, concise, and reasonably particularized. For example, a request for "each and every document supporting your claim" is objectionably broad in most cases.

2 - *Use of Form Requests.* An attorney shall review any standard form document request or subpoena *duces tecum* and modify it to apply to the facts and contentions of the particular case. A "boilerplate" request or subpoena not directed to the facts of the particular case shall not be used. Neither should burdensome "boilerplate" definitions or instructions be used in formulating a document request or subpoena. Words used in discovery normally should carry their plain and ordinary meaning unless the particular case requires a special or technical definition, which should be specified plainly and concisely by the party required to respond to the term(s).

3 - *Reading and Interpreting Requests for Documents.* An attorney receiving a request for documents or a subpoena *duces tecum* shall reasonably and naturally interpret it, recognizing that the attorney serving it generally does not have specific knowledge of the documents sought and that

the attorney receiving the request or subpoena generally has or can obtain pertinent knowledge from the client. Furthermore, attorneys are reminded that evasive or incomplete disclosures, answers, or responses may be sanctionable under the provisions of Rule 37, Federal Rules of Civil Procedure.

4 - <u>Contact With the Client When a Document Request Is Received.</u> Upon receiving a document request, counsel should promptly confer with the client and take reasonable steps to ensure that the client (i) understands what documents are requested, (ii) has adopted a reasonable plan to obtain documents in a timely and reasonable manner, and (iii) is purposefully implementing that plan in good faith.

5 - <u>Responding to a Document Request.</u> A party and counsel ordinarily have complied with the duty to respond to a document request if they have:

(a) Responded to the requests within the time set by the governing rule, stipulation, or court-ordered extension;

(b) Objected with specificity to objectionable requests;

(c) Produced the documents themselves (or copies), specifically identified those documents that are being or will be produced, or specified precisely where the documents can be found and when they can be reviewed;

(d) Stated specifically that no responsive documents have been found; and

(e) Ensured a reasonable inquiry with those persons and a reasonable search of those places likely to result in the discovery of responsive documents.

6 - <u>Objections.</u> Absent compelling circumstances, failure to assert an objection to a request for production within the time allowed for responding constitutes a waiver and will preclude a party from asserting the objection in response to a motion to compel. Objections to requests for production should be specific, not generalized, and should be in compliance with the provisions of Rule 34(b), Federal Rules of Civil Procedure. Objections to portions of a document request do not excuse the responding party from producing those documents to which there is no objection. Specific objections should be matched to specific requests. General or blanket objections should be used only when they apply to every request.

7 - <u>Producing Documents Subject to Objection.</u> When the scope of the document production is narrowed by one or more objections, this fact and the nature of the documents withheld should be asserted explicitly.

8 - <u>When Production Is Limited by Interpretation.</u> If a party objects to a request as overbroad when a narrower version of the request would not be objectionable, the documents responsive to the narrower version ordinarily should be produced without waiting for a resolution of the dispute over the scope of the request. When production is limited by a party's objection, the producing party should clearly describe the limitation in its response.

9 - <u>Supplementation of Document Production.</u> A party should promptly produce any responsive documents discovered after the original production.

10 - <u>Producing Business Records in Lieu of Answering Interrogatories.</u> Rule 33(d), Federal Rules of Civil Procedure, allows a party in very limited circumstances to produce business records in lieu of answering interrogatories. To avoid abuses of Rule 33(d), the party wishing to respond to interrogatories in the manner contemplated by Rule 33(d) should observe the following practice:

(a) Specify the documents to be produced in sufficient detail to permit the interrogating party to locate and identify the records and to ascertain the answer as readily as could the party from whom discovery is sought.

(b)   The producing party shall make its records available in a reasonable manner [i.e., with tables, chairs, lighting, air conditioning or heat, and the like if possible] during normal business hours, or, in lieu of agreement, from 8:00 a.m. to 5:00 p.m., Monday through Friday, excluding holidays.

(c)   The producing party shall designate one of its regular employees to instruct the interrogating party on the use of the records retention system involved. That person shall be one who is fully familiar with the records system and, if a question concerning the records arises and the designated person cannot answer, the producing party should act reasonably and cooperatively in locating someone who knows the answer to the question.

(d)   The producing party shall make available any computerized information or summaries that it either possesses or can produce by a reasonably efficient procedure.

(e)   The producing party shall provide any relevant compilations, abstracts, or summaries, either in its custody or reasonably obtainable by it, not prepared in anticipation of litigation. If it has any documents arguably subject to this clause but which it declines to produce for some reason, the producing party shall call the circumstances to the attention of the opposing party, who may move to compel.

(f)   All of the actual clerical data extraction work shall be performed by the interrogating party unless agreed to the contrary, or unless, after actually beginning the effort, it appears that the task could be performed more efficiently by the producing party. In that event, the interrogating party may ask the Court to review the propriety of Rule 33(d) election. In other words, it behooves the producing party to make the document search as simple as possible, or the producing party may be required to answer the interrogatory in full.

11 - Oral Requests for Production of Documents. As a practical matter, many lawyers produce or exchange documents upon informal request, often confirmed by letter. A lawyer's promise that documents will be produced should be honored. Requests for production of documents and responses may be made on the record at depositions but usually should be confirmed in writing to avoid uncertainty. Attorneys are reminded that informal requests may not support a motion to compel.

B.   Procedures Governing Manner of Production

Production of Documents. Rule 34, Federal Rules of Civil Procedure, sets forth the procedures required for responding to a request for production of documents. Rule 34 also defines the term "document." In addition, the following general guidelines, although varied to suit the needs of each case, are normally followed:

1 -   Place of Production. As a matter of convenience, the request may suggest production at the office of either counsel. The Court expects the lawyers to reasonably accommodate one another with respect to the place of production of documents.

2 -   Manner of Production. Rule 34, Federal Rules of Civil Procedure, requires that a party producing documents for inspection produce them as they are maintained in the usual course of business or organize and label them to correspond with the categories in the request. In addition, if feasible, all of the documents should be made available simultaneously, and the party inspecting can determine the desired order of review. While the inspection is in progress, the inspecting party shall have the right to review again any documents which have already been examined during the inspection.

If the documents are produced as they are kept in the usual course of business, the producing party has an obligation to explain the general scheme of record-keeping to the inspecting party. The objective is to acquaint the inspecting party generally with how and where the documents are maintained. If the documents are produced to correspond with the categories in the request, some reasonable effort should be made to identify certain groups of the produced documents with particular categories of the request or to provide some meaningful description of the documents produced. The producing party is not obligated to rearrange or reorganize the documents.

3 - Listing or Marking. The producing party is encouraged to list or mark the documents which have been produced. This will prevent later confusion or dispute about which documents were produced. For relatively few documents, a list prepared by the inspecting attorney (which should be exchanged with opposing counsel) may be appropriate; when more documents are involved, the inspecting attorney may want to number each document. The producing party should allow such numbering so long as marking the document does not materially interfere with its intended use. Documents that would be materially altered by marking (e.g., promissory notes) should be listed rather than marked. Alternatively, copies of the documents (rather than originals) may be marked.

4 - Copying. Photocopies of the original documents are often prepared by the producing party for the inspecting party as a matter of convenience. However, the inspecting party has the right to insist on inspecting the original documents.

The photocopying of documents will generally be the responsibility of the inspecting party, but the producing party must render reasonable assistance and cooperation depending on its staffing and facilities. In a case with a manageable number of documents, the producing party should allow its personnel and its photocopying equipment to be used with the understanding that the inspecting party will pay reasonable charges. If a large quantity of documents is produced, it may be reasonable for the inspecting party to furnish personnel to make copies on the producing party's equipment or it may be reasonable for the inspecting party to furnish both the personnel and the photocopying equipment. On occasion it may be reasonable for the documents to be photocopied at another location or by an outside professional copy service.

5 - Scanning. The producing party should cooperate reasonably if the inspecting party wishes to scan rather than copy documents. The inspecting party must pay for all expenses associated with the scanning.

6 - Later Inspection. The inspecting party's right to inspect the documents again at a later date (after having completed the entire initial inspection) must be determined on a case-by-case basis, but permission should not be unreasonably withheld.

7 - Objections. Rule 34, Federal Rules of Civil Procedure, requires that if a request for production is objectionable only in part, production should be afforded with respect to the unobjectionable portions of the request. Objections to the production of documents based on generalized claims of privilege will be rejected. A claim of privilege must be supported by a statement of particulars sufficient to enable the Court to assess its validity. For a more detailed discussion of the invocation of privilege see Section V of this handbook. The procedures for invoking privilege set forth in Section V also apply to document production (which often requires the production of a "privilege log" containing the information requested in Section V).

8 - General. The Court expects lawyers to reach agreements regarding the production of documents based upon considerations of reasonableness, convenience, and common sense. Lawyers and parties can expect the Court to deal appropriately with a lawyer or party who acts unreasonably to thwart the discovery process.

IV.   Interrogatories

A.   Preparation and Answering of Interrogatories

1 -   <u>Informal Requests.</u> Whenever possible, counsel should try to exchange information informally. The results of such exchanges, to the extent relevant, may then be included in the record by requests for admissions or stipulations.

2 -   <u>Number and Scope of Interrogatories.</u> Rule 33(a), Federal Rules of Civil Procedure, restricts to 25 (including all parts and subparts) the number of interrogatories a party may serve on any other party. Leave of court, which is not routinely given absent stipulation, is required to serve more than 25 interrogatories cumulatively. Pursuant to Rule 26(g), counsel's signature on interrogatories constitutes a certification of compliance with those limitations. Interrogatories should be brief, simple, particularized, unambiguous, and capable of being understood by jurors when read in conjunction with the answer. They should not be argumentative nor should they impose unreasonable burdens on the responding party.

3 -   <u>Responses.</u> Rule 33(b), Federal Rules of Civil Procedure, requires the respondent to answer an interrogatory separately and fully in writing and under oath, unless the respondent objects, in which event the party objecting shall state the reasons for objection and shall answer to the extent the interrogatory is not objectionable. Interrogatories should be interpreted reasonably, in good faith, and according to the meaning the plain language of the interrogatory would naturally import. When in doubt about the meaning of an interrogatory, the responding party should give it a reasonable interpretation (which may be specified in the response) and offer an answer designed to provide, rather than deny, information.

4 -   <u>Objections.</u> Absent compelling circumstances, failure to assert objections to an interrogatory within the time for answers constitutes a waiver and will preclude a party from asserting the objection in a response to a motion to compel. All grounds for an objection must be stated with specificity. Specific objections should be matched to specific interrogatories. General or blanket objections should be used only when they apply to every interrogatory. When an answer is narrowed by one or more objections, this fact and the nature of the information withheld should be specified in the response itself.

5 -   <u>Assertions of Privilege.</u> Generalized assertions of privilege will be rejected. A claim of privilege must be supported by a statement of particulars sufficient to enable the Court to assess its validity. For a more detailed discussion of the invocation of privilege, see Section V dealing with privilege. The procedures for invoking privilege set forth in Section V also apply to interrogatory answers.

6 -   <u>Interrogatory Responses.</u> A party and counsel ordinarily have complied with their obligation to respond to interrogatories if they have:

   (a)   Responded to the interrogatories within the time set by the governing rule, stipulation, or court-ordered extension;

   (b)   Ensured a reasonable inquiry, including a review of documents likely to have information necessary to respond to interrogatories;

   (c)   Objected specifically to objectionable interrogatories; and

   (d)   Provided responsive answers to other interrogatories.

7 -   <u>Form Interrogatories.</u> There are certain kinds of cases which lend themselves to interrogatories which may be markedly similar from case to case, for example, employment discrimination and maritime cargo damage suits or diversity actions in which form interrogatories have been approved by state law. Aside from such cases, the use of "form" interrogatories is ordinarily

132

inappropriate. Carefully review interrogatories to ensure that they are tailored to the individual case; "boilerplate" is to be avoided.

8 - <u>Contention Interrogatories.</u> Interrogatories that generally require the responding party to state the basis of particular claims, defenses, or contentions in pleadings or other documents should be used sparingly and, if used, should be designed (1) to target claims, defenses, or contentions that the propounding attorney reasonably suspects may be the proper subject of early dismissal or resolution or (2) to identify and narrow the scope of unclear claims, defenses, and contentions. Interrogatories that purport to require a detailed narrative of the opposing parties' case are generally improper because they are overbroad and oppressive.

9 - <u>Reference to Deposition or Document.</u> Because a party is entitled to discovery both by deposition and interrogatory, it is ordinarily insufficient to answer an interrogatory by reference to an extrinsic matter, such as "see deposition of James Smith" or "see insurance claim." For example, a corporation may be required to state its official, corporate response even though one of its high-ranking officers has been deposed, because the testimony of an officer may not necessarily represent a complete or express corporate answer. Similarly, a reference to a single document is not necessarily a full answer, and the information in the document—unlike the interrogatory answer—is not ordinarily set forth under oath.

In rare circumstances, it may be appropriate for a corporation or partnership to answer a complex interrogatory by saying something such as "Acme Roofing Company adopts as its answer to this interrogatory the deposition testimony of James Smith, its Secretary, on pages 127-145 of his deposition transcript." This may suffice when an individual has already fully answered an interrogatory in the course of a previous deposition and the party agrees to be bound by this testimony. However, counsel are reminded, as provided in Rule 37(a)(3), Federal Rules of Civil Procedure, that for purposes of discovery sanctions, "an evasive or incomplete answer is to be treated as a failure to answer."

10 - <u>Interrogatories Should Be Reasonably Particularized.</u> Interrogatories designed to force an exhaustive or oppressive catalogue of information are generally improper. For example, an interrogatory such as "identify each and every document upon which you rely in support of your claim in Count Two" is objectionably overbroad in a typical case, although it may be appropriate in, for example, a simple suit on a note. While there is no simple and reliable test, common sense and good faith usually suggest whether such an interrogatory is proper.

11 - <u>Rule 33(d).</u> Rule 33(d), Federal Rules of Civil Procedure, allows a party in very limited circumstances to produce business records in lieu of answering interrogatories. Please refer to Section III A 10 for a detailed discussion of this option.

12 - <u>Answering Objectionable Interrogatories.</u> If any interrogatory is objectionable because of overbreadth, the responding party, although objecting, must answer the interrogatory to the extent that the interrogatory is not overbroad. In other words, an objection for overbreadth does not relieve the duty to respond to an extent that is not overbroad, while a party awaits a judicial determination.

V.   PRIVILEGE

A.   Invocation of Privilege

1 - <u>Claims of Privilege or Protection of Trial Preparation Materials.</u> A party who responds to or objects to discovery requests and who withholds information otherwise discoverable, asserting that the information is privileged or subject to protection as trial preparation material, must assert the claim expressly and must describe the nature of the documents, communications, or things not

produced or disclosed, such that, without revealing the privileged or protected information itself, the description will enable other parties to assess the applicability of the privilege or protection. See Rule 26(b)(5), Federal Rules of Civil Procedure. Withholding materials without notice is contrary to Rule 26 and may result in sanctions.

2 - <u>Procedure for Invocation of Privilege During a Deposition.</u> Rule 30(d), Federal Rules of Civil Procedure, permits objection during a deposition but requires a concise statement of the objection. Argumentative and suggestive objections or responses are improper. Rule 30(d) allows a person to instruct a deponent not to answer if necessary to preserve a privilege. While Rule 30(d) provides certain protections, counsel should be mindful that abuse of these protections is sanctionable. If a claim of privilege is asserted during a deposition and information is not provided on the basis of such assertion:

(a) The attorney asserting the privilege shall identify during the deposition the nature of the claimed privilege (including work product) and, if the privilege is asserted in connection with a claim or defense governed by state law, specify the claimed state law privilege; and

(b) At the time the privilege is asserted, the deposing attorney may seek and the deposed party must provide, if sought (unless divulgence of the information would cause disclosure of privileged information):

  (i) For documents, to the extent the information is readily obtainable from the witness being deposed or otherwise:

    (1) the type of document, e.g., letter or memorandum;

    (2) the general subject matter of the document;

    (3) the date of the document; and

    (4) other information sufficient to identify the document for a subpoena *duces tecum*, including, if appropriate, the author, addressee, and any other recipient of the document, and, unless apparent, the relationship to each other of the author, addressee, and any other recipient;

  (ii) For oral communications:

    (1) the name of the person making the communication and the names of persons present when the communication occurred, and unless apparent, the relationship of the persons present during the communication;

    (2) the date and place of communication; and

    (3) the general subject matter of the communication.

  (iii) Objection on the ground of privilege asserted during a deposition may be amplified by the objecting party subsequent to the objection.

(c) After a claim of privilege has been asserted, the attorney seeking disclosure shall have reasonable latitude during the deposition to question the witness to establish other relevant information concerning the assertion of the privilege, unless divulgence of such information would cause disclosure of privileged information, including:

  (i) the applicability of the particular privilege being asserted;

  (ii) the circumstances which may constitute an exception to the assertion of the privilege;

  (iii) the circumstances which may result in the privilege having been waived; and

  (iv) the circumstances which may overcome a claim of qualified privilege.

VI. MOTIONS TO COMPEL, FOR A PROTECTIVE ORDER, OR TO QUASH

A. Reference to Local Rule 3.04

The procedures and guidelines governing the filing of motions to compel and for protective orders require certification of a good faith conference before any discovery motion is filed, is strictly enforced. Many potential discovery disputes are resolved (or the differences narrowed or clarified) when counsel confer in good faith, preferably in person or by telephone.

B. Effect of Filing a Motion for a Protective Order

The mere filing of a motion for a protective order does not, absent an order of the Court granting the motion, excuse the moving party from complying with the requested or scheduled discovery. Upon receipt of objectionable discovery, a party has a duty to seek relief immediately, i.e., without waiting until the discovery is due or almost due. Upon receipt of a motion for a protective order, the Court may issue a temporary stay of discovery pending resolution of the motion. However, a party's diligence in seeking relief is a principal factor in the decision whether to grant a stay. Of course, a conference with opposing counsel must precede a motion for a protective order.

VII. TECHNOLOGY

A. Preserving and Producing Electronic Information

1 - Document Request. Unless otherwise stated in a request, a request for "documents" should be construed as also asking for information contained or stored in an electronic medium or format.

2 - Document Production. Upon request, a party serving written discovery requests or responses should provide the other party or parties with a diskette or other electronic version of the requests or responses (if reasonably available).

3 - Preserving Electronic Information. Unless the requesting party can demonstrate a substantial need, a party does not ordinarily have a duty to take steps to try to restore electronic information that has been deleted or discarded in the regular course of business but may not have been completely erased from computer memory.

4 - Discovery of Electronic Information.

(a) A party may request the production of electronic information, if reasonable, in hard copy, in electronic form, or in both forms. A party may also ask for the production of ancillary electronic information that relates to relevant electronic documents, such as information that would indicate (i) whether and when electronic mail was sent or opened by its recipient(s) or (ii) whether and when information was created or edited. A party also may request the software necessary to retrieve, read, or interpret electronic information.

(b) In resolving a motion seeking to compel or protect against the production of electronic information or related software, the Court will consider such factors as (i) the burden and expense of the discovery, (ii) the need for the discovery, (iii) the complexity of the case, (iv) the need to protect an applicable privilege, (v) whether the information or the software needed to access the information is proprietary or constitutes confidential business information, (vi) the breadth of the discovery request, and (vii) the relative resources of the parties.

(c) The discovering party generally should bear any special expenses incurred by the responding party in producing requested electronic information. The responding party generally need not incur undue burden or expense in producing electronic information, including the cost of acquiring or creating software needed to retrieve responsive electronic information for production to the other side.

(d) Where the parties are unable to agree on who bears the costs of producing electronic information, the Court's resolution will consider, among other factors: (i) whether the cost of producing it is disproportional to the anticipated benefit of requiring its production, (ii) the relative expense and burden on each side of producing it, (iii) the relative benefit to the parties of producing it, and (iv) whether the responding party has any special or customized system for storing or retrieving the information.

(e) The parties are encouraged to stipulate to the authenticity and identifying characteristics (date, author, etc.) of electronic information that is not self-authenticating.

5 - <u>Using Technology to Facilitate Discovery.</u> In appropriate cases, the parties may agree to, or the Court may direct, the production of some or all discovery materials, at least in the first instance, in an electronic format and allocate the resulting expenses among the parties.

SAMPLE STANDING ORDER REGARDING DISCOVERY OF ELECTRONICALLY STORED INFORMATION

[Adapted from Orders and Rules for various U.S. District Courts]

1. **Introduction.** The court expects the parties to cooperatively reach agreement on how to conduct e-discovery. In the event that such agreement has not been reached by the time of the Fed. R. Civ. P. 16 scheduling conference, the following default standards shall apply until such time, if ever, the parties reach agreement and conduct e-discovery on a consensual basis.

2. **Definitions.** In this Order, the following definitions will apply:

    a. "Metadata" means: (i) information embedded in a Native File that is not ordinarily viewable or printable from the application that generated, edited, or modified such Native File; and (ii) information generated automatically by the operation of a computer or other information technology system when a Native File is created, modified, transmitted, deleted or otherwise manipulated by a user of such system. Metadata is a subset of ESI.

    b. "Native File(s)" means ESI in the electronic format of the application in which such ESI is normally created, viewed and/or modified. Native Files are a subset of ESI.

    c. "Static Image(s)" means a representation of ESI produced by converting a Native File into a standard image format capable of being viewed and printed on standard computer systems. In the absence of agreement of the parties or order of Court, a Static Image should be provided in either Tagged Image File Format (TIFF, or .TIF files) or Portable Document Format (PDF). If load files were created in the process of converting Native Files to Static Images, or if load files may be created without undue burden or cost, load files should be produced together with Static Images.

3. **Before the discovery conference.** Prior to the Rule 26(f) conference, the parties shall exchange the following information:

    a. A list of the most likely custodians of relevant electronically stored information ("identified custodians"), including a brief description of each person's title and responsibilities.

    b. A list of each relevant electronic system that has been in place at all relevant times and a general description of each system, including the nature, scope, character, organization, and formats employed in each system, and whether the information contained on that system is of limited accessibility. Electronically stored information of limited accessibility may include those created or used by electronic media no longer in use, maintained in redundant electronic storage media, or for which retrieval involves substantial cost.

    c. The name of the party's "retention coordinator," the individual designated by the party as being most knowledgeable regarding that party's electronic document retention policies.

    d. The name of the party's designated "e-discovery coordinator," who serves as the individual through whom all e-discovery requests and responses are coordinated. Regardless of whether the e-discovery coordinator is an attorney (in-house or outside counsel), a third party consultant, or an employee of the party, he or she must be

        i. Familiar with the party's electronic systems and capabilities in order to explain these systems and answer relevant questions.

        ii. Knowledgeable about the technical aspects of e-discovery, including electronic document storage, organization, and format issues.

        iii. Prepared to participate in e-discovery dispute resolutions.

To the extent that the state of the pleadings does not permit a meaningful discussion of the above by the time of the Rule 26(f) conference, the parties shall either agree on a date by which this information will be mutually exchanged or submit the issue for resolution by the court at the Rule 16 scheduling conference.

Prior to the Fed. R. Civ. P. 26(f) Conference of Parties, Counsel for the parties must:

a. Advise their clients of the substantive principles governing the preservation of relevant or discoverable ESI while the lawsuit is pending, taking into account the considerations enumerated in Schedule A, attached hereto.

b. Become reasonably familiar with their clients' current and relevant past ESI, if any, or alternatively, identify a person who can participate in the Fed. R. Civ. P. 26(f) Conference of Parties and who is familiar with the subjects enumerated in Schedule B, attached hereto.

4. At the discovery conference. The following topics, if applicable, should be discussed at the Fed. R. Civ. P. 26(f) conference:

a. The anticipated scope of requests for, and objections to, production of ESI, as well as the form of production of ESI and, specifically, but without limitation, whether production will be of the Native File, Static Image, or other searchable or non-searchable formats.

   i. If the parties are unable to reach agreement on the format for production, ESI should be produced to the Requesting Party as Static Images. When the Static Image is produced, the Producing Party should maintain a separate file as a Native File and, in that separate file, it should not modify the Native File in a manner that materially changes the file and the Metadata. After initial production in Static Images is complete, a party seeking production of Native File ESI should demonstrate particularized need.

b. Whether production of some or all ESI in paper format is agreeable in lieu of production in electronic format, and whether Metadata is requested for some or all ESI and, if so, the volume and costs of producing and reviewing said ESI.

c. Preservation of ESI during the pendency of the lawsuit, specifically, but without limitation, applicability of the "safe harbor" provision of Fed. R. Civ. P. 37, preservation of Metadata, preservation of deleted ESI, back up or archival ESI, ESI contained in dynamic systems, ESI destroyed or overwritten by the routine operation of systems, and offsite and offline ESI (including ESI stored on home or personal computers). This discussion should include whether the parties can agree on methods of review of ESI by the responding party in a manner that does not unacceptably change Metadata.

   i. If Counsel are able to agree, the terms of an agreed-upon preservation order may be submitted to the Court;

   ii. If Counsel are unable to agree, each party may submit a narrowly tailored, proposed preservation order to the Court for its consideration.

d. Post-production assertion, and preservation or waiver of, the attorney-client privilege, work product doctrine, and/or other privileges in light of "clawback," "quick peek," or testing or sampling procedures.

e. Identification of ESI that is not reasonably accessible without undue burden or cost, specifically, and without limitation, the identity of such sources and the reasons for a contention that the ESI is or is not reasonably accessible without undue burden or cost, the methods of storing and retrieving that ESI, and the anticipated costs and efforts involved in retrieving that ESI.

f. Because identifying information may not be placed on ESI as easily as Bates stamping paper documents, methods of identifying pages or segments of ESI produced in discovery should be discussed, and, specifically, and without limitation, the following alternatives may be considered by the parties: electronically paginating Native File ESI pursuant to a stipulated agreement that the alteration does not affect admissibility; renaming Native Files using bates-type numbering systems, e.g., ABC0001, ABC0002, ABC0003, with some method of referring to unnumbered "pages" within each file; using software that produces "hash marks" or "hash values" for each Native File; placing pagination on Static Images; or any other practicable method. The parties are encouraged to discuss the use of a digital notary for producing Native Files.

g. The method and manner of redacting information from ESI if only part of the ESI is discoverable. If Metadata is redacted from a file, written notice of such redaction, and the scope of that redaction, should be provided.

h. The nature of information systems used by the party or person or entity served with a subpoena requesting ESI.

i. Specific facts related to the costs and burdens of preservation, retrieval, and use of ESI.

j. Cost sharing for the preservation, retrieval and/or production of ESI, including any discovery database, differentiating between ESI that is reasonably accessible and ESI that is not reasonably accessible; provided however that absent a contrary showing of good cause, e.g., Fed. R. Civ. P. 26(b)(2)(C), the parties should generally presume that the Producing Party bears all costs as to reasonably accessible ESI and, provided further, the parties should generally presume that there will be cost sharing or cost shifting as to ESI that is not reasonably accessible. The parties may choose to discuss the use of an Application Service Provider that is capable of establishing a central repository of ESI for all parties.

k. Search methodologies for retrieving or reviewing ESI such as identification of the systems to be searched; identification of systems that will not be searched; restrictions or limitations on the search; factors that limit the ability to search; the use of key word searches, with an agreement on the words or terms to be searched; using sampling to search rather than searching all of the records; limitations on the time frame of ESI to be searched; limitations on the fields or document types to be searched; limitations regarding whether back up, archival, legacy or deleted ESI is to be searched; the number of hours that must be expended by the searching party or person in conducting the search and compiling and reviewing ESI; and the amount of pre-production review that is reasonable for the Producing Party to undertake in light of the considerations set forth in Fed. R. Civ. P. 26(b)(2)(C).

l. Preliminary depositions of information systems personnel, and limits on the scope of such depositions. Counsel should specifically consider whether limitations on the scope of such depositions should be submitted to the Court with a proposed order that, if entered, would permit Counsel to instruct a witness not to answer questions beyond the scope of the limitation, pursuant to Fed. R. Civ. P. 30(d)(1).

m. The need for two-tier or staged discovery of ESI, considering whether ESI initially can be produced in a manner that is more cost-effective, while reserving the right to request or to oppose additional more comprehensive production in a latter stage or stages.

n. The need for any protective orders or confidentiality orders, in conformance with the Local Rules and substantive principles governing such orders.

o. Any request for sampling or testing of ESI; the parameters of such requests; the time, manner, scope, and place limitations that will voluntarily or by Court order be placed on such processes; the persons to be involved; and the dispute resolution mechanism, if any, agreed-upon by the parties.

p. Any agreement concerning retention of an agreed-upon Court expert, retained at the cost of the parties, to assist in the resolution of technical issues presented by ESI.

5. Timing of e-discovery. Discovery of relevant electronically stored information shall proceed in a sequenced fashion.

a. After receiving requests for document production, the parties shall search their documents, other than those identified as limited accessibility electronically stored information, and produce relevant responsive electronically stored information in accordance with Fed. R. Civ. P. 26(b)(2).

b. Electronic searches of documents identified as of limited accessibility shall not be conducted until the initial electronic document search has been completed. Requests for information expected to be found in limited accessibility documents must be narrowly focused with some basis in fact supporting the request.

c. On-site inspections of electronic media under Fed. R. Civ. P. 34(b) shall not be permitted absent exceptional circumstances, where good cause and specific need have been demonstrated.

d. Absent the parties' agreement or a court order upon a showing of good cause by the requesting party, the categories of ESI identified in Schedule C attached hereto need not be preserved.

6. Search methodology. If the parties intend to employ an electronic search to locate relevant electronically stored information, the parties shall disclose any restrictions as to scope and method which might affect their ability to conduct a complete electronic search of the electronically stored information. The parties shall reach agreement as to the method of searching, and the words, terms, and phrases to be searched with the assistance of the respective e-discovery coordinators, who are charged with familiarity with the parties' respective systems. The parties also shall reach agreement as to the timing and conditions of any additional searches which may become necessary in the normal course of discovery. To minimize the expense, the parties may consider limiting the scope of the electronic search (*e.g.*, time frames, fields, document types).

7. Format. If, during the course of the Rule 26(f) conference, the parties cannot agree to the format for document production, electronically stored information shall be produced to the requesting party as image files (*e.g.*, PDF or TIFF). When the image file is produced, the producing party must preserve the integrity of the electronic document's contents, *i.e.*, the original formatting of the document, its metadata and, where applicable, its revision history. After initial production in image file format is complete, a party must demonstrate particularized need for production of electronically stored information in their native format.

8. Retention. Within the first thirty (30) days of discovery, the parties should work toward an agreement (akin to the standard protective order) that outlines the steps each party shall take to segregate and preserve the integrity of all relevant electronically stored information. In order to avoid later accusations of spoliation, a Fed. R. Civ. P. 30(b)(6) deposition of each party's retention coordinator may be appropriate.

The retention coordinators shall:

a. Take steps to ensure that relevant e-mail of identified custodians shall not be permanently deleted in the ordinary course of business and that relevant electronically stored information maintained by the individual custodians shall not be altered.

b. Provide notice as to the criteria used for spam and/or virus filtering of e-mail and attachments; e-mails and attachments filtered out by such systems shall be deemed non-responsive so long as the criteria underlying the filtering are reasonable.

9. Privilege. Electronically stored information that contains privileged information or attorney-work product shall be immediately returned if the documents appear on their face to have been inadvertently produced or if there is notice of the inadvertent production within thirty (30) days of such. In all other circumstances, Fed. R. Civ. P. 26(b)(5)(B) shall apply.

10. Costs. Generally, the costs of discovery shall be borne by each party. However, the court will apportion the costs of electronic discovery upon a showing of good cause.

11. Metadata. The production of Metadata apart from its Native File may impose substantial costs, either in the extraction of such Metadata from the Native Files, or in its review for purposes of redacting non-discoverable information contained in such Metadata. The persons involved in the discovery process are expected to be cognizant of those costs in light of the various factors established in Fed. R. Civ. P. 26(b)(2)(C). The following principles should be utilized in determining whether Metadata may be discovered:

a. Metadata is part of ESI. Such Metadata, however, may not be relevant to the issues presented or, if relevant, not be reasonably subject to discovery given the Rule 26(b)(2)(C) cost-benefit factors. Therefore, it may be subject to cost-shifting under Fed. R. Civ. P. 26(b)(2)(C).

b. Metadata may generally be viewed as System Metadata, Substantive Metadata, or Embedded Metadata. System Metadata is data that is automatically generated by a computer system. For example, System Metadata often includes information such as the author, date and time of creation, and the date a document was modified. Substantive Metadata is data that reflects the substantive changes made to the document by the user. For example, it may include the text of actual changes to a document. While no generalization is universally applicable, System Metadata is less likely to involve issues of work product and/or privilege.

c. Metadata, especially Substantive Metadata, need not be routinely produced, except upon agreement of the requesting and producing litigants, or upon a showing of good cause in a motion filed by the Requesting Party.

d. If a Producing Party produces ESI without some or all of the Metadata that was contained in the ESI, the Producing Party should inform all other parties of this fact, in writing, at or before the time of production.

e. Some Native Files contain, in addition to Substantive Metadata and/or System Metadata, Embedded Metadata, which means the text, numbers, content, data, or other information that is directly or indirectly inputted into a Native File by a user and which is not typically visible to the user viewing the output display of the Native File on screen or as a print out. Examples of Embedded Metadata include, but are not limited to, spreadsheet formulas (which display as the result of the formula operation), hidden columns, externally or internally linked files (*e.g.*, sound files in Powerpoint presentations), references to external files and content (*e.g.*, hyperlinks to HTML files or URLs), references and fields (*e.g.*, the field codes for an auto-numbered document), and certain database information if the data is part of a database (*e.g.*, a date field in a database will display as a formatted date, but its actual value is typically a long integer). Subject to the other provisions of this Protocol related to the costs and benefits of preserving and producing Metadata (see generally Paragraph 8), subject to potential redaction of Substantive Metadata, and subject to reducing the scope of production of Embedded Metadata, Embedded Metadata is generally discoverable and in appropriate cases, see Fed. R. Civ. P. 26(b)(2)(C), should be produced as a matter of course.

f. In the absence of an agreement or court order to the contrary, and subject to Paragraph "e" above regarding Embedded Metadata, the parties are only obligated to provide the following metadata for all ESI produced, to the extent such metadata exists: Custodian, File Path, Email Subject, Conversation Index, From, To, CC, BCC, Date Sent, Time Sent, Date Received, Time Received, Filename, Author, Date Created, Date Modified, MD5 Hash, File Size, File Extension, Control Number Begin, Control Number End, Attachment Range, Attachment Begin, and Attachment End (or the equivalent thereof).

SCHEDULE A

Considerations Regarding Preservation Obligations

1) Scope of the "litigation hold," including:

   a) A determination of the categories of potentially discoverable information to be segregated and preserved;

   b) Identification of "key persons," and likely witnesses and persons with knowledge regarding relevant events;

   c) The relevant time period for the litigation hold.

2) Analysis of what needs to be preserved, including:

   a) The nature of specific types of ESI, including, email and attachments, word processing documents, spreadsheets, graphics and presentation documents, images, text files, hard drives, databases, instant messages, transaction logs, audio and video files, voicemail, Internet data, computer logs, text messages, or backup materials, and Native Files, and how it should be preserved;

   b) the extent to which Metadata, deleted data, or fragmented data, will be subject to litigation hold;

   c) paper documents that are exact duplicates of ESI;

   d) any preservation of ESI that has been deleted but not purged.

3) Determination of where ESI subject to the litigation hold is maintained, including:

   a) format, location, structure, and accessibility of active storage, backup, and archives;

   b) servers;

   c) computer systems, including legacy systems;

   d) remote and third-party locations;

   e) back-up media (for disasters) vs. back-up media for archival purposes/record retention laws;

   f) network, intranet, and shared areas (public folders, discussion databases, departmental drives, and shared network folders);

   g) desktop computers and workstations;

   h) portable media; laptops; personal computers; PDAs; paging devices; mobile telephones; and flash drives;

   i) tapes, discs, drives, cartridges and other storage media;

   j) home computers (to the extent, if any, they are used for business purposes);

   k) paper documents that represent ESI.

4) Distribution of the notification of the litigation hold:

   a) to parties and potential witnesses;

   b) to persons with records that are potentially discoverable;

   c) to persons with control over discoverable information;

d) to third parties (contractors and vendors who provide IT services).

5) Instructions to be contained in a litigation hold notice, including that:

a) there will be no deletion or modification of ESI subject to the litigation hold;

b) the recipient should advise whether specific categories of ESI subject to the litigation hold require particular actions (*e.g.*, printing paper copies of email and attachments) or transfer into "read only" media;

c) loading of new software that materially impacts ESI subject to the hold may occur only upon prior written approval from designated personnel;

d) where metadata, or data that has been deleted but not purged, is to be preserved, either a method to preserve such data before running compression, disk defragmentation or other computer optimization or automated maintenance programs or scripts of any kind ("File and System Maintenance Procedures"), or the termination of all File and System Maintenance Procedures during the pendency of the litigation hold;

e) reasonably safeguarding and preserving all portable or removable electronic storage media containing potentially relevant ESI;

f) maintaining hardware that has been removed from active production, if such hardware contains legacy systems with relevant ESI and there is no reasonably available alternative that preserves access to the Native Files on such hardware.

6) Monitoring compliance with the notification of litigation hold, including:

a) identifying contact person who will address questions regarding preservation duties;

b) identifying personnel with responsibility to confirm that compliance requirements are met;

c) determining whether data of "key persons" requires special handling (*e.g.*, imaging/cloning hard drives);

d) periodic checks of logs or memoranda detailing compliance;

e) issuance of periodic reminders that the litigation hold is still in effect.

SCHEDULE B

Subjects Within Knowledge of E-Discovery Representative

1) Email systems; blogs; instant messaging; Short Message Service (SMS) systems; word processing systems; spreadsheet and database systems; system history files, cache files, and cookies; graphics, animation, or document presentation systems; calendar systems; voice mail systems, including specifically, whether such systems include ESI; data files; program files; internet systems; and, intranet systems. This may include information concerning the specific version of software programs and may include information stored on electronic bulletin boards, regardless of whether they are maintained by the party, authorized by the party, or officially sponsored by the party, as long as such information is in the possession, custody, or control of such party. To the extent reasonably possible, this includes the database program used over the relevant time, its database dictionary, and the manner in which such program records transactional history in respect to deleted records.

2) Storage systems, including whether ESI is stored on servers, individual hard drives, home computers, "laptop" or "notebook" computers, personal digital assistants, pagers, mobile telephones,

or removable/portable storage devices, such as CD-Roms, DVDs, "floppy" disks, zip drives, tape drives, external hard drives, flash, thumb or "key" drives, or external service providers.

3) Back up and archival systems, including those that are onsite, offsite, or maintained using one or more third-party vendors. This may include a reasonable inquiry into the back-up routine, application, and process and location of storage media, and requires inquiry into whether ESI is reasonably accessible without undue burden or cost, whether it is compressed, encrypted, and the type of device on which it is recorded (*e.g.*, whether it uses sequential or random access), and whether software that is capable of rendering it into usable form without undue expense is within the client's possession, custody, or control.

4) Obsolete or "legacy" systems containing ESI and the extent, if any, to which such ESI was copied or transferred to new or replacement systems.

5) Current and historical website information, including any potentially relevant or discoverable statements contained on that or those site(s), as well as systems to back up, archive, store, or retain superseded, deleted, or removed web pages, and policies regarding allowing third parties' sites to archive client website data.

6) Event data records automatically created by the operation, usage, or polling of software or hardware (such as recorded by a motor vehicle's GPS or other internal computer prior to an occurrence), if any and if applicable, in automobiles, trucks, aircraft, vessels, or other vehicles or equipment.

7) Communication systems, if any and if applicable, such as ESI records of radio transmissions, telephones, personal digital assistants, or GPS systems.

8) ESI erasure, modification, or recovery mechanisms, such as metadata scrubbers or programs that repeatedly overwrite portions of storage media in order to preclude data recovery, and policies regarding the use of such processes and software, as well as recovery programs;

9) Policies regarding records management, including the retention or destruction of ESI prior to the client receiving knowledge that a claim is reasonably anticipated.

10) "Litigation hold" policies that are instituted when a claim is reasonably anticipated, including all such policies that have been instituted, and the date on which they were instituted.

11) The identity of custodians of key ESI, including "key persons" and related staff members, and the information technology or information systems personnel, vendors, or subcontractors who are best able to describe the client's information technology system.

12) The identity of vendors or subcontractors who store ESI for, or provide services or applications to, the client or a key person; the nature, amount, and a description of the ESI stored by those vendors or subcontractors; contractual or other agreements that permit the client to impose a "litigation hold" on such ESI; whether or not such a "litigation hold" has been placed on such ESI; and, if not, why not.

SCHEDULE C

ESI Not Subject to Preservation Without Heightened Showing

1) Deleted, slack, fragmented, or other data only accessible by forensics.

2) Random access memory (RAM), temporary files, or other ephemeral data that are difficult to preserve without disabling the operating system.

3) On-line access data such as temporary Internet files, history, cache, cookies, and the like.

4) Data in metadata fields that are frequently updated automatically, such as last-opened dates.

5) Back-up data that are substantially duplicative of data that are more accessible elsewhere.

6) Voice messages.

7) Instant messages that are not ordinarily printed or maintained in a server dedicated to instant messaging.

8) Electronic mail or pin-to-pin messages sent to or from mobile devices (e.g., iPhone and Blackberry devices), provided that a copy of such mail is routinely saved elsewhere.

9) Other electronic data stored on a mobile device, such as calendar or contact data or notes, provided that a copy of such information is routinely saved elsewhere.

10) Logs of calls made from mobile devices.

11) Server, system or network logs.

12) Electronic data temporarily stored by laboratory equipment or attached electronic equipment, provided that such data is not ordinarily preserved as part of a laboratory report.

13) Data remaining from systems no longer in use and that is unintelligible on the systems in use.

FEDERAL RULES OF EVIDENCE

(With all amendments through December 1, 2015)

ARTICLE I. GENERAL PROVISIONS

Rule 101. Scope; Definitions

(a) **Scope.** These rules apply to proceedings in United States courts. The specific courts and proceedings to which the rules apply, along with exceptions, are set out in Rule 1101.

(b) **Definitions.** In these rules:

    (1) "civil case" means a civil action or proceeding;

    (2) "criminal case" includes a criminal proceeding;

    (3) "public office" includes a public agency;

    (4) "record" includes a memorandum, report, or data compilation;

    (5) a "rule prescribed by the Supreme Court" means a rule adopted by the Supreme Court under statutory authority; and

    (6) a reference to any kind of written material or any other medium includes electronically stored information.

Rule 102. Purpose

These rules should be construed so as to administer every proceeding fairly, eliminate unjustifiable expense and delay, and promote the development of evidence law, to the end of ascertaining the truth and securing a just determination.

Rule 103. Rulings on Evidence

(a) **Preserving a Claim of Error.** A party may claim error in a ruling to admit or exclude evidence only if the error affects a substantial right of the party and:

    (1) if the ruling admits evidence, a party, on the record:

        (A) timely objects or moves to strike; and

        (B) states the specific ground, unless it was apparent from the context; or

    (2) if the ruling excludes evidence, a party informs the court of its substance by an offer of proof, unless the substance was apparent from the context.

(b) **Not Needing to Renew an Objection or Offer of Proof.** Once the court rules definitively on the record — either before or at trial — a party need not renew an objection or offer of proof to preserve a claim of error for appeal.

(c) **Court's Statement About the Ruling; Directing an Offer of Proof.** The court may make any statement about the character or form of the evidence, the objection made, and the ruling. The court may direct that an offer of proof be made in question-and-answer form.

(d) Preventing the Jury from Hearing Inadmissible Evidence. To the extent practicable, the court must conduct a jury trial so that inadmissible evidence is not suggested to the jury by any means.

(e) Taking Notice of Plain Error. A court may take notice of a plain error affecting a substantial right, even if the claim of error was not properly preserved.

Rule 104. Preliminary Questions

(a) In General. The court must decide any preliminary question about whether a witness is qualified, a privilege exists, or evidence is admissible. In so deciding, the court is not bound by evidence rules, except those on privilege.

(b) Relevance That Depends on a Fact. When the relevance of evidence depends on whether a fact exists, proof must be introduced sufficient to support a finding that the fact does exist. The court may admit the proposed evidence on the condition that the proof be introduced later.

(c) Conducting a Hearing So That the Jury Cannot Hear It. The court must conduct any hearing on a preliminary question so that the jury cannot hear it if:

(1) the hearing involves the admissibility of a confession;

(2) a defendant in a criminal case is a witness and so requests; or

(3) justice so requires.

(d) Cross-Examining a Defendant in a Criminal Case. By testifying on a preliminary question, a defendant in a criminal case does not become subject to cross-examination on other issues in the case.

(e) Evidence Relevant to Weight and Credibility. This rule does not limit a party's right to introduce before the jury evidence that is relevant to the weight or credibility of other evidence.

Rule 105. Limiting Evidence That Is Not Admissible Against Other Parties or for Other Purposes

If the court admits evidence that is admissible against a party or for a purpose — but not against another party or for another purpose — the court, on timely request, must restrict the evidence to its proper scope and instruct the jury accordingly.

Rule 106. Remainder of or Related Writings or Recorded Statements

If a party introduces all or part of a writing or recorded statement, an adverse party may require the introduction, at that time, of any other part — or any other writing or recorded statement — that in fairness ought to be considered at the same time.

ARTICLE II. JUDICIAL NOTICE

Rule 201. Judicial Notice of Adjudicative Facts

(a) Scope. This rule governs judicial notice of an adjudicative fact only, not a legislative fact.

(b) Kinds of Facts That May Be Judicially Noticed. The court may judicially notice a fact that is not subject to reasonable dispute because it:

(1) is generally known within the trial court's territorial jurisdiction; or

(2) can be accurately and readily determined from sources whose accuracy cannot reasonably be questioned.

(c) Taking Notice. The court:

(1) may take judicial notice on its own; or

(2) must take judicial notice if a party requests it and the court is supplied with the necessary information.

(d) Timing. The court may take judicial notice at any stage of the proceeding.

(e) Opportunity to Be Heard. On timely request, a party is entitled to be heard on the propriety of taking judicial notice and the nature of the fact to be noticed. If the court takes judicial notice before notifying a party, the party, on request, is still entitled to be heard.

(f) Instructing the Jury. In a civil case, the court must instruct the jury to accept the noticed fact as conclusive. In a criminal case, the court must instruct the jury that it may or may not accept the noticed fact as conclusive.

ARTICLE III. PRESUMPTIONS IN CIVIL CASES

Rule 301.   Presumptions in Civil Cases Generally

In a civil case, unless a federal statute or these rules provide otherwise, the party against whom a presumption is directed has the burden of producing evidence to rebut the presumption. But this rule does not shift the burden of persuasion, which remains on the party who had it originally.

Rule 302.   Applying State Law to Presumptions in Civil Cases

In a civil case, state law governs the effect of a presumption regarding a claim or defense for which state law supplies the rule of decision.

ARTICLE IV. RELEVANCE AND ITS LIMITS

Rule 401.   Test for Relevant Evidence

Evidence is relevant if:

(a) it has any tendency to make a fact more or less probable than it would be without the evidence; and

(b) the fact is of consequence in determining the action.

Rule 402.   General Admissibility of Relevant Evidence

Relevant evidence is admissible unless any of the following provides otherwise:

- the United States Constitution;
- federal statute;

- these rules; or

- other rules prescribed by the Supreme Court.

Irrelevant evidence is not admissible.

Rule 403.   Excluding Relevant Evidence for Prejudice, Confusion, Waste of Time, or Other Reasons

The court may exclude relevant evidence if its probative value is substantially outweighed by a danger of one or more of the following: unfair prejudice, confusing the issues, misleading the jury, undue delay, wasting time, or needlessly presenting cumulative evidence.

Rule 404.   Character Evidence; Crimes or Other Acts

(a) Character Evidence.

(1) *Prohibited Uses*. Evidence of a person's character or character trait is not admissible to prove that on a particular occasion the person acted in accordance with the character or trait.

(2) *Exceptions for a Defendant or Victim in a Criminal Case*. The following exceptions apply in a criminal case:

(A) a defendant may offer evidence of the defendant's pertinent trait, and if the evidence is admitted, the prosecutor may offer evidence to rebut it;

(B) subject to the limitations in Rule 412, a defendant may offer evidence of an alleged victim's pertinent trait, and if the evidence is admitted, the prosecutor may:

(i) offer evidence to rebut it; and

(ii) offer evidence of the defendant's same trait; and

(C) in a homicide case, the prosecutor may offer evidence of the alleged victim's trait of peacefulness to rebut evidence that the victim was the first aggressor.

(1) *Exceptions for a Witness*. Evidence of a witness's character may be admitted under Rules 607, 608, and 609.

(b) Crimes, Wrongs, or Other Acts.

(1) *Prohibited Uses*. Evidence of a crime, wrong, or other act is not admissible to prove a person's character in order to show that on a particular occasion the person acted in accordance with the character.

(2) *Permitted Uses; Notice in a Criminal Case*. This evidence may be admissible for another purpose, such as proving motive, opportunity, intent, preparation, plan, knowledge, identity, absence of mistake, or lack of accident. On request by a defendant in a criminal case, the prosecutor must:

(A) provide reasonable notice of the general nature of any such evidence that the prosecutor intends to offer at trial; and

(B) do so before trial — or during trial if the court, for good cause, excuses lack of pretrial notice.

Rule 405. Methods of Proving Character

(a) By Reputation or Opinion. When evidence of a person's character or character trait is admissible, it may be proved by testimony about the person's reputation or by testimony in the form of an opinion. On cross-examination of the character witness, the court may allow an inquiry into relevant specific instances of the person's conduct.

(b) By Specific Instances of Conduct. When a person's character or character trait is an essential element of a charge, claim, or defense, the character or trait may also be proved by relevant specific instances of the person's conduct.

Rule 406. Habit; Routine Practice

Evidence of a person's habit or an organization's routine practice may be admitted to prove that on a particular occasion the person or organization acted in accordance with the habit or routine practice. The court may admit this evidence regardless of whether it is corroborated or whether there was an eyewitness.

Rule 407. Subsequent Remedial Measures

When measures are taken that would have made an earlier injury or harm less likely to occur, evidence of the subsequent measures is not admissible to prove:

- negligence;

- culpable conduct;

- a defect in a product or its design; or

- a need for a warning or instruction.

But the court may admit this evidence for another purpose, such as impeachment or — if disputed — proving ownership, control, or the feasibility of precautionary measures.

Rule 408. Compromise Offers and Negotiations

(a) Prohibited Uses. Evidence of the following is not admissible — on behalf of any party — either to prove or disprove the validity or amount of a disputed claim or to impeach by a prior inconsistent statement or a contradiction:

    (1) furnishing, promising, or offering — or accepting, promising to accept, or offering to accept — a valuable consideration in compromising or attempting to compromise the claim; and

    (2) conduct or a statement made during compromise negotiations about the claim — except when offered in a criminal case and when the negotiations related to a claim by a public office in the exercise of its regulatory, investigative, or enforcement authority.

(b) Exceptions. The court may admit this evidence for another purpose, such as proving a witness's bias or prejudice, negating a contention of undue delay, or proving an effort to obstruct a criminal investigation or prosecution.

Rule 409.   Offers to Pay Medical and Similar Expenses

Evidence of furnishing, promising to pay, or offering to pay medical, hospital, or similar expenses resulting from an injury is not admissible to prove liability for the injury.

Rule 410.   Pleas, Plea Discussions, and Related Statements

(a) Prohibited Uses. In a civil or criminal case, evidence of the following is not admissible against the defendant who made the plea or participated in the plea discussions:

   (1) a guilty plea that was later withdrawn;

   (2) a nolo contendere plea;

   (3) a statement made during a proceeding on either of those pleas under Federal Rule of Criminal Procedure 11 or a comparable state procedure; or

   (4) a statement made during plea discussions with an attorney for the prosecuting authority if the discussions did not result in a guilty plea or they resulted in a later-withdrawn guilty plea.

(b) Exceptions. The court may admit a statement described in Rule 410(a)(3) or (4):

   (1) in any proceeding in which another statement made during the same plea or plea discussions has been introduced, if in fairness the statements ought to be considered together; or

   (2) in a criminal proceeding for perjury or false statement, if the defendant made the statement under oath, on the record, and with counsel present.

Rule 411.   Liability Insurance

Evidence that a person was or was not insured against liability is not admissible to prove whether the person acted negligently or otherwise wrongfully. But the court may admit this evidence for another purpose, such as proving a witness's bias or prejudice or proving agency, ownership, or control.

Rule 412.   Sex-Offense Cases: The Victim's Sexual Behavior or Predisposition

(a) Prohibited Uses. The following evidence is not admissible in a civil or criminal proceeding involving alleged sexual misconduct:

   (1) evidence offered to prove that a victim engaged in other sexual behavior; or

   (2) evidence offered to prove a victim's sexual predisposition.

(b) Exceptions.

   (1) *Criminal Cases*. The court may admit the following evidence in a criminal case:

      (A) evidence of specific instances of a victim's sexual behavior, if offered to prove that someone other than the defendant was the source of semen, injury, or other physical evidence;

      (B) evidence of specific instances of a victim's sexual behavior with respect to the person accused of the sexual misconduct, if offered by the defendant to prove consent or if offered by the prosecutor; and

      (C) evidence whose exclusion would violate the defendant's constitutional rights.

(2) *Civil Cases*. In a civil case, the court may admit evidence offered to prove a victim's sexual behavior or sexual predisposition if its probative value substantially outweighs the danger of harm to any victim and of unfair prejudice to any party. The court may admit evidence of a victim's reputation only if the victim has placed it in controversy.

(c) Procedure to Determine Admissibility.

(1) *Motion*. If a party intends to offer evidence under Rule 412(b), the party must:

(A) file a motion that specifically describes the evidence and states the purpose for which it is to be offered;

(B) do so at least 14 days before trial unless the court, for good cause, sets a different time;

(C) serve the motion on all parties; and

(D) notify the victim or, when appropriate, the victim's guardian or representative.

(2) *Hearing*. Before admitting evidence under this rule, the court must conduct an in camera hearing and give the victim and parties a right to attend and be heard. Unless the court orders otherwise, the motion, related materials, and the record of the hearing must be and remain sealed.

(d) Definition of "Victim." In this rule, "victim" includes an alleged victim.

ARTICLE V. PRIVILEGES

Rule 501. Privilege in General

The common law — as interpreted by United States courts in the light of reason and experience — governs a claim of privilege unless any of the following provides otherwise:

- the United States Constitution;
- a federal statute; or
- rules prescribed by the Supreme Court.

But in a civil case, state law governs privilege regarding a claim or defense for which state law supplies the rule of decision.

Rule 502. Attorney-Client Privilege and Work Product; Limitations on Waiver

The following provisions apply, in the circumstances set out, to disclosure of a communication or information covered by the attorney-client privilege or work-product protection.

(a) Disclosure Made in a Federal Proceeding or to a Federal Office or Agency; Scope of a Waiver. When the disclosure is made in a federal proceeding or to a federal office or agency and waives the attorney-client privilege or work-product protection, the waiver extends to an undisclosed communication or information in a federal or state proceeding only if:

(1) the waiver is intentional;

(2) the disclosed and undisclosed communications or information concern the same subject matter; and

(3) they ought in fairness to be considered together.

(b) Inadvertent Disclosure. When made in a federal proceeding or to a federal office or agency, the disclosure does not operate as a waiver in a federal or state proceeding if:

(1) the disclosure is inadvertent;

(2) the holder of the privilege or protection took reasonable steps to prevent disclosure; and

(3) the holder promptly took reasonable steps to rectify the error, including (if applicable) following Federal Rule of Civil Procedure 26(b)(5)(B).

(c) Disclosure Made in a State Proceeding. When the disclosure is made in a state proceeding and is not the subject of a state-court order concerning waiver, the disclosure does not operate as a waiver in a federal proceeding if the disclosure:

(1) would not be a waiver under this rule if it had been made in a federal proceeding; or

(2) is not a waiver under the law of the state where the disclosure occurred.

(d) Controlling Effect of a Court Order. A federal court may order that the privilege or protection is not waived by disclosure connected with the litigation pending before the court — in which event the disclosure is also not a waiver in any other federal or state proceeding.

(e) Controlling Effect of a Party Agreement. An agreement on the effect of disclosure in a federal proceeding is binding only on the parties to the agreement, unless it is incorporated into a court order.

(f) Controlling Effect of this Rule. Notwithstanding Rules 101 and 1101, this rule applies to state proceedings and to federal court-annexed and federal court-mandated arbitration proceedings, in the circumstances set out in the rule. And notwithstanding Rule 501, this rule applies even if state law provides the rule of decision.

(g) Definitions. In this rule:

(1) "attorney-client privilege" means the protection that applicable law provides for confidential attorney-client communications; and

(2) "work-product protection" means the protection that applicable law provides for tangible material (or its intangible equivalent) prepared in anticipation of litigation or for trial.

ARTICLE VI. WITNESSES

Rule 601. Competency to Testify in General

Every person is competent to be a witness unless these rules provide otherwise. But in a civil case, state law governs the witness's competency regarding a claim or defense for which state law supplies the rule of decision.

Rule 602. Need for Personal Knowledge

A witness may testify to a matter only if evidence is introduced sufficient to support a finding that the witness has personal knowledge of the matter. Evidence to prove personal knowledge may consist of the witness's own testimony. This rule does not apply to a witness's expert testimony under Rule 703.

Rule 603.   Oath or Affirmation to Testify Truthfully

Before testifying, a witness must give an oath or affirmation to testify truthfully. It must be in a form designed to impress that duty on the witness's conscience.

Rule 604.   Interpreter

An interpreter must be qualified and must give an oath or affirmation to make a true translation.

Rule 605.   Judge's Competency as a Witness

The presiding judge may not testify as a witness at the trial. A party need not object to preserve the issue.

Rule 606. Juror's Competency as a Witness

(a) At the Trial. A juror may not testify as a witness before the other jurors at the trial. If a juror is called to testify, the court must give a party an opportunity to object outside the jury's presence.

(b) During an Inquiry into the Validity of a Verdict or Indictment.

   (1) *Prohibited Testimony or Other Evidence.* During an inquiry into the validity of a verdict or indictment, a juror may not testify about any statement made or incident that occurred during the jury's deliberations; the effect of anything on that juror's or another juror's vote; or any juror's mental processes concerning the verdict or indictment. The court may not receive a juror's affidavit or evidence of a juror's statement on these matters.

   (2) *Exceptions.* A juror may testify about whether:

   (A) extraneous prejudicial information was improperly brought to the jury's attention;

   (B) an outside influence was improperly brought to bear on any juror; or

   (C) a mistake was made in entering the verdict on the verdict form.

Rule 607.   Who May Impeach a Witness

Any party, including the party that called the witness, may attack the witness's credibility.

Rule 608.   A Witness's Character for Truthfulness or Untruthfulness

(a) Reputation or Opinion Evidence. A witness's credibility may be attacked or supported by testimony about the witness's reputation for having a character for truthfulness or untruthfulness, or by testimony in the form of an opinion about that character. But evidence of truthful character is admissible only after the witness's character for truthfulness has been attacked.

(b) Specific Instances of Conduct. Except for a criminal conviction under Rule 609, extrinsic evidence is not admissible to prove specific instances of a witness's conduct in order to attack or support the witness's character for truthfulness. But the court may, on cross-examination, allow them to be inquired into if they are probative of the character for truthfulness or untruthfulness of:

(1) the witness; or

(2) another witness whose character the witness being cross-examined has testified about.

By testifying on another matter, a witness does not waive any privilege against self-incrimination for testimony that relates only to the witness's character for truthfulness.

Rule 609.   Impeachment by Evidence of a Criminal Conviction

(a) **In General.** The following rules apply to attacking a witness's character for truthfulness by evidence of a criminal conviction:

    (1) for a crime that, in the convicting jurisdiction, was punishable by death or by imprisonment for more than one year, the evidence:

        (A) must be admitted, subject to Rule 403, in a civil case or in a criminal case in which the witness is not a defendant; and

        (B) must be admitted in a criminal case in which the witness is a defendant, if the probative value of the evidence outweighs its prejudicial effect to that defendant; and

    (2) for any crime regardless of the punishment, the evidence must be admitted if the court can readily determine that establishing the elements of the crime required proving — or the witness's admitting — a dishonest act or false statement.

(b) **Limit on Using the Evidence After 10 Years.** This subdivision (b) applies if more than 10 years have passed since the witness's conviction or release from confinement for it, whichever is later. Evidence of the conviction is admissible only if:

    (1) its probative value, supported by specific facts and circumstances, substantially outweighs its prejudicial effect; and

    (2) the proponent gives an adverse party reasonable written notice of the intent to use it so that the party has a fair opportunity to contest its use.

(c) **Effect of a Pardon, Annulment, or Certificate of Rehabilitation.** Evidence of a conviction is not admissible if:

    (1) the conviction has been the subject of a pardon, annulment, certificate of rehabilitation, or other equivalent procedure based on a finding that the person has been rehabilitated, and the person has not been convicted of a later crime punishable by death or by imprisonment for more than one year; or

    (2) the conviction has been the subject of a pardon, annulment, or other equivalent procedure based on a finding of innocence.

(d) **Juvenile Adjudications.** Evidence of a juvenile adjudication is admissible under this rule only if:

    (1) it is offered in a criminal case;

    (2) the adjudication was of a witness other than the defendant;

    (3) an adult's conviction for that offense would be admissible to attack the adult's credibility; and

    (4) admitting the evidence is necessary to fairly determine guilt or innocence.

(e) **Pendency of an Appeal.** A conviction that satisfies this rule is admissible even if an appeal is pending. Evidence of the pendency is also admissible.

Rule 610. Religious Beliefs or Opinions

Evidence of a witness's religious beliefs or opinions is not admissible to attack or support the witness's credibility.

Rule 611. Mode and Order of Examining Witnesses and Presenting Evidence

(a) **Control by the Court; Purposes.** The court should exercise reasonable control over the mode and order of examining witnesses and presenting evidence so as to:

    (1) make those procedures effective for determining the truth;

    (2) avoid wasting time; and

    (3) protect witnesses from harassment or undue embarrassment.

(b) **Scope of Cross-Examination.** Cross-examination should not go beyond the subject matter of the direct examination and matters affecting the witness's credibility. The court may allow inquiry into additional matters as if on direct examination.

(c) **Leading Questions.** Leading questions should not be used on direct examination except as necessary to develop the witness's testimony. Ordinarily, the court should allow leading questions:

    (1) on cross-examination; and

    (2) when a party calls a hostile witness, an adverse party, or a witness identified with an adverse party.

Rule 612. Writing Used to Refresh a Witness's Memory

(a) **Scope.** This rule gives an adverse party certain options when a witness uses a writing to refresh memory:

    (1) while testifying; or

    (2) before testifying, if the court decides that justice requires the party to have those options.

(b) **Adverse Party's Options; Deleting Unrelated Matter.** Unless 18 U.S.C. § 3500 provides otherwise in a criminal case, an adverse party is entitled to have the writing produced at the hearing, to inspect it, to cross-examine the witness about it, and to introduce in evidence any portion that relates to the witness's testimony. If the producing party claims that the writing includes unrelated matter, the court must examine the writing in camera, delete any unrelated portion, and order that the rest be delivered to the adverse party. Any portion deleted over objection must be preserved for the record.

(c) **Failure to Produce or Deliver the Writing.** If a writing is not produced or is not delivered as ordered, the court may issue any appropriate order. But if the prosecution does not comply in a criminal case, the court must strike the witness's testimony or — if justice so requires — declare a mistrial.

Rule 613. Witness's Prior Statement

(a) **Showing or Disclosing the Statement During Examination.** When examining a witness about the witness's prior statement, a party need not show it or disclose its contents to the witness. But the party must, on request, show it or disclose its contents to an adverse party's attorney.

(b) Extrinsic Evidence of a Prior Inconsistent Statement. Extrinsic evidence of a witness's prior inconsistent statement is admissible only if the witness is given an opportunity to explain or deny the statement and an adverse party is given an opportunity to examine the witness about it, or if justice so requires. This subdivision (b) does not apply to an opposing party's statement under Rule 801(d)(2).

Rule 614.   Court's Calling or Examining a Witness

(a) Calling. The court may call a witness on its own or at a party's request. Each party is entitled to cross-examine the witness.

(b) Examining. The court may examine a witness regardless of who calls the witness.

(c) Objections. A party may object to the court's calling or examining a witness either at that time or at the next opportunity when the jury is not present.

Rule 615.   Excluding Witnesses

At a party's request, the court must order witnesses excluded so that they cannot hear other witnesses' testimony. Or the court may do so on its own. But this rule does not authorize excluding:

(a) a party who is a natural person;

(b) an officer or employee of a party that is not a natural person, after being designated as the party's representative by its attorney;

(c) a person whose presence a party shows to be essential to presenting the party's claim or defense; or

(d) a person authorized by statute to be present.

ARTICLE VII. OPINIONS AND EXPERT TESTIMONY

Rule 701.   Opinion Testimony by Lay Witnesses

If a witness is not testifying as an expert, testimony in the form of an opinion is limited to one that is:

(a) rationally based on the witness's perception;

(b) helpful to clearly understanding the witness's testimony or to determining a fact in issue; and

(c) not based on scientific, technical, or other specialized knowledge within the scope of Rule 702.

Rule 702.   Testimony by Expert Witnesses

A witness who is qualified as an expert by knowledge, skill, experience, training, or education may testify in the form of an opinion or otherwise if:

(a) the expert's scientific, technical, or other specialized knowledge will help the trier of fact to understand the evidence or to determine a fact in issue;

(b) the testimony is based on sufficient facts or data;

(c) the testimony is the product of reliable principles and methods; and

(d) the expert has reliably applied the principles and methods to the facts of the case.

Rule 703. Bases of an Expert's Opinion Testimony

An expert may base an opinion on facts or data in the case that the expert has been made aware of or personally observed. If experts in the particular field would reasonably rely on those kinds of facts or data in forming an opinion on the subject, they need not be admissible for the opinion to be admitted. But if the facts or data would otherwise be inadmissible, the proponent of the opinion may disclose them to the jury only if their probative value in helping the jury evaluate the opinion substantially outweighs their prejudicial effect.

Rule 704. Opinion on an Ultimate Issue

(a) **In General — Not Automatically Objectionable.** An opinion is not objectionable just because it embraces an ultimate issue.

(b) **Exception.** In a criminal case, an expert witness must not state an opinion about whether the defendant did or did not have a mental state or condition that constitutes an element of the crime charged or of a defense. Those matters are for the trier of fact alone.

Rule 705. Disclosing the Facts or Data Underlying an Expert's Opinion

Unless the court orders otherwise, an expert may state an opinion — and give the reasons for it — without first testifying to the underlying facts or data. But the expert may be required to disclose those facts or data on cross-examination.

Rule 706. Court-Appointed Expert Witnesses

(a) **Appointment Process.** On a party's motion or on its own, the court may order the parties to show cause why expert witnesses should not be appointed and may ask the parties to submit nominations. The court may appoint any expert that the parties agree on and any of its own choosing. But the court may only appoint someone who consents to act.

(b) **Expert's Role.** The court must inform the expert of the expert's duties. The court may do so in writing and have a copy filed with the clerk or may do so orally at a conference in which the parties have an opportunity to participate. The expert:

(1) must advise the parties of any findings the expert makes;

(2) may be deposed by any party;

(3) may be called to testify by the court or any party; and

(4) may be cross-examined by any party, including the party that called the expert.

(c) **Compensation.** The expert is entitled to a reasonable compensation, as set by the court. The compensation is payable as follows:

(1) in a criminal case or in a civil case involving just compensation under the Fifth Amendment, from any funds that are provided by law; and

(2) in any other civil case, by the parties in the proportion and at the time that the court directs — and the compensation is then charged like other costs.

(d) **Disclosing the Appointment to the Jury.** The court may authorize disclosure to the jury that the court appointed the expert.

(e) **Parties' Choice of Their Own Experts.** This rule does not limit a party in calling its own experts.

ARTICLE VIII. HEARSAY

Rule 801. Definitions That Apply to this Article; Exclusions from Hearsay

(a) Statement. "Statement" means a person's oral assertion, written assertion, or nonverbal conduct, if the person intended it as an assertion.

(b) Declarant. "Declarant" means the person who made the statement.

(c) Hearsay. "Hearsay" means a statement that:

    (1) the declarant does not make while testifying at the current trial or hearing; and

    (2) a party offers in evidence to prove the truth of the matter asserted in the statement.

(d) Statements That Are Not Hearsay. A statement that meets the following conditions is not hearsay:

    (1) *A Declarant-Witness's Prior Statement.* The declarant testifies and is subject to cross-examination about a prior statement, and the statement:

        (A) is inconsistent with the declarant's testimony and was given under penalty of perjury at a trial, hearing, or other proceeding or in a deposition;

        (B) is consistent with the declarant's testimony and is offered:

            (i) to rebut an express or implied charge that the declarant recently fabricated it or acted from a recent improper influence or motive in so testifying; or

            (ii) to rehabilitate the declarant's credibility as a witness when attacked on another ground; or

        (C) identifies a person as someone the declarant perceived earlier.

    (2) *An Opposing Party's Statement.* The statement is offered against an opposing party and:

        (A) was made by the party in an individual or representative capacity;

        (B) is one the party manifested that it adopted or believed to be true;

        (C) was made by a person whom the party authorized to make a statement on the subject;

        (D) was made by the party's agent or employee on a matter within the scope of that relationship and while it existed; or

        (E) was made by the party's coconspirator during and in furtherance of the conspiracy.

    The statement must be considered but does not by itself establish the declarant's authority under (C); the existence or scope of the relationship under (D); or the existence of the conspiracy or participation in it under (E).

Rule 802. The Rule Against Hearsay

Hearsay is not admissible unless any of the following provides otherwise:

- a federal statute;
- these rules; or
- other rules prescribed by the Supreme Court.

Rule 803. Exceptions to the Rule Against Hearsay – Regardless of Whether the Declarant Is Available as a Witness

The following are not excluded by the rule against hearsay, regardless of whether the declarant is available as a witness:

(1) ***Present Sense Impression.*** A statement describing or explaining an event or condition, made while or immediately after the declarant perceived it.

(2) ***Excited Utterance.*** A statement relating to a startling event or condition, made while the declarant was under the stress of excitement that it caused.

(3) ***Then-Existing Mental, Emotional, or Physical Condition.*** A statement of the declarant's then-existing state of mind (such as motive, intent, or plan) or emotional, sensory, or physical condition (such as mental feeling, pain, or bodily health), but not including a statement of memory or belief to prove the fact remembered or believed unless it relates to the validity or terms of the declarant's will.

(4) ***Statement Made for Medical Diagnosis or Treatment.*** A statement that:

(A) is made for—and is reasonably pertinent to—medical diagnosis or treatment; and

(B) describes medical history; past or present symptoms or sensations; their inception; or their general cause.

(5) ***Recorded Recollection.*** A record that:

(A) is on a matter the witness once knew about but now cannot recall well enough to testify fully and accurately;

(B) was made or adopted by the witness when the matter was fresh in the witness's memory; and

(C) accurately reflects the witness's knowledge.

If admitted, the record may be read into evidence but may be received as an exhibit only if offered by an adverse party.

(6) ***Records of a regularly conducted activity.*** A record of an act, event, condition, opinion, or diagnosis if:

(A) the record was made at or near the time by—or from information transmitted by—someone with knowledge;

(B) the record was kept in the course of a regularly conducted activity of a business, organization, occupation, or calling, whether or not for profit;

(C) making the record was a regular practice of that activity;

(D) all these conditions are shown by the testimony of the custodian or another qualified witness, or by a certification that complies with Rule 902(11) or (12) or with a statute permitting certification; and

(E) the opponent does not show that the source of information or the method or circumstances of preparation indicate a lack of trustworthiness.

(7) ***Absence of a record of a regularly conducted activity.*** Evidence that a matter is not included in a record described in paragraph (6) if:

(A) the evidence is admitted to prove that the matter did not occur or exist;

(B) a record was regularly kept for a matter of that kind; and

(C) the opponent does not show that the possible source of the information or other circumstances indicate a lack of trustworthiness.

(8) *Public records.* A record or statement of a public office if:

(A) it sets out:

(i) the offices activities;

(ii) a matter observed while under a legal duty to report, but not including, in a criminal case, a matter observed by law-enforcement personnel; or

(iii) in a civil case or against the government in a criminal case, factual findings from a legally authorized investigation; and

(B) the opponent does not show that the source of information or other circumstances indicate a lack of trustworthiness.

(9) *Public Records of Vital Statistics.* A record of a birth, death, or marriage, if reported to a public office in accordance with a legal duty.

(10) *Absence of a Public Record.* Testimony—or a certification under Rule 902—that a diligent search failed to disclose a public record or statement if:

(A) the testimony or certification is admitted to prove that

(i) the record or statement does not exist; or

(ii) a matter did not occur or exist, if a public office regularly kept a record or statement for a matter of that kind; and

(B) in a criminal case, a prosecutor who intends to offer a certification provides written notice of that intent at least 14 days before trial, and the defendant does not object in writing within 7 days of receiving the notice—unless the court sets a different time for the notice or the objection.

(11) *Records of Religious Organizations Concerning Personal or Family History.* A statement of birth, legitimacy, ancestry, marriage, divorce, death, relationship by blood or marriage, or similar facts of personal or family history, contained in a regularly kept record of a religious organization.

(12) *Certificates of Marriage, Baptism, and Similar Ceremonies.* A statement of fact contained in a certificate:

(A) made by a person who is authorized by a religious organization or by law to perform the act certified;

(B) attesting that the person performed a marriage or similar ceremony or administered a sacrament; and

(C) purporting to have been issued at the time of the act or within a reasonable time after it.

(13) *Family Records.* A statement of fact about personal or family history contained in a family record, such as a Bible, genealogy, chart, engraving on a ring, inscription on a portrait, or engraving on an urn or burial marker.

(14) *Records of Documents That Affect an Interest in Property.* The record of a document that purports to establish or affect an interest in property if:

(A) the record is admitted to prove the content of the original recorded document, along with its signing and its delivery by each person who purports to have signed it;

(B) the record is kept in a public office; and

(C) a statute authorizes recording documents of that kind in that office.

(15) *Statements in Documents That Affect an Interest in Property.* A statement contained in a document that purports to establish or affect an interest in property if the matter stated was relevant to the document's purpose—unless later dealings with the property are inconsistent with the truth of the statement or the purport of the document.

(16) *Statements in Ancient Documents.* A statement in a document that is at least 20 years old and whose authenticity is established.

(17) *Market Reports and Similar Commercial Publications.* Market quotations, lists, directories, or other compilations that are generally relied on by the public or by persons in particular occupations.

(18) *Statements in Learned Treatises, Periodicals, or Pamphlets.* A statement contained in a treatise, periodical, or pamphlet if:

(A) the statement is called to the attention of an expert witness on cross-examination or relied on by the expert on direct examination; and

(B) the publication is established as a reliable authority by the expert's admission or testimony, by another expert's testimony, or by judicial notice.

If admitted, the statement may be read into evidence but not received as an exhibit.

(19) *Reputation Concerning Personal or Family History.* A reputation among a person's family by blood, adoption, or marriage—or among a person's associates or in the community—concerning the person's birth, adoption, legitimacy, ancestry, marriage, divorce, death, relationship by blood, adoption, or marriage, or similar facts of personal or family history.

(20) *Reputation Concerning Boundaries or General History.* A reputation in a community—arising before the controversy—concerning boundaries of land in the community or customs that affect the land, or concerning general historical events important to that community, state, or nation.

(21) *Reputation Concerning Character.* A reputation among a person's associates or in the community concerning the person's character.

(22) *Judgment of a Previous Conviction.* Evidence of a final judgment of conviction if:

(A) the judgment was entered after a trial or guilty plea, but not a nolo contendere plea;

(B) the conviction was for a crime punishable by death or by imprisonment for more than a year;

(C) the evidence is admitted to prove any fact essential to the judgment; and

(D) when offered by the prosecutor in a criminal case for a purpose other than impeachment, the judgment was against the defendant.

The pendency of an appeal may be shown but does not affect admissibility.

(23) *Judgments Involving Personal, Family, or General History, or a Boundary.* A judgment that is admitted to prove a matter of personal, family, or general history, or boundaries, if the matter:

(A) was essential to the judgment; and

(B) could be proved by evidence of reputation.

(24) *[Other Exceptions.]* [Transferred to Rule 807.]

Rule 804. Exceptions — When the Declarant Is Unavailable as a Witness

(a) Criteria for Being Unavailable. A declarant is considered to be unavailable as a witness if the declarant:

    (1) is exempted from testifying about the subject matter of the declarant's statement because the court rules that a privilege applies;

    (2) refuses to testify about the subject matter despite a court order to do so;

    (3) testifies to not remembering the subject matter;

    (4) cannot be present or testify at the trial or hearing because of death or a then-existing infirmity, physical illness, or mental illness; or

    (5) is absent from the trial or hearing and the statement's proponent has not been able, by process or other reasonable means, to procure:

        (A) the declarant's attendance, in the case of a hearsay exception under Rule 804(b)(1) or (6); or

        (B) the declarant's attendance or testimony, in the case of a hearsay exception under Rule 804(b)(2), (3), or (4).

But this subdivision (a) does not apply if the statement's proponent procured or wrongfully caused the declarant's unavailability as a witness in order to prevent the declarant from attending or testifying.

(b) The Exceptions. The following are not excluded by the rule against hearsay if the declarant is unavailable as a witness:

    (1) *Former Testimony*. Testimony that:

        (A) was given as a witness at a trial, hearing, or lawful deposition, whether given during the current proceeding or a different one; and

        (B) is now offered against a party who had — or, in a civil case, whose predecessor in interest had — an opportunity and similar motive to develop it by direct, cross-, or redirect examination.

    (2) *Statement Under the Belief of Imminent Death*. In a prosecution for homicide or in a civil case, a statement that the declarant, while believing the declarant's death to be imminent, made about its cause or circumstances.

    (3) *Statement Against Interest*. A statement that:

        (A) a reasonable person in the declarant's position would have made only if the person believed it to be true because, when made, it was so contrary to the declarant's proprietary or pecuniary interest or had so great a tendency to invalidate the declarant's claim against someone else or to expose the declarant to civil or criminal liability; and

        (B) is supported by corroborating circumstances that clearly indicate its trustworthiness, if it is offered in a criminal case as one that tends to expose the declarant to criminal liability.

    (4) *Statement of Personal or Family History*. A statement about:

        (A) the declarant's own birth, adoption, legitimacy, ancestry, marriage, divorce, relationship by blood, adoption, or marriage, or similar facts of personal or family history, even though the declarant had no way of acquiring personal knowledge about that fact; or

        (B) another person concerning any of these facts, as well as death, if the declarant was related to the person by blood, adoption, or marriage or was so intimately associated with the person's family that the declarant's information is likely to be accurate.

(5) [*Other Exceptions.*] [Transferred to Rule 807.]

(6) ***Statement Offered Against a Party That Wrongfully Caused the Declarant's Unavailability***. A statement offered against a party that wrongfully caused — or acquiesced in wrongfully causing — the declarant's unavailability as a witness, and did so intending that result.

Rule 805.   Hearsay Within Hearsay

Hearsay within hearsay is not excluded by the rule against hearsay if each part of the combined statements conforms with an exception to the rule.

Rule 806.   Attacking and Supporting the Declarant's Credibility

When a hearsay statement — or a statement described in Rule 801(d)(2)(C), (D), or (E) — has been admitted in evidence, the declarant's credibility may be attacked, and then supported, by any evidence that would be admissible for those purposes if the declarant had testified as a witness. The court may admit evidence of the declarant's inconsistent statement or conduct, regardless of when it occurred or whether the declarant had an opportunity to explain or deny it. If the party against whom the statement was admitted calls the declarant as a witness, the party may examine the declarant on the statement as if on cross-examination.

Rule 807.   Residual Exception

(a) **In General.** Under the following circumstances, a hearsay statement is not excluded by the rule against hearsay even if the statement is not specifically covered by a hearsay exception in Rule 803 or 804:

   (1) the statement has equivalent circumstantial guarantees of trustworthiness;

   (2) it is offered as evidence of a material fact;

   (3) it is more probative on the point for which it is offered than any other evidence that the proponent can obtain through reasonable efforts; and

   (4) admitting it will best serve the purposes of these rules and the interests of justice.

(b) **Notice.** The statement is admissible only if, before the trial or hearing, the proponent gives an adverse party reasonable notice of the intent to offer the statement and its particulars, including the declarant's name and address, so that the party has a fair opportunity to meet it.

ARTICLE IX. AUTHENTICATION AND IDENTIFICATION

Rule 901.   Authenticating or Identifying Evidence

(a) **In General.** To satisfy the requirement of authenticating or identifying an item of evidence, the proponent must produce evidence sufficient to support a finding that the item is what the proponent claims it is.

(b) **Examples.** The following are examples only — not a complete list — of evidence that satisfies the requirement:

(1) *Testimony of a Witness with Knowledge*. Testimony that an item is what it is claimed to be.

(2) *Nonexpert Opinion About Handwriting*. A nonexpert's opinion that handwriting is genuine, based on a familiarity with it that was not acquired for the current litigation.

(3) *Comparison by an Expert Witness or the Trier of Fact*. A comparison with an authenticated specimen by an expert witness or the trier of fact.

(4) *Distinctive Characteristics and the Like*. The appearance, contents, substance, internal patterns, or other distinctive characteristics of the item, taken together with all the circumstances.

(5) *Opinion About a Voice*. An opinion identifying a person's voice — whether heard firsthand or through mechanical or electronic transmission or recording — based on hearing the voice at any time under circumstances that connect it with the alleged speaker.

(6) *Evidence About a Telephone Conversation*. For a telephone conversation, evidence that a call was made to the number assigned at the time to:

    (A) a particular person, if circumstances, including self-identification, show that the person answering was the one called; or

    (B) a particular business, if the call was made to a business and the call related to business reasonably transacted over the telephone.

(7) *Evidence About Public Records*. Evidence that:

    (A) a document was recorded or filed in a public office as authorized by law; or

    (B) a purported public record or statement is from the office where items of this kind are kept.

(8) *Evidence About Ancient Documents or Data Compilations*. For a document or data compilation, evidence that it:

    (A) is in a condition that creates no suspicion about its authenticity;

    (B) was in a place where, if authentic, it would likely be; and

    (C) is at least 20 years old when offered.

(9) *Evidence About a Process or System*. Evidence describing a process or system and showing that it produces an accurate result.

(10) *Methods Provided by a Statute or Rule*. Any method of authentication or identification allowed by a federal statute or a rule prescribed by the Supreme Court.

Rule 902. Evidence That Is Self-Authenticating

The following items of evidence are self-authenticating; they require no extrinsic evidence of authenticity in order to be admitted:

    (1) *Domestic Public Documents That Are Sealed and Signed*. A document that bears:

        (A) a seal purporting to be that of the United States; any state, district, commonwealth, territory, or insular possession of the United States; the former Panama Canal Zone; the Trust Territory of the Pacific Islands; a political subdivision of any of these entities; or a department, agency, or officer of any entity named above; and

        (B) a signature purporting to be an execution or attestation.

(2) ***Domestic Public Documents That Are Not Sealed but Are Signed and Certified.*** A document that bears no seal if:

    (A) it bears the signature of an officer or employee of an entity named in Rule 902(1)(A); and

    (B) another public officer who has a seal and official duties within that same entity certifies under seal — or its equivalent — that the signer has the official capacity and that the signature is genuine.

(3) ***Foreign Public Documents.*** A document that purports to be signed or attested by a person who is authorized by a foreign country's law to do so. The document must be accompanied by a final certification that certifies the genuineness of the signature and official position of the signer or attester — or of any foreign official whose certificate of genuineness relates to the signature or attestation or is in a chain of certificates of genuineness relating to the signature or attestation. The certification may be made by a secretary of a United States embassy or legation; by a consul general, vice consul, or consular agent of the United States; or by a diplomatic or consular official of the foreign country assigned or accredited to the United States. If all parties have been given a reasonable opportunity to investigate the document's authenticity and accuracy, the court may, for good cause, either:

    (A) order that it be treated as presumptively authentic without final certification; or

    (B) allow it to be evidenced by an attested summary with or without final certification.

(4) ***Certified Copies of Public Records.*** A copy of an official record — or a copy of a document that was recorded or filed in a public office as authorized by law — if the copy is certified as correct by:

    (A) the custodian or another person authorized to make the certification; or

    (B) a certificate that complies with Rule 902(1), (2), or (3), a federal statute, or a rule prescribed by the Supreme Court.

(5) ***Official Publications.*** A book, pamphlet, or other publication purporting to be issued by a public authority.

(6) ***Newspapers and Periodicals.*** Printed material purporting to be a newspaper or periodical.

(7) ***Trade Inscriptions and the Like.*** An inscription, sign, tag, or label purporting to have been affixed in the course of business and indicating origin, ownership, or control.

(8) ***Acknowledged Documents.*** A document accompanied by a certificate of acknowledgment that is lawfully executed by a notary public or another officer who is authorized to take acknowledgments.

(9) ***Commercial Paper and Related Documents.*** Commercial paper, a signature on it, and related documents, to the extent allowed by general commercial law.

(10) ***Presumptions Under a Federal Statute.*** A signature, document, or anything else that a federal statute declares to be presumptively or prima facie genuine or authentic.

(11) ***Certified Domestic Records of a Regularly Conducted Activity.*** The original or a copy of a domestic record that meets the requirements of Rule 803(6)(A)-(C), as shown by a certification of the custodian or another qualified person that complies with a federal statute or a rule prescribed by the Supreme Court. Before the trial or hearing, the proponent must give an adverse party reasonable written notice of the intent to offer the record — and must make the record and certification available for inspection — so that the party has a fair opportunity to challenge them.

(12) ***Certified Foreign Records of a Regularly Conducted Activity.*** In a civil case, the original or a copy of a foreign record that meets the requirements of Rule 902(11), modified as follows: the certification, rather than complying with a federal statute or Supreme Court rule, must be signed in a manner that, if falsely made, would subject the maker to a criminal penalty in the country where the certification is signed. The proponent must also meet the notice requirements of Rule 902(11).

Rule 903. Subscribing Witness's Testimony

A subscribing witness's testimony is necessary to authenticate a writing only if required by the law of the jurisdiction that governs its validity.

ARTICLE X. CONTENTS OF WRITINGS, RECORDINGS, AND PHOTOGRAPHS

Rule 1001.   Definitions That Apply to This Article

In this article:

(a) A "writing" consists of letters, words, numbers, or their equivalent set down in any form.

(b) A "recording" consists of letters, words, numbers, or their equivalent recorded in any manner.

(c) A "photograph" means a photographic image or its equivalent stored in any form.

(d) An "original" of a writing or recording means the writing or recording itself or any counterpart intended to have the same effect by the person who executed or issued it. For electronically stored information, "original" means any printout — or other output readable by sight — if it accurately reflects the information. An "original" of a photograph includes the negative or a print from it.

(e) A "duplicate" means a counterpart produced by a mechanical, photographic, chemical, electronic, or other equivalent process or technique that accurately reproduces the original.

Rule 1002.   Requirement of the Original

An original writing, recording, or photograph is required in order to prove its content unless these rules or a federal statute provides otherwise.

Rule 1003.   Admissibility of Duplicates

A duplicate is admissible to the same extent as the original unless a genuine question is raised about the original's authenticity or the circumstances make it unfair to admit the duplicate.

Rule 1004.   Admissibility of Other Evidence of Content

An original is not required and other evidence of the content of a writing, recording, or photograph is admissible if:

(a) all the originals are lost or destroyed, and not by the proponent acting in bad faith;

(b) an original cannot be obtained by any available judicial process;

(c) the party against whom the original would be offered had control of the original; was at that time put on notice, by pleadings or otherwise, that the original would be a subject of proof at the trial or hearing; and fails to produce it at the trial or hearing; or

(d) the writing, recording, or photograph is not closely related to a controlling issue.

Rule 1005. Copies of Public Records to Prove Content

The proponent may use a copy to prove the content of an official record — or of a document that was recorded or filed in a public office as authorized by law — if these conditions are met: the record or document is otherwise admissible; and the copy is certified as correct in accordance with Rule 902(4) or is testified to be correct by a witness who has compared it with the original. If no such copy can be obtained by reasonable diligence, then the proponent may use other evidence to prove the content.

Rule 1006. Summaries to Prove Content

The proponent may use a summary, chart, or calculation to prove the content of voluminous writings, recordings, or photographs that cannot be conveniently examined in court. The proponent must make the originals or duplicates available for examination or copying, or both, by other parties at a reasonable time and place. And the court may order the proponent to produce them in court.

Rule 1007. Testimony or Statement of a Party to Prove Content

The proponent may prove the content of a writing, recording, or photograph by the testimony, deposition, or written statement of the party against whom the evidence is offered. The proponent need not account for the original.

Rule 1008. Functions of the Court and Jury

Ordinarily, the court determines whether the proponent has fulfilled the factual conditions for admitting other evidence of the content of a writing, recording, or photograph under Rule 1004 or 1005. But in a jury trial, the jury determines — in accordance with Rule 104(b) — any issue about whether:

(a) an asserted writing, recording, or photograph ever existed;

(b) another one produced at the trial or hearing is the original; or

(c) other evidence of content accurately reflects the content.

ARTICLE XI. MISCELLANEOUS RULES

Rule 1101. Applicability of the Rules

(a) To Courts and Judges. These rules apply to proceedings before:

United States district courts;

United States bankruptcy and magistrate judges;

United States courts of appeals;

the United States Court of Federal Claims; and

the district courts of Guam, the Virgin Islands, and the Northern Mariana Islands.

(b) To Cases and Proceedings. These rules apply in:

civil cases and proceedings, including bankruptcy, admiralty, and maritime cases;

criminal cases and proceedings; and

contempt proceedings, except those in which the court may act summarily.

(c) Rules on Privilege. The rules on privilege apply to all stages of a case or proceeding.

(d) Exceptions. These rules — except for those on privilege — do not apply to the following:

(1) the court's determination, under Rule 104(a), on a preliminary question of fact governing admissibility;

(2) grand-jury proceedings; and

(3) miscellaneous proceedings such as:

extradition or rendition;

issuing an arrest warrant, criminal summons, or search warrant;

a preliminary examination in a criminal case;

sentencing;

granting or revoking probation or supervised release; and

considering whether to release on bail or otherwise.

(e) Other Statutes and Rules. A federal statute or a rule prescribed by the Supreme Court may provide for admitting or excluding evidence independently from these rules.

SELECTED INDIANA RULES OF PROFESSIONAL CONDUCT

[Including Amendments made through October 1, 2015]

PREAMBLE: A LAWYER'S RESPONSIBILITIES

[1]   A lawyer, as a member of the legal profession, is a representative of clients, an officer of the legal system and a public citizen having special responsibility for the quality of justice. Whether or not engaging in the practice of law, lawyers should conduct themselves honorably.

[2]   As a representative of clients, a lawyer performs various functions. As advisor, a lawyer provides a client with an informed understanding of the client's legal rights and obligations and explains their practical implications. As advocate, a lawyer asserts the client's position under the rules of the adversary system. As negotiator, a lawyer seeks a result advantageous to the client but consistent with requirements of honest dealings with others. As intermediary between clients, a lawyer seeks to reconcile their divergent interests as an advisor and, to a limited extent, as a spokesperson for each client. As an evaluator, a lawyer acts by examining a client's legal affairs and reporting about them to the client or to others.

[4]   In all professional functions a lawyer should be competent, prompt and diligent. A lawyer should maintain communication with a client concerning the representation. A lawyer should keep in confidence information relating to representation of a client except so far as disclosure is required or permitted by the Rules of Professional Conduct or other law.

[5]   A lawyer's conduct should conform to the requirements of the law, both in professional service to clients and in the lawyer's business and personal affairs. A lawyer should use the law's procedures only for legitimate purposes and not to harass or intimidate others. A lawyer should demonstrate respect for the legal system and for those who serve it, including judges, other lawyers and public officials. While it is a lawyer's duty, when necessary, to challenge the rectitude of official action, it is also a lawyer's duty to uphold legal process.

[6]   As a public citizen, a lawyer should seek improvement of the law, access to the legal system, the administration of justice and the quality of service rendered by the legal profession. As a member of a learned profession, a lawyer should cultivate knowledge of the law beyond its use for clients, employ that knowledge in reform of the law and work to strengthen legal education. In addition, a lawyer should further the public's understanding of and confidence in the rule of law and the justice system because legal institutions in a constitutional democracy depend on popular participation and support to maintain their authority. A lawyer should be mindful of deficiencies in the administration of justice and of the fact that the poor, and sometimes persons who are not poor, cannot afford adequate legal assistance. Therefore, all lawyers should devote professional time and resources and use civic influence to ensure equal access to our system of justice for all those who because of economic or social barriers cannot afford or secure adequate legal counsel. A lawyer should aid the legal profession in pursuing these objectives and should help the bar regulate itself in the public interest.

[7]   Many of a lawyer's professional responsibilities are prescribed in the Rules of Professional Conduct, as well as substantive and procedural law. However, a lawyer is also guided by personal conscience and the approbation of professional peers. A lawyer should strive to attain the highest level of skill, to improve the law and the legal professional and to exemplify the legal profession's ideals of public service.

[8]   A lawyer's responsibilities as a representative of clients, an officer of the legal system and a public citizen are usually harmonious. Thus, when an opposing party is well represented, a lawyer can be an effective advocate on behalf of a client and at the same time assume that justice is being done.

So also, a lawyer can be sure that preserving client confidences ordinarily serves the public interest because people are more likely to seek legal advice, and thereby heed their legal obligations, when they know their communications will be private.

[9]   In the nature of law practice, however, conflicting responsibilities are encountered. Virtually all difficult ethical problems arise from conflict between a lawyer's responsibilities to clients, to the legal system and to the lawyer's own interest in remaining an ethical person while earning a satisfactory living. The Rules of Professional Conduct often prescribe terms for resolving such conflicts. Within the framework of these Rules, however, many difficult issues of professional discretion can arise. Such issues must be resolved through the exercise of sensitive professional and moral judgment guided by the basic principles underlying the Rules. These principles include the lawyer's obligation to protect and pursue a client's legitimate interests, within the bounds of the law, while maintaining a professional, courteous and civil attitude toward all persons involved in the legal system.

[10] The legal profession is largely self-governing. Although other professions also have been granted powers of self-government, the legal profession is unique in this respect because of the close relationship between the profession and the processes of government and law enforcement. This connection is manifested in the fact that ultimate authority over the legal profession is vested largely in the courts.

[11] To the extent that lawyers meet the obligations of their professional calling, the occasion for government regulation is obviated. Self-regulation also helps maintain the legal profession's independence from government domination. An independent legal profession is an important force in preserving government under law, for abuse of legal authority is more readily challenged by a profession whose members are not dependent on government for the right to practice.

[12] The legal profession's relative autonomy carries with it special responsibilities of self-government. The profession has a responsibility to assure that its regulations are conceived in the public interest and not in furtherance of parochial or self-interested concerns of the bar. Every lawyer is responsible for observance of the Rules of Professional Conduct. A lawyer should also aid in securing their observance by other lawyers. Neglect of these responsibilities compromises the independence of the profession and the public interest which it serves.

[13] Lawyers play a vital role in the preservation of society. The fulfillment of this role requires an understanding by lawyers of their relationship to our legal system. The Rules of Professional Conduct, when properly applied, serve to define that relationship.

SCOPE

[14] The Rules of Professional Conduct are rules of reason. They should be interpreted with reference to the purposes of legal representation and of the law itself. Some of the Rules are imperatives, cast in the terms "shall" or "shall not." These define proper conduct for purposes of professional discipline. Others, generally cast in the term "may," are permissive and define areas under the Rules in which the lawyer has discretion to exercise professional judgment. No disciplinary action should be taken when the lawyer chooses not to act or acts within the bounds of such discretion. Other Rules define the nature of relationships between the lawyer and others. The Rules are thus partly obligatory and disciplinary and partly constitutive and descriptive in that they define a lawyer's professional role. Many of the Comments use the term "should." Comments do not add obligations to the Rules but provide guidance for practicing in compliance with the Rules.

[15] The Rules presuppose a larger legal context shaping the lawyer's role. That context includes court rules and statutes relating to matters of licensure, laws defining specific obligations of lawyers and substantive and procedural law in general. The Comments are sometimes used to alert lawyers to their responsibilities under such other law.

[16] Compliance with the Rules, as with all law in an open society, depends primarily upon understanding and voluntary compliance, secondarily upon reinforcement by peer and public opinion and finally, when necessary, upon enforcement through disciplinary proceedings. The Rules do not, however, exhaust the moral and ethical considerations that should inform a lawyer, for no worthwhile human activity can be completely defined by legal rules. The Rules simply provide a framework for the ethical practice of law.

[17] Furthermore, for purposes of determining the lawyer's authority and responsibility, principles of substantive law external to these Rules determine whether a client-lawyer relationship exists. Most of the duties flowing from the client-lawyer relationship attach only after the client has requested the lawyer to render legal services and the lawyer has agreed to do so. But there are some duties, such as that of confidentiality under Rule 1.6, that attach when the lawyer agrees to consider whether a client-lawyer relationship shall be established. See Rule 1.18. Whether a client-lawyer relationship exists for any specific purpose can depend on the circumstances and may be a question of fact.

[19] Failure to comply with an obligation or prohibition imposed by a Rule is a basis for invoking the disciplinary process. The Rules presuppose that disciplinary assessment of a lawyer's conduct will be made on the basis of the facts and circumstances as they existed at the time of the conduct in question and in recognition of the fact that a lawyer often has to act upon uncertain or incomplete evidence of the situation. Moreover, the Rules presuppose that whether or not discipline should be imposed for a violation, and the severity of a sanction, depend on all the circumstances, such as the willfulness and seriousness of the violation, extenuating factors and whether there have been previous violations.

Rule 1.0. Terminology

(a) "Belief" or "believes" denotes that the person involved actually supposed the fact in question to be true. A person's belief may be inferred from circumstances.

(b) "Confirmed in writing," when used in reference to the informed consent of a person, denotes informed consent that is given in writing by the person or a writing that a lawyer promptly transmits to the person confirming an oral informed consent. See paragraph (n) for the definition of "writing." See paragraph (e) for the definition of "informed consent." If it is not feasible to obtain or transmit the writing at the time the person gives informed consent, then the lawyer must obtain or transmit it within a reasonable time thereafter.

(c) "Firm" or "law firm" denotes a lawyer or lawyers in a law partnership, professional corporation, sole proprietorship or other association authorized to practice law; or lawyers employed in a legal services organization or the legal department of a corporation or other organization.

(d) "Fraud" or "fraudulent" denotes conduct that is fraudulent under the substantive or procedural law of the applicable jurisdiction and has a purpose to deceive.

(e) "Informed consent" denotes the agreement by a person to a proposed course of conduct after the lawyer has communicated adequate information and explanation about the material risks of and reasonably available alternatives to the proposed course of conduct.

(f) "Knowingly," "known," or "knows" denotes actual knowledge of the fact in question. A person's knowledge may be inferred from circumstances.

(g) "Partner" denotes a member of a partnership, a shareholder in a law firm organized as a professional corporation, or a member of an association authorized to practice law.

(h) "Reasonable" or "reasonably" when used in relation to conduct by a lawyer denotes the conduct of a reasonably prudent and competent lawyer.

(i) "Reasonable belief" or "reasonably believes" when used in reference to a lawyer denotes that the lawyer believes the matter in question and that the circumstances are such that the belief is reasonable.

(j) "Reasonably should know" when used in reference to a lawyer denotes that a lawyer of reasonable prudence and competence would ascertain the matter in question.

(k) "Screened" denotes the isolation of a lawyer from any participation in a matter through the timely imposition of procedures within a firm that are reasonably adequate under the circumstances to protect information that the isolated lawyer is obligated to protect under these Rules or other law.

(l) "Substantial" when used in reference to degree or extent denotes a material matter of clear and weighty importance.

(m) "Tribunal" denotes a court, an arbitrator, or any other neutral body or neutral individual making a decision, based on evidence presented and the law applicable to that evidence, which decision is binding on the parties involved.

(n) "Writing" or "written" denotes a tangible or electronic record of a communication or representation, including handwriting, typewriting, printing, photostatting, photography, audio or videorecording or e-mail. A "signed" writing includes an electronic sound, symbol or process attached to or logically associated with a writing and executed or adopted by a person with the intent to sign the writing.

Rule 1.1. Competence

A lawyer shall provide competent representation to a client. Competent representation requires the legal knowledge, skill, thoroughness and preparation reasonably necessary for the representation.

Rule 1.2. Scope of Representation and Allocation of Authority Between Client and Lawyer

(a) Subject to paragraphs (c) and (d), a lawyer shall abide by a client's decisions concerning the objectives of representation and, as required by Rule 1.4, shall consult with the client as to the means by which they are to be pursued. A lawyer may take such action on behalf of the client as is impliedly authorized to carry out the representation. A lawyer shall abide by a client's decision whether to settle a matter. In a criminal case, the lawyer shall abide by the client's decision, after consultation with the lawyer, as to a plea to be entered, whether to waive jury trial and whether the client will testify.

(b) A lawyer's representation of a client, including representation by appointment, does not constitute an endorsement of the client's political, economic, social or moral views or activities.

(c) A lawyer may limit the scope and objectives of the representation if the limitation is reasonable under the circumstances and the client gives informed consent.

(d) A lawyer shall not counsel a client to engage, or assist a client, in conduct that the lawyer knows is criminal or fraudulent, but a lawyer may discuss the legal consequences of any proposed course of conduct with a client and may counsel or assist a client to make a good faith effort to determine the validity, scope, meaning or application of the law.

Rule 1.3. Diligence

A lawyer shall act with reasonable diligence and promptness in representing a client.

Rule 1.4. Communication

(a) A lawyer shall:

    (1) promptly inform the client of any decision or circumstance with respect to which the client's informed consent, as defined in Rule 1.0(e), is required by these Rules;

    (2) reasonably consult with the client about the means by which the client's objectives are to be accomplished;

    (3) keep the client reasonably informed about the status of the matter;

    (4) promptly comply with reasonable requests for information; and

    (5) consult with the client about any relevant limitation on the lawyer's conduct when the lawyer knows that the client expects assistance not permitted by the Rules of Professional Conduct or other law or assistance limited under Rule 1.2(c).

(b) A lawyer shall explain a matter to the extent reasonably necessary to permit the client to make informed decisions regarding the representation.

Rule 1.5. Fees

(a) A lawyer shall not make an agreement for, charge, or collect an unreasonable fee or an unreasonable amount for expenses. The factors to be considered in determining the reasonableness of a fee include the following:

    (1) the time and labor required, the novelty and difficulty of the questions involved, and the skill requisite to perform the legal service properly;

    (2) the likelihood, if apparent to the client, that the acceptance of the particular employment will preclude other employment by the lawyer;

    (3) the fee customarily charged in the locality for similar legal services;

    (4) the amount involved and the results obtained;

    (5) the time limitations imposed by the client or by the circumstances;

    (6) the nature and length of the professional relationship with the client;

    (7) the experience, reputation, and ability of the lawyer or lawyers performing the services; and

    (8) whether the fee is fixed or contingent.

(b) The scope of the representation and the basis or rate of the fee and expenses for which the client will be responsible shall be communicated to the client, preferably in writing, before or within a reasonable time after commencing the representation, except when the lawyer will charge a regularly represented client on the same basis or rate. Any changes in the basis or rate of the fee or expenses shall also be communicated to the client.

(c) A fee may be contingent on the outcome of the matter for which the service is rendered, except in a matter in which a contingent fee is prohibited by paragraph (d) or other law. A contingent fee agreement shall be in a writing signed by the client and shall state the method by which the fee is to be determined, including the percentage or percentages that shall accrue to the lawyer in the event of settlement, trial or appeal; litigation and other expenses to be deducted from the recovery; and whether such expenses are to be deducted before or after the contingent fee is calculated. The agreement must clearly notify the client of any expenses for which the client will be liable whether or not the client is the prevailing party. Upon conclusion of a contingent fee matter, the lawyer shall provide the client with a written statement stating the outcome of the matter and, if there is a recovery, showing the remittance to the client and the method of its determination.

(d) A lawyer shall not enter into an arrangement for, charge, or collect:

    (1) any fee in a domestic relations matter, the payment or amount of which is contingent upon the securing of a dissolution or upon the amount of maintenance, support, or property settlement, or obtaining custody of a child; or

    (2) a contingent fee for representing a defendant in a criminal case.

This provision does not preclude a contract for a contingent fee for legal representation in a domestic relations post-judgment collection action, provided the attorney clearly advises his or her client in writing of the alternative measures available for the collection of such debt and, in all other particulars, complies with Prof.Cond.R. 1.5(c).

(e) A division of a fee between lawyers who are not in the same firm may be made only if:

    (1) the division is in proportion to the services performed by each lawyer or each lawyer assumes joint responsibility for the representation;

    (2) the client agrees to the arrangement, including the share each lawyer will receive, and the agreement is confirmed in writing; and

    (3) the total fee is reasonable.

Rule 1.6. Confidentiality of Information

(a) A lawyer shall not reveal information relating to representation of a client unless the client gives informed consent, the disclosure is impliedly authorized in order to carry out the representation or the disclosure is permitted by paragraph (b).

(b) A lawyer may reveal information relating to the representation of a client to the extent the lawyer reasonably believes necessary:

    (1) to prevent reasonably certain death or substantial bodily harm;

    (2) to prevent the client from committing a crime or from committing fraud that is reasonably certain to result in substantial injury to the financial interests or property of another and in furtherance of which the client has used or is using the lawyer's services;

    (3) to prevent, mitigate or rectify substantial injury to the financial interests or property of another that is reasonably certain to result or has resulted from the client's commission of a crime or fraud in furtherance of which the client has used the lawyer's services;

    (4) to secure legal advice about the lawyer's compliance with these Rules;

    (5) to establish a claim or defense on behalf of the lawyer in a controversy between the lawyer and the client, to establish a defense to a criminal charge or civil claim against the lawyer

based upon conduct in which the client was involved, or to respond to allegations in any proceeding concerning the lawyer's representation of the client; or

(6) to comply with other law or a court order.

(c) In the event of a lawyer's physical or mental disability or the appointment of a guardian or conservator of an attorney's client files, disclosure of a client's names and files is authorized to the extent necessary to carry out the duties of the person managing the lawyer's files.

Rule 1.7. Conflict of Interest: Current Clients

(a) Except as provided in paragraph (b), a lawyer shall not represent a client if the representation involves a concurrent conflict of interest. A concurrent conflict of interest exists if:

(1) the representation of one client will be directly adverse to another client; or

(2) there is a significant risk that the representation of one or more clients will be materially limited by the lawyer's responsibilities to another client, a former client or a third person or by a personal interest of the lawyer.

(b) Notwithstanding the existence of a concurrent conflict of interest under paragraph (a), a lawyer may represent a client if:

(1) the lawyer reasonably believes that the lawyer will be able to provide competent and diligent representation to each affected client;

(2) the representation is not prohibited by law;

(3) the representation does not involve the assertion of a claim by one client against another client represented by the lawyer in the same litigation or other proceeding before a tribunal; and

(4) each affected client gives informed consent, confirmed in writing.

Rule 1.8. Conflict of Interest: Current Clients: Specific Rules

(a) A lawyer shall not enter into a business transaction with a client or knowingly acquire an ownership, possessory, security or other pecuniary interest adverse to a client unless:

(1) the transaction and terms on which the lawyer acquires the interest are fair and reasonable to the client and are fully disclosed and transmitted in writing in a manner that can be reasonably understood by the client;

(2) the client is advised in writing of the desirability of seeking and is given a reasonable opportunity to seek the advice of independent legal counsel on the transaction; and

(3) the client gives informed consent, in a writing signed by the client, to the essential terms of the transaction and the lawyer's role in the transaction, including whether the lawyer is representing the client in the transaction.

(b) A lawyer shall not use information relating to representation of a client to the disadvantage of the client unless the client gives informed consent, except as permitted or required by these Rules.

(c) A lawyer shall not solicit any substantial gift from a client, including a testamentary gift, or prepare on behalf of a client an instrument giving the lawyer or a person related to the lawyer any substantial gift unless the lawyer or other recipient of the gift is related to the client.

For purposes of this paragraph, related persons include a spouse, child, grandchild, parent, grandparent or other relative or individual with whom the lawyer or the client maintains a close, familial relationship.

(d) Prior to the conclusion of representation of a client, a lawyer shall not make or negotiate an agreement giving the lawyer literary or media rights to a portrayal or account based in substantial part on information relating to the representation.

(e) A lawyer shall not provide financial assistance to a client in connection with pending or contemplated litigation, except that:

    (1) a lawyer may advance court costs and expenses of litigation, the repayment of which may be contingent on the outcome of the matter; and

    (2) a lawyer representing an indigent client may pay court costs and expenses of litigation on behalf of the client.

(f) A lawyer shall not accept compensation for representing a client from one other than the client unless:

    (1) the client gives informed consent;

    (2) there is no interference with the lawyer's independence of professional judgment or with the client-lawyer relationship; and

    (3) information relating to representation of a client is protected as required by Rule 1.6.

(g) A lawyer who represents two or more clients shall not participate in making an aggregate settlement of the claims of or against the clients, or in a criminal case an aggregated agreement as to guilty or nolo contendere pleas, unless each client gives informed consent, in a writing signed by the client. The lawyer's disclosure shall include the existence and nature of all the claims or pleas involved and of the participation of each person in the settlement.

(h) A lawyer shall not:

    (1) make an agreement prospectively limiting the lawyer's liability to a client for malpractice unless the client is independently represented in making the agreement; or

    (2) settle a claim or potential claim for such liability with an unrepresented client or former client unless that person is advised in writing of the desirability of seeking and is given a reasonable opportunity to seek the advice of independent legal counsel in connection therewith.

(i) A lawyer shall not acquire a proprietary interest in the cause of action or subject matter of litigation the lawyer is conducting for a client, except that the lawyer may:

    (1) acquire a lien authorized by law to secure the lawyer's fee or expenses; and

    (2) contract with a client for a reasonable contingent fee in a civil case.

(j) A lawyer shall not have sexual relations with a client unless a consensual sexual relationship existed between them when the client-lawyer relationship commenced.

(k) While lawyers are associated in a firm, a prohibition in paragraphs (a) through (i) and (l) that applies to any one of them shall apply to all of them.

(l) A part-time prosecutor or deputy prosecutor authorized by statute to otherwise engage in the practice of law shall refrain from representing a private client in any matter wherein exists an issue upon which said prosecutor has statutory prosecutorial authority or responsibilities. This restriction is not intended to prohibit representation in tort cases in which investigation and any prosecution of infractions has terminated, nor to prohibit representation in family law matters involving no issue subject to prosecutorial authority or responsibilities. Upon a prior, express written limitation of responsibility to exclude prosecutorial authority in matters related to family law, a part-time deputy prosecutor may fully represent private clients in cases involving family law.

Rule 1.9. Duties to Former Clients

(a) A lawyer who has formerly represented a client in a matter shall not thereafter represent another person in the same or a substantially related matter in which that person's interests are materially adverse to the interests of the former client unless the former client gives informed consent, confirmed in writing.

(b) A lawyer shall not knowingly represent a person in the same or a substantially related matter in which a firm with which the lawyer formerly was associated had previously represented a client

   (1) whose interests are materially adverse to that person; and

   (2) about whom the lawyer had acquired information protected by Rules 1. 6 and 1.9(c) that is material to the matter; unless the former client gives informed consent, confirmed in writing.

(c) A lawyer who has formerly represented a client in a matter or whose present or former firm has formerly represented a client in a matter shall not thereafter:

   (1) use information relating to the representation to the disadvantage of the former client except as these Rules would permit or require with respect to a client, or when the information has become generally known; or

   (2) reveal information relating to the representation except as these Rules would permit or require with respect to a client.

Rule 1.10. Imputation of Conflicts of Interest: General Rule

(a) While lawyers are associated in a firm, none of them shall knowingly represent a client when any one of them practicing alone would be prohibited from doing so by Rules 1.7, 1.9, or 2.2 unless the prohibition is based on a personal interest of the prohibited lawyer and does not present a significant risk of materially limiting the representation of the client by the remaining lawyers in the firm.

(b) When a lawyer has terminated an association with a firm, the firm is not prohibited from thereafter representing a person with interests materially adverse to those of a client represented by the formerly associated lawyer and not currently represented by the firm unless:

   (1) the matter is the same or substantially related to that in which the formerly associated lawyer represented the client; and

   (2) any lawyer remaining in the firm has information protected by Rules 1.6 and 1.9(c) that is material to the matter.

(c) When a lawyer becomes associated with a firm, no lawyer associated in the firm shall knowingly represent a person in a matter in which that lawyer is disqualified under Rule 1.9 unless:

   (1) the personally disqualified lawyer did not have primary responsibility for the matter that causes the disqualification under Rule 1.9;

    (2)   the personally disqualified lawyer is timely screened from any participation in the matter and is apportioned no part of the fee therefrom; and

    (3)   written notice is promptly given to any affected former client to enable it to ascertain compliance with the provisions of this rule.

(d)   A disqualification prescribed by this rule may be waived by the affected client under the conditions stated in Rule 1.7.

(e)   The disqualification of lawyers associated in a firm with former or current government lawyers is governed by Rule 1.11.

Rule 1.13. Organization as Client

(a)   A lawyer employed or retained by an organization represents the organization acting through its duly authorized constituents.

(b)   If a lawyer for an organization knows that an officer, employee or other person associated with the organization is engaged in action, intends to act or refuses to act in a matter related to the representation that is a violation of a legal obligation to the organization, or a violation of law which reasonably might be imputed to the organization, and that is likely to result in substantial injury to the organization, then the lawyer shall proceed as is reasonably necessary in the best interest of the organization. Unless the lawyer reasonably believes that it is not necessary in the best interest of the organization to do so, the lawyer shall refer the matter to higher authority in the organization, including, if warranted by the circumstances to the highest authority that can act on behalf of the organization as determined by applicable law.

(c)   Except as provided in paragraph (d), if

    (1)   despite the lawyer's efforts in accordance with paragraph (b) the highest authority that can act on behalf of the organization insists upon or fails to address in a timely and appropriate manner an action, or a refusal to act, that is clearly a violation of law and

    (2)   the lawyer reasonably believes that the violation is reasonably certain to result in substantial injury to the organization, then the lawyer may reveal information relating to the representation whether or not Rule 1.6 permits such disclosure, but only if and to the extent the lawyer reasonably believes necessary to prevent substantial injury to the organization.

(d)   Paragraph (c) shall not apply with respect to information relating to a lawyer's representation of an organization to investigate an alleged violation of law, or to defend the organization or an officer, employee or other constituent associated with the organization against a claim arising out of an alleged violation of law.

(e)   A lawyer who reasonably believes that he or she has been discharged because of the lawyer's actions taken pursuant to paragraphs (b) or (c), or who withdraws under circumstances that require or permit the lawyer to take action under either of those paragraphs, shall proceed as the lawyer reasonably believes necessary to assure that the organization's highest authority is informed of the lawyer's discharge or withdrawal.

(f)   In dealing with an organization's directors, officers, employees, members, shareholders or other constituents, a lawyer shall explain the identity of the client when the lawyer knows or reasonably should know that the organization's interests are adverse to those of the constituents with whom the lawyer is dealing.

(g) A lawyer representing an organization may also represent any of its directors, officers, employees, members, shareholders or other constituents, subject to the provisions of Rule 1.7. If the organization's consent to the dual representation is required by Rule 1.7, the consent shall be given by an appropriate official of the organization other than the individual who is to be represented, or by the shareholders.

Rule 1.16. Declining or Terminating Representation

(a) Except as stated in paragraph (c), a lawyer shall not represent a client or, where representation has commenced, shall withdraw from the representation of a client if:

    (1) the representation will result in violation of the Rules of Professional Conduct or other law;

    (2) the lawyer's physical or mental condition materially impairs the lawyer's ability to represent the client; or

    (3) the lawyer is discharged.

(b) Except as stated in paragraph (c), a lawyer may withdraw from representing a client if:

    (1) withdrawal can be accomplished without material adverse effect on the interests of the client;

    (2) the client persists in a course of action involving the lawyer's services that the lawyer reasonably believes is criminal or fraudulent;

    (3) the client has used the lawyer's services to perpetrate a crime or fraud;

    (4) a client insists upon taking action that the lawyer considers repugnant or with which the lawyer has a fundamental disagreement;

    (5) the client fails substantially to fulfill an obligation to the lawyer regarding the lawyer's services and has been given reasonable warning that the lawyer will withdraw unless the obligation is fulfilled;

    (6) the representation will result in an unreasonable financial burden on the lawyer or has been rendered unreasonably difficult by the client; or

    (7) other good cause for withdrawal exists.

(c) A lawyer must comply with applicable law requiring notice to or permission of a tribunal when terminating a representation. When ordered to do so by a tribunal, a lawyer shall continue representation notwithstanding good cause for terminating the representation.

(d) Upon termination of representation, a lawyer shall take steps to the extent reasonably practicable to protect a client's interests, such as giving reasonable notice to the client, allowing time for employment of other counsel, surrendering papers and property to which the client is entitled and refunding any advance payment of fee or expense that has not been earned or incurred. The lawyer may retain papers relating to the client to the extent permitted by other law.

Rule 1.18. Duties to Prospective Client

(a) A person who discusses with a lawyer the possibility of forming a client-lawyer relationship with respect to a matter is a prospective client.

(b) Even when no client-lawyer relationship ensues, a lawyer who has had discussions with a prospective client shall not use or reveal information learned in the consultation, except as Rule 1.9 would permit with respect to information of a former client.

(c) A lawyer subject to paragraph (b) shall not represent a client with interests materially adverse to those of a prospective client in the same or a substantially related matter if the lawyer received information from the prospective client that could be significantly harmful to that person in the matter, except as provided in paragraph (d). If a lawyer is disqualified from representation under this paragraph, no lawyer in a firm with which that lawyer is associated may knowingly undertake or continue representation in such a matter, except as provided in paragraph (d).

(d) When a lawyer has received disqualifying information as defined in paragraph (c), representation is permissible if:

(1) both the affected client and the prospective client have given informed consent, confirmed in writing, or:

(2) the lawyer who received the information took reasonable measures to avoid exposure to more disqualifying information than was reasonably necessary to determine whether to represent the prospective client; and

(i) the disqualified lawyer is timely screened from any participation in the matter and is apportioned no part of the fee therefrom; and

(ii) written notice is promptly given to the prospective client.

Rule 2.1. Advisor

In representing a client, a lawyer shall exercise independent professional judgment and render candid advice. In rendering advice, a lawyer may refer not only to law but to other considerations such as moral, economic, social and political factors, that may be relevant to the client's situation.

Rule 3.1. Meritorious Claims and Contentions

A lawyer shall not bring or defend a proceeding, or assert or controvert an issue therein, unless there is a basis in law and fact for doing so that is not frivolous, which includes a good faith argument for an extension, modification or reversal of existing law. A lawyer for the defendant in a criminal proceeding, or the respondent in a proceeding that could result in incarceration, may nevertheless so defend the proceeding as to require that every element of the case be established.

Rule 3.2. Expediting Litigation

A lawyer shall make reasonable efforts to expedite litigation consistent with the interests of the client.

Rule 3.3. Candor Toward the Tribunal

(a) A lawyer shall not knowingly:

(1) make a false statement of fact or law to a tribunal or fail to correct a false statement of material fact or law previously made to the tribunal by the lawyer;

    (2) fail to disclose to the tribunal legal authority in the controlling jurisdiction known to the lawyer to be directly adverse to the position of the client and not disclosed by opposing counsel; or

    (3) offer evidence that the lawyer knows to be false. If a lawyer, the lawyer's client, or a witness called by the lawyer, has offered material evidence and the lawyer comes to know of its falsity, the lawyer shall take reasonable remedial measures, including, if necessary, disclosure to the tribunal. A lawyer may refuse to offer evidence, other than the testimony of a defendant in a criminal matter, that the lawyer reasonably believes is false.

(b) A lawyer who represents a client in an adjudicative proceeding and who knows that a person intends to engage, is engaging or has engaged in criminal or fraudulent conduct related to the proceeding shall take reasonable remedial measures, including, if necessary, disclosure to the tribunal.

(c) The duties stated in paragraphs (a) and (b) continue to the conclusion of the proceeding, and apply even if compliance requires disclosure of information otherwise protected by Rule 1.6.

(d) In an ex parte proceeding, a lawyer shall inform the tribunal of all material facts known to the lawyer which will enable the tribunal to make an informed decision, whether or not the facts are adverse.

Rule 3.4. Fairness to Opposing Party and Counsel

A lawyer shall not:

(a) unlawfully obstruct another party's access to evidence or unlawfully alter, destroy or conceal a document or other material having potential evidentiary value. A lawyer shall not counsel or assist another person to do any such act;

(b) falsify evidence, counsel or assist a witness to testify falsely, or offer an inducement to a witness that is prohibited by law;

(c) knowingly disobey an obligation under the rules of a tribunal except for an open refusal based on an assertion that no valid obligation exists;

(d) in pretrial procedure, make a frivolous discovery request or fail to make reasonably diligent effort to comply with a legally proper discovery request by an opposing party;

(e) in trial, allude to any matter that the lawyer does not reasonably believe is relevant or that will not be supported by admissible evidence, assert personal knowledge of facts in issue except when testifying as a witness, or state a personal opinion as to the justness of a cause, the credibility of a witness, the culpability of a civil litigant or the guilt or innocence of an accused; or

(f) request a person other than a client to refrain from voluntarily giving relevant information to another party unless:

    (1) the person is a relative or an employee or other agent of a client; and

    (2) the lawyer reasonably believes that the person's interests will not be adversely affected by refraining from giving such information.

Rule 3.5. Impartiality and Decorum of the Tribunal

A lawyer shall not:

(a) seek to influence a judge, juror, prospective juror or other official by means prohibited by law;

(b) communicate ex parte with such a person during the proceeding unless authorized to do so by law or court order;

   (c) communicate with a juror or prospective juror after discharge of the jury if:

       (1) the communication is prohibited by law or court order;

       (2) the juror has made known to the lawyer a desire not to communicate; or

       (3) the communication involves misrepresentation, coercion, duress or harassment.

   (d) engage in conduct intended to disrupt a tribunal.

Rule 3.7. Lawyer as Witness

   (a) A lawyer shall not act as advocate at a trial in which the lawyer is likely to be a necessary witness unless:

       (1) the testimony relates to an uncontested issue;

       (2) the testimony relates to the nature and value of legal services rendered in the case; or

       (3) disqualification of the lawyer would work substantial hardship on the client.

   (b) A lawyer may act as advocate in a trial in which another lawyer in the lawyer's firm is likely to be called as a witness unless precluded from doing so by Rule 1.7 or Rule 1.9.

Rule 4.1. Truthfulness in Statements to Others

In the course of representing a client a lawyer shall not knowingly:

   (a) make a false statement of material fact or law to a third person; or

   (b) fail to disclose a material fact to a third person when disclosure is necessary to avoid assisting a criminal or fraudulent act by a client, unless disclosure is prohibited by Rule 1.6.

Rule 4.2. Communication with Person Represented by Counsel

In representing a client, a lawyer shall not communicate about the subject of the representation with a person the lawyer knows to be represented by another lawyer in the matter, unless the lawyer has the consent of the other lawyer or is authorized by law or a court order.

Rule 4.3. Dealing with Unrepresented Persons

In dealing on behalf of a client with a person who is not represented by counsel, a lawyer shall not state or imply that the lawyer is disinterested. When the lawyer knows or reasonably should know that the unrepresented person misunderstands the lawyer's role in the matter, the lawyer shall make reasonable efforts to correct the misunderstanding. The lawyer shall not give legal advice to an unrepresented person, other than the advice to secure counsel, if the lawyer knows or reasonably should know that the interests of such person are or have a reasonable possibility of being in conflict with the interests of the client.

Rule 4.4. Respect for Rights of Third Persons

   (a) In representing a client, a lawyer shall not use means that have no substantial purpose other than to embarrass, delay, or burden a third person, or use methods of obtaining evidence that violate the legal rights of such a person.

(b) A lawyer who receives a document relating to the representation of the lawyer's client and knows or reasonably should know that the document was inadvertently sent shall promptly notify the sender.

Rule 7.1. Communications Concerning a Lawyer's Services

A lawyer shall not make a false or misleading communication about the lawyer or the lawyer's services. A communication is false or misleading if it contains a material misrepresentation of fact or law, or omits a fact necessary to make the statement considered as a whole not materially misleading.

Rule 7.2. Advertising

(a) Subject to the requirements of this rule, lawyers and law firms may advertise their professional services and law related services. The term "advertise" as used in these Indiana Rules of Professional Conduct refers to any manner of public communication partly or entirely intended or expected to promote the purchase or use of the professional services of a lawyer, law firm, or any employee of either involving the practice of law or law-related services.

(b) A lawyer shall not give anything of value to a person for recommending or advertising the lawyer's services except that a lawyer may:

    (1) pay the reasonable costs of advertisements or communications permitted by this Rule;

    (2) pay the usual charges of a legal service plan or a not-for-profit or qualified lawyer referral service described in Rule 7.3(d);

    (3) pay for a law practice in accordance with Rule 1.17; and

    (4) refer clients to another lawyer or a non-lawyer professional pursuant to an agreement not otherwise prohibited under these Rules that provides for the other person to refer clients or customers to the lawyer, if

        (i) the reciprocal referral agreement is not exclusive, and

        (ii) the client is informed of the existence and nature of the agreement.

(c) Any communication subject to this rule shall include the name and office address of at least one lawyer or law firm responsible for its content. The lawyer or law firm responsible for the content of any communication subject to this rule shall keep a copy or recording of each such communication for six years after its dissemination.

Rule 7.4. Communication of Fields of Practice and Specialization

(a) A lawyer may communicate the fact that the lawyer does or does not practice in particular fields of law.

(b) A lawyer admitted to engage in patent practice before the United States Patent and Trademark Office may use the designation "Patent Attorney" or a substantially similar designation.

(c) A lawyer engaged in Admiralty practice may use the designation "Admiralty," "Proctor in Admiralty" or a substantially similar designation.

(d) A lawyer shall not state or imply that the lawyer is a specialist in a particular field of law, unless:

(1) The lawyer has been certified as a specialist by an Independent Certifying Organization accredited by the Indiana Commission for Continuing Legal Education pursuant to Admission and Discipline Rule 30; and,

(2) The certifying organization is identified in the communication.

(e) Pursuant to rule-making powers inherent in its ability and authority to police and regulate the practice of law by attorneys admitted to practice law in the State of Indiana, the Indiana Supreme Court hereby vests exclusive authority for accreditation of Independent Certifying Organizations that certify specialists in legal practice areas and fields in the Indiana Commission for Continuing Legal Education. The Commission shall be the exclusive accrediting body in Indiana, for purposes of Rule 7.4(d)(1), above; and shall promulgate rules and guidelines for accrediting Independent Certifying Organizations that certify specialists in legal practice areas and fields. The rules and guidelines shall include requirements of practice experience, continuing legal education, objective examination; and, peer review and evaluation, with the purpose of providing assurance to the consumers of legal services that the attorneys attaining certification within areas of specialization have demonstrated extraordinary proficiency within those areas of specialization. The Supreme Court shall retain review oversight with respect to the Commission, its requirements, and its rules and guidelines. The Supreme Court retains the power to alter or amend such requirements, rules and guidelines; and, to review the actions of the Commission in respect to this Rule 7.4.

Rule 7.5. Firm Names and Letterheads

(a) Firm names, letterheads, and other professional designations are subject to the following requirements:

(1) A lawyer shall not use a firm name, letterhead or other professional designation that violates Rule 7.1.

(2) The name of a professional corporation, professional association, limited liability partnership, or limited liability company may contain, "P.C.", "P.A.," "LLP," or "LLC" or similar symbols indicating the nature of the organization.

(3) If otherwise lawful a firm may use as, or continue to include in, its name, the name or names of one or more deceased or retired members of the firm or of a predecessor firm in a continuing line of succession. See Admission & Discipline Rule 27.

(4) A trade name may be used by a lawyer in private practice subject to the following requirements:

(i) the name shall not imply a connection with a government agency or with a public or charitable legal services organization and shall not otherwise violate Rule 7.1.

(ii) the name shall include the name of a lawyer (or the name of a deceased or retired member of the firm, or of a predecessor firm in a manner that complies with subparagraph (2) above).

(iii) the name shall not include words other than words that comply with clause (ii) above and words that:

(A) identify the field of law in which the firm concentrates its work, or

(B) describe the geographic location of its offices, or

(C) indicate a language fluency.

(b) A law firm with offices in more than one jurisdiction may use the same name or other professional designation in Indiana if the name or other designation does not violate paragraph (a) and the identification of the lawyers in an office of the firm indicates the jurisdictional limitations on those not licensed to practice in Indiana.

(c) The name of a lawyer holding a public office shall not be used in the name of a law firm, or in communications on its behalf, during any substantial period in which the lawyer is not actively and regularly practicing with the firm. A member of a part-time legislative body such as the General Assembly, a county or city council, or a school board is not subject to this rule.

(d) Lawyers may state or imply that they practice in a partnership or other organization only when they in fact do so.

Rule 8.3. Reporting Professional Misconduct

(a) A lawyer who knows that another lawyer has committed a violation of the Rules of Professional Conduct that raises a substantial question as to that lawyer's honesty, trustworthiness or fitness as a lawyer in other respects, shall inform the appropriate professional authority.

(b) A lawyer who knows that a judge has committed a violation of applicable rules of judicial conduct that raises a substantial question as to the judge's fitness for office shall inform the appropriate authority.

(c) This Rule does not require reporting of a violation or disclosure of information if such action would involve disclosure of information that is otherwise protected by Rule 1.6, or is gained by a lawyer while providing advisory opinions or telephone advice on legal ethics issues as a member of a bar association committee or similar entity formed for the purposes of providing such opinions or advice and designated by the Indiana Supreme Court.

(d) The relationship between lawyers or judges acting on behalf of a judges or lawyers assistance program approved by the Supreme Court, and lawyers or judges who have agreed to seek assistance from and participate in any such programs, shall be considered one of attorney and client, with its attendant duty of confidentiality and privilege from disclosure.

Rule 8.4. Misconduct

It is professional misconduct for a lawyer to:

(a) violate or attempt to violate the Rules of Professional Conduct, knowingly assist or induce another to do so, or do so through the acts of another;

(b) commit a criminal act that reflects adversely on the lawyer's honesty, trustworthiness or fitness as a lawyer in other respects;

(c) engage in conduct involving dishonesty, fraud, deceit or misrepresentation;

(d) engage in conduct that is prejudicial to the administration of justice;

(e) state or imply an ability to influence improperly a government agency or official or to achieve results by means that violate the Rules of Professional Conduct or other law;

(f) knowingly assist a judge or judicial officer in conduct that is a violation of applicable rules of judicial conduct or other law; or

(g) engage in conduct, in a professional capacity, manifesting, by words or conduct, bias or prejudice based upon race, gender, religion, national origin, disability, sexual orientation, age, socioeconomic status, or similar factors. Legitimate advocacy respecting the foregoing factors does not violate this subsection. A trial judge's finding that preemptory challenges were exercised on a discriminatory basis does not alone establish a violation of this Rule.

GUIDELINES FOR LITIGATION CONDUCT

Local Rules of the U.S. District Court,
District of New Jersey, Appendix R

Preamble

A lawyer's conduct should be characterized at all times by personal courtesy and professional integrity in the fullest sense of those terms. In fulfilling our duty to represent a client vigorously as lawyers, we will be mindful of our obligations to the administration of justice, which is a truth-seeking process designed to resolve human and societal problems in a rational, peaceful, and efficient manner.

A judge's conduct should be characterized at all times by courtesy and patience toward all participants. As judges, we owe to all participants in a legal proceeding respect, diligence, punctuality, and protection against unjust and improper criticism or attack.

Conduct that may be characterized as uncivil, abrasive, abusive, hostile, or obstructive impedes the fundamental goal of resolving disputes rationally, peacefully, and efficiently. Such conduct tends to delay and often to deny justice.

The following Guidelines are designed to encourage us, judges and lawyers, to meet our obligations to each other, to litigants and to the system of justice, and thereby achieve the twin goals of civility and professionalism, but of which are hallmarks of a learned profession dedicated to public service.

We encourage judges, lawyers, and clients to make a mutual and firm commitment to these Guidelines.

We support the principles espoused in the following Guidelines, but under no circumstances should these Guidelines be used as a basis for litigation or for sanctions or penalties.

Lawyer's Duties to Other Counsel

1.   We will practice our profession with a continuing awareness that our role is to zealously advance the legitimate interests of our clients. In our dealings with others we will not reflect the ill feelings of our clients. We will treat all other counsel, parties, and witnesses in a civil and courteous manner, not only in court, but also in all other written and oral communications. We will refrain from acting upon or manifesting bias or prejudice based upon race, sex, religion, national origin, disability, age, sexual orientation or socioeconomic status toward any participant in the legal process.

2.   We will not, even when called upon by a client to do so, abuse or indulge in offensive conduct directed to other counsel, parties, or witnesses. We will abstain from disparaging personal remarks or acrimony toward other counsel, parties, or witnesses. We will treat adverse witnesses and parties with fair consideration.

3.   We will not encourage or knowingly authorize any person under our control to engage in conduct that would be improper if we were to engage in such conduct.

4.   We will not, absent good cause, attribute bad motives or improper conduct to other counsel.

5.   We will not lightly seek court sanctions.

6.   We will in good faith adhere to all express promises and to agreements with other counsel, whether oral or in writing, and to all agreements implied by the circumstances or local customs.

7.   When we reach an oral understanding on a proposed agreement or a stipulation and decide to commit it to writing, the drafter will endeavor in good faith to state the oral understanding accurately

and completely. The drafter will provide other counsel the opportunity to review the writing. As drafts are exchanged between or among counsel, changes from prior drafts will be identified in the draft or otherwise explicitly brought to other counsel's attention. We will not include in a draft matters to which there has been no agreement without explicitly advising other counsel in writing of the addition.

8. We will endeavor to confer early with other counsel to assess settlement possibilities. We will not falsely hold out the possibility of settlement to obtain unfair advantage.

9. In civil actions, we will stipulate to relevant matters if they are undisputed and if no good faith advocacy basis exists for not stipulating.

10. We will not use any form of discovery or discovery scheduling as a means of harassment.

11. Whenever circumstances allow, we will make good faith efforts to resolve by agreement objections before presenting them to the court.

12. We will not time the filing or service of motions or pleadings in any way that unfairly limits another party's opportunity to respond.

13. We will not request an extension of time solely for the purpose of unjustified delay or to obtain unfair advantage.

14. We will consult other counsel regarding scheduling matters in a good faith effort to avoid scheduling conflicts.

15. We will endeavor to accommodate previously scheduled dates for hearings, depositions, meetings, conferences, vacations, seminars, or other functions that produce good faith calendar conflicts on the part of other counsel.

16. We will promptly notify other counsel and, if appropriate, the court or other persons, when hearings, depositions, meetings, or conferences are to be canceled or postponed.

17. We will agree to reasonable requests for extensions of time and for waiver of procedural formalities, provided our clients' legitimate rights will not be materially or adversely affected.

18. We will not cause any default or dismissal to be entered without first notifying opposing counsel, when we know his or her identity.

19. We will take depositions only when actually needed. We will not take depositions for the purposes of harassment or other improper purpose.

20. We will not engage in any conduct during a deposition that would not be appropriate in the presence of a judge.

21. We will not obstruct questioning during a deposition or object to deposition questions unless permitted under applicable law.

22. During depositions we will ask only those questions we reasonably believe are necessary, and appropriate, for the prosecution or defense of an action.

23. We will carefully craft document production requests so they are limited to those documents we reasonably believe are necessary, and appropriate, for the prosecution or defense of an action. We will not design production requests to place an undue burden or expense on a party, or for any other improper purpose.

24. We will respond to document requests reasonably and not strain to interpret requests in an artificially restrictive manner to avoid disclosure of relevant and non-privileged documents. We will not produce documents in a manner designed to hide or obscure the existence of particular documents, or to accomplish any other improper purpose.

25. We will carefully craft interrogatories so they are limited to those matters we reasonably believe are necessary, and appropriate, for the prosecution or defense of an action, and we will not design them to place an undue burden or expense on a party, or for any other improper purpose.

26. We will respond to interrogatories reasonably and will not strain to interpret them in an artificially restrictive manner to avoid disclosure of relevant and non-privileged information, or for any other improper purpose.

27. We will base our discovery objections on a good faith belief in their merit and will not object solely for the purpose of withholding or delaying the disclosure or relevant information, or for any other improper purpose.

28. When a draft order is to be prepared by counsel to reflect a court ruling, we will draft an order that accurately and completely reflects the court's ruling. We will promptly prepare and submit a proposed order to other counsel and attempt to reconcile any differences before the draft order is presented to the court.

29. We will not ascribe a position to another counsel that counsel has not taken.

30. Unless permitted or invited by the court, we will not send copies of correspondence between counsel to the court.

31. Nothing contained in these Guidelines is intended or shall be construed to inhibit vigorous advocacy, including vigorous cross-examination.

Lawyer's Duties to the Court

1. We will speak and write civilly and respectfully in all communications with the court.

2. We will be punctual and prepared for all court appearances so that all hearings, conferences, and trial may commence on time; if delayed, we will notify the court and counsel, if possible.

3. We will be considerate of the time constraints and pressures on the court and court staff inherent in their efforts to administer justice.

4. We will not engage in any conduct that brings disorder or disruption to the courtroom. We will advise our clients and witnesses appearing in court of the proper conduct expected and required there and, to the best of our ability, prevent our clients and witnesses from creating disorder or disruption.

5. We will not knowingly misrepresent, mis-characterize, misquote, or mis-cite facts or authorities in any oral or written communication to the court.

6. We will not write letters to the court in connection with a pending action, unless invited or permitted by the court.

7. Before dates for hearings or trials are set, or if that is not feasible, immediately after such date has been set, we will attempt to verify the availability of necessary participants and witnesses so we can promptly notify the court of any likely problems.

8. We will act and speak civilly to court marshals, clerks, court reporters, secretaries, and law clerks with an awareness that they, too, are an integral part of the judicial system.

U.S. DISTRICT COURT ELECTRONIC CASE FILING ADMINISTRATIVE POLICIES AND PROCEDURES MANUAL

[Adapted from ECF Manual for the Southern District of California]

Section 1: The Electronic Filing System

a. Authorization for Electronic Filing

All attorneys admitted in this district must file documents with the court electronically, over the Internet, through the court's Case Management/Electronic Case Filing (CM/ECF) system.

Electronic transmission of a document to the CM/ECF system, together with the transmission of a Notice of Electronic Filing from the court, constitutes filing of the document for purposes of Rule 5(d) of the Federal Rules of Civil Procedure and Rule 49(d) of the Federal Rules of Criminal Procedure, and constitutes entry of the document on the docket kept by the Clerk of Court under Rules 58 and 79 of the Federal Rules of Civil Procedure. The following court policies govern electronic filing in this district unless, due to extraordinary circumstances, in a particular case, a judicial officer determines that these policies should be modified in the interest of justice.

b. Scope of Electronic Filing

Except as prescribed by local rule, order, or other procedure, the court has designated all cases to be assigned to the Electronic Filing System. Unless otherwise expressly provided in these rules or in exceptional circumstances preventing a registered user from filing electronically, all petitions, motions, memoranda of law, or other pleadings and documents required to be filed with the court by a registered user in connection with a case assigned to the Electronic Filing System must be electronically filed.

Case initiating documents in civil cases, including but not limited to the civil Complaint and Notice of Removal, may be filed electronically. All sealed case initiating documents in civil cases must be filed in paper format. All case initiating documents in criminal cases, including the criminal Complaint, Information, Indictment and Superseding Information or Indictment, must be filed in paper format at the Clerk's Office. All subsequent documents must be filed by registered users electronically except as provided in these rules or as ordered by the court.

c. The Official Record and Maintenance of Original Paper Documents

The official court record will be the electronic file maintained on the court's servers. This includes information transmitted to the Court in electronic format, as well as documents filed in paper form, scanned, and made a part of the electronic record to the extent permitted by the court's policies. The official record will also include any documents or exhibits that may be impractical to scan. The electronic file maintained on the court's servers must contain a reference to any such documents filed with the court. For cases initiated prior to the implementation of the Electronic Filing System, the official court record will include both the pre-implementation paper file maintained by the Clerk, as well as the post-implementation electronic files maintained on the court's servers. The Clerk's Office will not maintain a paper court file in any case initiated on or after the effective date of these procedures except as otherwise provided in these procedures.

If an original pleading has some intrinsic value, the filing party must retain the original paper document for a period of five years from the date the document is signed, or for one year after the expiration of all time periods for appeal, whichever period is greater, and must provide the original paper document to the court upon request.

d. Definitions

CASE MANAGEMENT/ELECTRONIC CASE FILING SYSTEM, referred to in these procedures as the system or CM/ECF, means the Internet-based system for filing documents and maintaining court case files in this district.

DOCUMENT means pleadings, motions, exhibits, declarations, affidavits, memoranda, papers, orders, notices, and any other filing by or with the court.

ELECTRONIC FILING means uploading a document directly from the registered user's computer in "Portable Document Format" (.pdf), using the CM/ECF system to file that document in the court's case file. Individual .pdf documents must not exceed ten (10) megabytes (MB) in size. Sending a document or pleading to the court via e-mail other than as described below does not constitute "electronic filing."

NOTICE OF ELECTRONIC FILING, referred to in these procedures as NEF, is a notice automatically generated by the CM/ECF system at the time a document is filed with the court. The notice sets forth the time of filing, the name of the attorney and/or party filing the document, the type of document, the text of the docket entry, the name of the party and/or attorney receiving the notice, and an electronic link (hyperlink) to the filed document which allows recipients to retrieve the document automatically.

.pdf refers to Portable Document Format, a proprietary file format developed by Adobe Systems, Inc. A document file created with a word processor, or a paper document which has been scanned, must be converted to Portable Document Format to be electronically filed with the court. Converted files contain the extension ".pdf". Documents which exist only in paper form may be scanned into .pdf for electronic filing. The Court recommends scanner settings at 400 pixels per inch (ppi). Electronic documents must be converted to .pdf directly from a word processing program (e.g., Microsoft Word® or Corel WordPerfect®) and must be searchable.

REGISTERED USER is an individual who has been issued a login and password by the court to electronically file documents.

PACER (Public Access to Court Electronic Records) is an automated system that allows a subscriber to view, print and download court case file information over the Internet for a fee.

e. System Availability

The CM/ECF system is designed to provide service 24 hours a day. The parties, however, are encouraged to file documents in advance of filing deadlines and during normal business hours. The Clerk's Office has established a Help Desk (866-555-5555) to respond to questions regarding CM/ECF and the registration process. The Help Desk will be staffed during normal business hours. Information can also be obtained on the court web site.

f. Registration and Attorney Responsibilities

Registration in the CM/ECF system for the purpose of electronic service of pleadings and other papers is mandatory for attorneys.

All attorneys in good standing must register for the CM/ECF system by obtaining a user name and password from the court clerk or by completing the on-line registration form available on the court's web site.

Registration constitutes consent to electronic service of documents by e-mail, as provided by the Federal Rules of Civil Procedure. An attorney may register up to two (2) additional e-mail addresses.

An attorney whose e-mail address, mailing address, telephone or fax number has changed must timely update the information with the court. Attorneys employed by federal, state, and local government agencies are responsible for updating their attorney information upon their appointment and separation from their respective agency.

A filing party must maintain an electronic mailbox of sufficient capacity, with the appropriate e-mail permissions, to receive electronic notice of case-related transmissions.

An attorney may apply to the court for permission to file documents in paper form. Attorneys must show good cause to file and serve using non-electronic filing. Permission for non-electronic filing may be withdrawn at any time by the court and the attorney may be required to file documents using the CM/ECF system.

If an attorney, without leave of court, fails to file electronically, he or she must also file a "Notice of Non-Compliance with Mandatory Electronic Filing" setting forth the reason(s) for filing in non-electronic form and seeking leave of the court to file in non-electronic form.

After leave to appear pro hac vice has been granted, attorneys will have five (5) days to register for electronic filing.

g. Logins and Passwords

Each attorney who completes registration will be issued one login and password. Documents filed under an attorney's login and password will constitute that attorney's signature for purposes of the Local Rules and Federal Rules of Civil and Criminal Procedure, including Rule 11 of the Federal Rules of Civil Procedure. Therefore, only one password will be issued and the attorney should not permit the password to be used by anyone other than an authorized agent. The attorney is responsible for all documents filed with his or her password.

If a registered user believes the security of an existing password has been compromised, the user must immediately notify the Clerk's Office and change the password through the CM/ECF system utility menu.

h. Privacy

Unless otherwise ordered by the court, parties must refrain from including, or must partially redact where inclusion is necessary, the following personal identifiers from all pleadings and documents filed with the court, including exhibits thereto:

1. Social Security numbers. If an individual's Social Security number must be included in a pleading or document, only the last four (4) digits of that number should be used.

2. Names of minor children. If the involvement of a minor child must be mentioned, only the initials of that child should be used.

3. Dates of birth. If an individual's date of birth must be included in a pleading or document, only the year should be used.

4. Financial account numbers. If financial account numbers are relevant, only the last four digits of these numbers should be used.

5. Home address. In criminal cases, if a home address must be included only the city and state should be listed.

The responsibility for redacting personal identifiers rests solely with the parties. The Clerk's Office will not review each document for compliance with this rule. A party filing a redacted document must retain the complete unredacted document for the duration of the case, including any period of appeal, unless instructed by the Court to file the complete unredacted document under seal.

Without a court order, the court will not provide public electronic access to the following documents:

a. Sealed documents.

b. Unexecuted warrants of any kind.

c. Pretrial bail reports and bond supporting documents. Only the conditions of release will be available to the public electronically.

d. Pre-Sentence reports and all sentencing materials including the statement of reasons related to the judgment of conviction. Only the judgment of conviction will be available to the public electronically.

e. Juvenile records.

f. Magistrate information sheets and financial affidavits submitted by an accused.

g. Pleadings and reports related to the competency or mental health of a defendant.

h. All abstracts of judgment so captioned in the document.

i. Applications for a writ of garnishment, a writ of garnishment, and a Clerk's notice of garnishment that are so captioned in the document.

j. Applications for a writ of execution, a writ of execution, and a Clerk's notice of execution that are so captioned in the document.

k. Civil settlement documents that contain personal identifiers listed above. It is the attorney's obligation to obtain an order sealing such documents.

i. Technical Specifications

Current technical specifications for CM/ECF can be found at the court's official web site. Specifications may change periodically. Registered users may refer to the web site for the most current requirements.

Section 2: Electronic Filing and Service of Documents

a. Filing

Electronically filed documents must meet the requirements of Fed. R. Civ. P. 10 (Form of Pleadings), and Local Civil Rule 5.1, as if they had been submitted on paper. Documents filed electronically are also subject to any page limitations set forth by Court order or by Local Civil Rule 7.1, Local Civil Rule 8.2, and Local Criminal Rule 47.1.

Unless otherwise expressly provided in these rules or in exceptional circumstances preventing a registered user from filing electronically, all applications, motions, memoranda of law, or other pleadings and documents required to be filed with the Court by a registered user in connection with a case assigned to the Electronic Filing System must be electronically filed.

E-mailing a document to the Clerk's Office or to the assigned judge does not constitute "filing" of the document.

The court may, upon the motion of a party or upon its own motion, strike any inappropriately filed document.

b. Pro Se Litigants

Unless otherwise authorized by the court, all documents submitted for filing to the Clerk's Office by parties appearing without an attorney must be in legible, paper form. The Clerk's Office will scan and electronically file the document.

A pro se party seeking leave to electronically file documents must file a motion and demonstrate the means to do so properly by stating their equipment and software capabilities in addition to agreeing to follow all rules and policies in the CM/ECF Administrative Policies and Procedures Manual. If granted leave to electronically file, the pro se party must register as a user with the Clerk's Office and as a subscriber to PACER within five (5) days.

A pro se party must seek leave to electronically file documents in each case filed. If an attorney enters an appearance on behalf of a pro se party, the attorney must advise the Clerk's Office to terminate the login and password for the pro se party.

c. Case Initiating Documents

Case initiating documents in civil cases, including but not limited to the civil Complaint and Notice of Removal, may be filed electronically. All sealed case initiating documents in civil cases must be filed in paper format. All case initiating documents in criminal cases, including but not limited to the criminal Complaint, Information, Indictment and Superseding Information or Indictment, must be filed in paper format at the Clerk's Office.

d. Service

1. Summons

The Clerk's Office will issue each summons, and the service of a summons must be effected pursuant to Rule 4 of the Federal Rules of Civil Procedure and the Federal Rules of Criminal Procedure.

After a summons has been served, or a waiver of service via summons has been received, the serving registered user must promptly scan the return of service or waiver and electronically file it. Non-registered filers may file the return of service or waiver with the Clerk's Office.

2. Service of Documents

Whenever a document is electronically filed in accordance with these procedures, the CM/ECF system will generate a "Notice of Electronic Filing" (NEF) to the filing party, the assigned judge and any registered user in the case. The NEF will constitute service of the document for purposes of the Federal Rules of Civil, Criminal and Appellate Procedure. Registration as a CM/ECF user constitutes consent to electronic service through the court's transmission facilities.

Each registered user of the CM/ECF system is responsible for assuring that the user's e-mail account is monitored regularly, and that e-mail notices are opened in a timely manner.

A certificate of service is required when a party electronically files a document. The certificate must state the manner in which service or notice was accomplished on each party. If the certificate of service is signed by someone other than a registered user, the filing party must scan and electronically file the original signed document as set forth in Section 2.f.2 below.

Any document that is not filed electronically must be served as a paper copy. A party who is not a registered participant of CM/ECF is entitled to service of a paper copy of any electronically filed document. The filing party must serve the non-registered party with the document according to the Federal Rules of Civil Procedure.

A non-registered filing party who files document(s) with the Clerk's Office for scanning and entry to CM/ECF must serve paper copies on all non-registered parties to the case. There will be some delay in the scanning, electronic filing and subsequent electronic noticing to registered users. If time is an issue, non-registered filers must provide a paper copy of the document(s) to all parties.

e. Courtesy Copies for Judicial Officers

Unless otherwise ordered by the court, parties must deliver to the Clerk's Office or mail directly to the judge's chambers, within 24 hours after filing, any criminal or civil case filing which exceeds 20 pages in length including attachments and exhibits. In addition, where a party makes multiple filings in a case on the same day, and those filings cumulatively exceed 20 pages, a courtesy copy must be provided to the assigned judicial officer. If the nature of the filing is such that the need for a judge's immediate attention is anticipated or desired, a courtesy copy must be delivered on the same day as the filing. A copy of the Notice of Electronic Filing must precede the first page of the courtesy copy. Courtesy copies are to be addressed to the attention of the assigned judicial officer.

f. Signatures

1. Registered Users

The registered user log-in and password required to submit documents to the CM/ECF system will serve as that registered user's signature for purposes of Rule 11 of the Federal Rules of Civil Procedure and for all other purposes under the Federal Rules of Civil, Criminal and Appellate Procedure and the Local Rules of this court. The name of the CM/ECF registered user under whose log-in and password the document is submitted must be preceded by a "s/" and typed in the space where the signature would otherwise appear. The correct format for an attorney signature is as follows:

s/Adam Attorney

Attorney for (Plaintiff/Defendant)

E-mail: adam.attorney@lawfirm.com

2. Non-Registered Signatories

If the original document requires the signature of a non-registered signatory, the filing party must scan and electronically file the original document. The electronically filed document maintained on the court's servers will constitute the official version of that record. The filing party must retain the original document for a period of five years from the date the document is signed, or for one year after the expiration of all time periods for appeal, whichever period is greater, and must provide the original paper document to the Court upon request.

3. Stipulations and Other Documents Requiring Multiple Signatures

All stipulations must be filed as joint motions. The filer of a joint motion need not obtain a hearing date prior to filing the joint motion. At the time a joint motion is filed, the filer must e-mail a proposed order to the e-mail address of the assigned judicial officer.

The filer of any joint motion or other document requiring more than one signature must certify that the content of the document is acceptable to all persons required to sign the document by obtaining either physical signatures or authorization for the electronic signatures of all parties on the document. Physical, facsimile or electronic signatures are permitted. The filer must electronically file the document indicating the signatories as "s/Jane Doe," "s/John Smith," etc., for each electronic signature.

Except as otherwise ordered, parties will have one business day to file an Objection to Electronic Filing if they object to contents of the joint motion or document that contains their signature. The assigned judicial officer will prepare an order, or enter a text order on the docket, following the filing of a joint motion.

g. Motions, Applications, or Other Requests for Ruling by the Court

1. Any supporting memorandum of points and authorities, declarations, and exhibits associated with motions, applications, or other requests for ruling by the Court, must be filed as attachments to the motion in the CM/ECF system.

2. Civil and criminal motions, and responses thereto, must be filed according to the deadlines set forth in the court's Local Rules.

3. A party wishing to file a motion or response on shortened time must file a motion for an order shortening time as required by the Local Rules. Counsel must e-mail a proposed order to the assigned judicial officer.

4. The Court may, upon its own motion, strike any inappropriately filed document.

h. Proposed Orders and Orders

Registered users SHOULD NOT FILE OR SUBMIT proposed orders within the electronic filing system. At the time of filing any joint motion, motion for continuance or extension of time, motion for an order shortening time, or similar non-dispositive procedural motion, the filer must also e-mail a separate proposed order to the assigned judicial officer, with a copy of the e-mail and proposed order also being sent to opposing counsel.

The proposed order must be in editable word processing format (i.e. WordPerfect or Microsoft Word), and not in .pdf format. The proposed order should not contain the name and law firm information of the filing party, and should not contain the word "proposed" in the caption.

The e-mail subject line should include the case number, followed by a short description of the attachment (i.e., 10cv1234 – Order Granting Motion for Continuance). Opposing counsel will have one business day to e-mail chambers any objections to the proposed order.

i. Ex Parte Documents

Ordinary *Ex Parte* motions, for which notice is to be provided to all parties, should be filed electronically. *Ex Parte* documents for which no notice is to be provided to opposing parties should be filed in paper format under seal. *Ex Parte* documents filed in the system will be served on all parties.

j. Sealed and Juvenile Documents

Sealed documents in civil cases are to be filed electronically in CM/ECF and served in paper format. Any document submitted for filing under seal in civil cases must be accompanied by a motion for an order authorizing such filing. In civil cases the motion to seal will be filed as a public document using the appropriate CM/ECF event located under the "Sealed Documents" category. The proposed document to be filed under seal must be lodged electronically using the "Sealed Lodged Proposed Document" event located under the "Sealed Documents" category.

If the motion to seal is granted, the judge will issue an order authorizing the electronic filing by the Clerk's Office of the lodged proposed document under seal. If the motion to seal is denied, the document will remain lodged under seal without further consideration absent contrary direction from the Court.

Electronic filing is not permitted in sealed cases. Documents intended for filing in sealed cases must be submitted in paper format. *Ex Parte* documents for which no notice is to be provided to opposing parties should be filed in paper format under seal.

1. Procedures for E-filing Sealed Documents in Civil Cases

    a. To e-file any sealed document in a civil case, including motions, responses, replies, declarations, etc., a filer must first e-file a motion to seal using the "Motion to File Document(s) Under Seal" event located in the civil events menu under "Sealed Documents." The motion will be a public entry on the docket and the document will be available to the public. All parties in the case will receive notice of the electronic filing. The proposed sealed documents should not be attached to this public filing.

    b. After filing the Motion to File Document(s) Under Seal, the filer shall immediately submit the proposed sealed documents in CM/ECF using the "Sealed Lodged Proposed Document" event located under the "Sealed Documents" category. The proposed document must include the notation "UNDER SEAL" in the caption. The proposed sealed documents will be unavailable for viewing by any attorney or member of the public. However, the docket text associated with the entry will be available for viewing by attorneys and the public. The docket entry will not contain specific information identifying the nature of the proposed sealed document. All parties in the case will receive notice of the electronic filing, however, the document itself will be unavailable. Counsel must serve copies on opposing counsel in a conventional manner.

  c. Counsel must e-mail a separate proposed order in word processing format to the assigned judicial officer. If the order is also to be filed under seal, it must so state.

  d. If counsel believes the motion for leave to file documents under seal itself should be filed under seal, counsel shall follow the same process to obtain leave to file that motion under seal.

k. Exhibits

Exhibits must be submitted electronically in CM/ECF as attachments. If the entire exhibit exceeds ten (10) megabytes, it must be submitted in multiple segments, not to exceed ten (10) megabytes each.

Exhibits must be paged in consecutive numerical order. Each document containing exhibits must have, as a cover page to the exhibits, a table of contents indicating the page number of each of the succeeding exhibits.

The filing party is required to verify the legibility of the scanned exhibits prior to electronically filing them with the court. Parties should scan documents in black and white, unless color is a critical feature of the information.

Original exhibits must be retained by the submitting party for the duration of the case, including any period of appeal.

A party may seek leave of the court to allow the non-electronic filing of exhibits when they are not convertible to electronic form (e.g. videotapes, maps, etc.). If leave is granted, the filing party must prepare a cover page in pleading format to be submitted with the exhibits. The cover page must contain a table of contents indicating the page number of each of the succeeding exhibits. The caption will state what document, if any, the exhibits are supporting. The actual exhibits must be tabbed and bound if appropriate.

Evidentiary and trial exhibits must be submitted directly to the appropriate courtroom deputy clerk and will not be filed with the court.

l. Hyperlinks

In order to preserve the integrity of the court record, attorneys wishing to insert hyperlinks in court filings should continue to use the traditional citation method for the cited authority, in addition to the hyperlink. The Judiciary's policy on hyperlinks is that a hyperlink contained in a filing is no more than a convenient mechanism for accessing material cited in the document. A hyperlink reference is extraneous to any filed document and is not part of the court's record.

m. Technical Failures

A registered user whose filing is made untimely as the result of a technical failure may seek appropriate relief from the court.

n. Correcting Filing or Docket Errors

  1. Once a document is submitted and becomes part of the case docket, corrections to the docket may be made only by the Clerk's Office. The CM/ECF system will not permit the filing party to make changes to the document or docket entry once the transaction has been accepted.

  2. The filing party should not attempt to re-file an incorrectly filed document.

  3. The filing party must contact the Clerk's Office CM/ECF Help Desk as soon as an error has been discovered and provide the case number and document number. If appropriate, the Clerk's

Office will make a docket entry indicating the document was filed in error. The filing party will be advised if the document needs to be re-filed.

4. If the Clerk's Office discovers filing or docketing errors, the filer will be advised of what further action, if any, is required to address the error. However, if the error is minor, the Clerk's Office may correct the error, with or without notifying the parties.

5. In the event it appears a document has been filed in the wrong case, the Clerk's Office will docket an entry indicating this possible error and notify the filing party. If it is confirmed as an error, the party will be directed to re-file the document in the correct case. The Clerk's Office will not delete any documents filed by a party unless ordered by the court.

o. Transcripts

The Judicial Conference has adopted a policy regarding electronic access to court transcripts. The following procedures apply as to transcripts:

Transcripts filed by contract court reporters or official transcribers will be submitted to the Clerk's Office in .pdf through e-mail to a designated e-mail address. Transcripts will be electronically filed and available for viewing at the Clerk's Office public terminal, but may NOT be copied or reproduced by the Clerk's Office for a period of 90 days. Registered users who have purchased the transcript during the 90 day period will be provided remote electronic access to the transcript in CM/ECF. The court reporter or official transcriber will notify the Clerk's Office when a registered user in a case has purchased the transcript so that access to the transcript can be given to the purchaser through the court's CM/ECF system.

Within 7 calendar days of the filing of the official transcript in CM/ECF, each party wishing to redact a transcript must electronically file a "Notice of Intent to Request Redaction." If no such notice is filed within the allotted time, the court will assume redaction of personal data identifiers from the transcript is not necessary. If redaction is requested, within 21 calendar days from the e-filing of the transcript with the Clerk, or longer by order of the Court, the parties must submit to the court reporter or official transcriber a redaction request statement indicating by page and line where personal identifiers appear in the transcript and how they are to be redacted. The responsibility for redacting personal identifiers rests solely with counsel and the parties. Personal identifiers are Social Security numbers, financial account numbers, names of minor children, dates of birth, and in criminal cases, home addresses.

p. Exceptions to Electronic Filing

The following documents must be submitted in paper form:

1. Abstract of Judgment

2. Sealed Criminal Documents or Sealed Civil Complaints

3. Indictment, Information, and Waiver of Indictment

4. Criminal Complaint

5. Financial Affidavit in Support of Request for Appointment of Counsel

6. Bond Documents

7. Affidavits Related to Criminal Complaints

8. Application for and Affidavit Supporting Warrants Issued

9. Writs Issued

10. Unless Available Electronically, the State Court Record in Habeas Corpus Cases Filed under 28 U.S.C.§2254

11. Application and Order for Pen Registers, Trap and Trace

12. Application for and Affidavit Supporting Wiretap Orders and 15-day Reports

13. Application for and Affidavit Supporting Trackers

14. Application and Order under 18 U.S.C. § 2703(d)

15. Reports of Medical or Mental Evaluations of Criminal Case Defendants

16. Probation and Pretrial Petitions

17. Plea Agreement

18. Stipulation of Fact and Joint Motion for Release of Material Witnesses (in Alien Smuggling Cases)

19. Civil Miscellaneous Cases Filed by Unregistered Attorneys

20. Any other document or filing that the court orders not to be electronically filed, imaged or maintained in the CM/ECF system.